True tales of the
old-time plains

True
Tales
of the
Old-Time
Plains

Key to location of stories

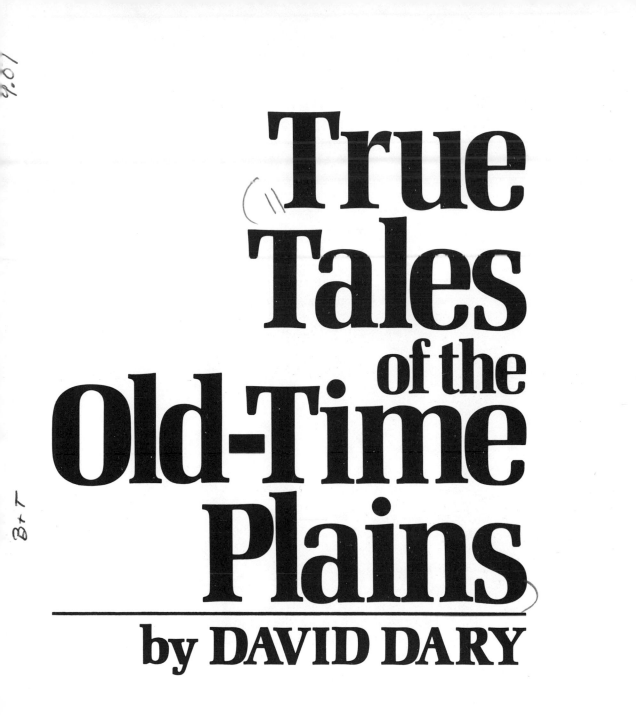

True Tales of the Old-Time Plains

by DAVID DARY

CROWN PUBLISHERS, INC. / NEW YORK

With appreciation to
JEFF AND MARTHA DYKES

When a land forgets its legends,
Sees but falsehoods in its past,
When a nation views its sires
In the light of fools and liars—
'Tis a sign of its decline,
And its glories cannot last.

—J. Fairfax-Blakesborough

Printed in the United States of America

Published simultaneously in Canada by
General Publishing Company Limited

Library of Congress Cataloging in Publication Data
Main entry under title:

True tales of the old-time plains.

A collection of articles appeared in the Kansas City Star.
Includes index.
1. Great Plains—History—Addresses, essays, lectures. 2. Frontier and pioneer life—Great Plains—Addresses, essays, lectures. 3. Pioneers—Great Plains—Biography—Addresses, essays, lectures. I. Dary, David. II. The Kansas City Star.
F591.T69 1979   978   78-31574
ISBN 0-517-53663-3

CONTENTS

PREFACE

This book is a collection of tales about people, animals and events in the Old West. Many of these stories hark back to a time when a man could ride his horse for a hundred miles or more across the unfenced, seemingly endless, windswept plains and when Indians, wild buffalo and mustangs had not yet been conquered by man. Other stories are set during the period when civilization, or what passed for it, had just moved onto the plains. Some of the stories span two centuries.

The characters in these stories are real. Many of them have unfamiliar names, but then there are William F. "Buffalo Bill" Cody, Abe Lincoln, Quantrill, Boston Corbett and Frederic Remington, whose fame as a western artist is well known but whose adventures on the plains are not. And there are the infamous Benders, Daltons and the Jayhawkers.

These stories are laid on the plains, that vast expanse of rolling open country stretching from north of the Canadian border south into Texas. Many of the tales occurred in what is today Kansas and the old territory of Kansas (1854–1861) that stretched from the Missouri River westward to the summit of the Rocky Mountains. It is this land, where my roots are deepest, that I know and love in spite of winters that can be unbearably cold and summers that can be horribly hot. The long springs and the usually colorful days of fall, with periods of delightful Indian summer, more than make up for the minor discomforts of the other seasons. But then it is my home.

Long before two of my great-grandfathers chose the western plains on which to build their homes and to raise their families—one homesteaded south of Abilene, Kansas, not far from the old Chisholm Trail, the other at the junction of the Kansas and Blue rivers—this land was labeled the "Great American Desert" by Zebulon M. Pike, who crossed the plains to the Rockies between 1805 and 1807. Others followed, including Stephen H. Long who gave the land the same label. The plains simply became territory that had to be crossed to get where you were going, whether it was the California or Kansas gold fields, the rich trading center of Santa Fe or that promised land somewhere on the other side of the Rockies.

Until the 1850s, most people in the East gave little thought of settling on the plains. For one thing, they felt uncomfortable. Many still do. The late John J. Ingalls of Kansas put it so aptly when he wrote, "Above the vague and receding horizons forever broods a pathetic solemnity, born of distance, silence and solitude."

The solitude of the plains undoubtedly accounted for the generally slow pace of life. It also accounted for frequent exaggerations. An English writer, Charles Wentworth Dilke, alluded to these traits after crossing the plains in 1866. In his book, *Greater Britain,* published in 1868, Dilke observed, "The singular wildness of Western thought, always verging on extravagance, is traceable to the width of Western land. The immensity of the continent produces a kind of intoxication; there is moral dram-drinking in the contemplation of the map. . . . Maps do not remove the impression produced by the views. The Arkansas River, which is born and dies within the limits of the plains, is two thousand miles in length. . . . The impression is not merely one of size. There is perfect beauty, wondrous fertility in the lonely steppe; no patriotism, no love of home, can prevent the traveler wishing here to end his days."

To the Easterner the plains and the American West in general appeared romantic. To many it still is. As Walter Prescott Webb observed, "The Easterner did not ride horses as did the Westerner. He did not wear a six-shooter . . . he did not herd cattle or wear boots or red handkerchiefs or spurs. . . . When the Easterner came in contact with this man of the West . . . the Easterner was at once impressed with the feeling that he had found something new in human beings."

Writing in 1931, Webb added that the significance of the plains on human life was that the "history of the white man in the Great Plains is the history of adjustments and modification, of giving up old things that would no longer function for new things that would, of giving up an old way of life for a new way in order that there might be *a* way."

Many of these stories reflect man's attempt to adjust to life on the plains. Others have been included simply because they are good stories and I enjoy telling them. If they are romantic, so be it. As a chronicler of life on the plains and prairie lands of the Old West, I find much enjoyment and satisfaction in discovering an old tale or legend, seeking to verify it if possible, uncovering new facts if they exist, sometimes visiting the area where the story was set and then telling the story in a fresh yet factual form.

Some of these stories are not jampacked with thrills and excitement. To artificially inject such material would hinder my attempt to reflect something of the true tempo of life on the old-time plains. That tempo was more often slow and plodding than fast and thrilling, in spite of the image often conveyed by western fiction writers and those people who have produced Hollywood westerns for theatres and television. Western fiction has never fascinated me. Reality is strange enough, especially as it relates to life on the western plains during the last century. The fact that these tales have endured the test of time is perhaps reason enough for retelling them between these covers.

I am indebted to many people whose names appear in the text and notes. And I owe a special debt of gratitude to Howard Turtle, retired editor of *Star,* the Sunday magazine of the *Kansas City Star,* who encouraged me in my search for tales and legends, and to Gene Murray, his successor, who did the same. Many of these stories first appeared in various forms under my byline in *Star* magazine. And I wish to thank Philip Winsor and Lurton Blassingame for their support and assistance and for believing that these stories should be preserved between the covers of a book.

David A. Dary

Lawrence, Kansas
Along the Kaw
1979

Part I

OVER THE TRAILS

Away, away from men and towns
To the silent wilderness.

—*Percy Bysshe Shelley*

Milt Bryan's Adventures on the Santa Fe Trail

On the first day of September 1828, Milt Bryan and twenty other men slowly rode out of the village of Santa Fe. They were going home. Bryan, an adventuresome young man of twenty-one, and the other traders were returning to Missouri after a successful trading venture in Santa Fe, then part of Mexico. Their caravan consisted of one hundred and fifty horses and mules herded loosely behind four horse-drawn wagons carrying supplies and several thousand dollars in Mexican silver coins, their trading profit. John Means, a seasoned plainsman, was captain of the caravan.

Only seven years earlier, William Becknell of Missouri had wandered into Santa Fe with a packtrain of Indian trade goods. The next year, 1822, Becknell returned with a few wagons loaded with goods intended for civilian trade and thereby established regular trade between Missouri and Santa Fe over what became known as the Santa Fe Trail.

Hearing wonderful stories of how profitable such trading was, Bryan had left his home in Boone County, Missouri, in the spring of 1828. He joined a party of traders at Independence, purchased some trading goods and traversed the nearly eight hundred miles of unsettled country between Missouri and Santa Fe. The trip was uneventful except for two days without water and a meeting with a band of apparently friendly Indians near where the trail crossed the Cimarron River in what is today the Oklahoma panhandle.

Milton Bryan as he appeared about the time of the Civil War. The exact date of this photo is unknown. *Author's collection*

Now, weeks later, Milt Bryan and the others were returning to Missouri. Bryan and the other men in the small caravan made good time their first day out of Santa Fe in spite of the obstinate nature of the mules they hoped to sell in Missouri. And nothing unusual happened for three or four days until the party reached Upper Cimarron Springs, where they intended to make camp for the night. As they went over a rise, they found themselves entering a large camp of Comanche Indians.

"We could neither turn back nor turn to either side, on account of the mountainous condition of the country," Bryan later wrote. "We realized too late that we were in a trap from which it would require both herculean and heroic efforts to escape."

There was only one road open to Bryan's party. It lay right through the Indian camp. With guns in readiness, the traders entered the camp. An Indian chief met them with smiles of welcome. "You must stay with us tonight," said the chief in Spanish, adding, "Our young men will guard your stock, and we have plenty of buffalo meat."

Captain Means, in charge of the caravan, turned down the Indian's invitation and gave the signal for the party to hurry through the camp. "Captain Means, Thomas Ellison and myself were a little behind the wagons and horses, on horseback, when they seized our bridle reins, and immediately began firing upon us," wrote Bryan.

Tom Ellison and Milt Bryan spurred their horses and got away, but Captain Means was hit and fell to the ground. He was dead.

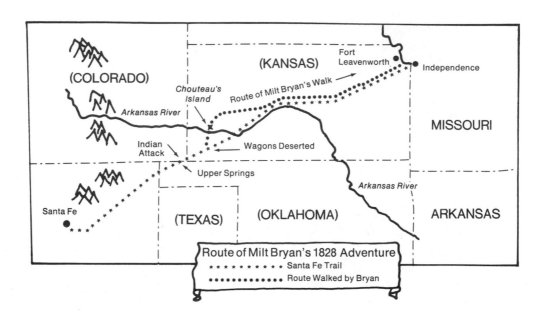

Route of Milt Bryan's 1828 Adventure
* * * * * * * * * Santa Fe Trail
● ● ● ● ● ● ● ● ● ● ● Route Walked by Bryan

As Bryan and the others raced away from the Indian camp, many Indians jumped on their ponies and gave chase. "We succeeded in fighting them off until we got about a half-mile from their camp. Since darkness was setting in, we decided to go into camp for the night. We tied our old gray bell mare to a stake, and whenever any of us could do so, we would go and jingle the bell, thereby keeping our horses from stampeding. We corralled our wagons for better protection and were kept busy all night resisting onslaughts from the Indians," wrote Bryan.

At daybreak the traders moved out on the trail only to suffer a new Indian attack. Throughout the day Indians, atop their ponies, charged into the caravan time and again. "We made but five miles of progress," wrote Bryan, adding, "It was a continuous fight, and we were harassed so greatly, it was very difficult for some of us to keep from falling into their hands."

Normally a caravan could make fifteen or more miles a day on the trail.

The next four days were a repeat of the first. Indians continued the harassment. "They would surround us, and then stop, as if renewing their strength, and they kept it up, until we were almost exhausted from fatigue and loss of sleep," observed Bryan.

But on the morning of the sixth day, as the traders moved onto the broad plains, there was no sign of the Indians. Some of the men talked as though the Indians had turned back. About midday, however, the Indians attacked. Yelling loudly they swept down on the traders. It was the largest group of Indians yet to attack the caravan. And before Bryan and the others knew what was happening, the Indians had stampeded the loose horses and mules—all one hundred and fifty.

Almost by instinct William Y Hitt, one of the traders, galloped after the animals. He was about to turn a few head of stampeding horses back toward the wagons when several Indians tried to capture him. He fought for his freedom from horseback and moments later escaped. But he was hurt. Bryan wrote that Hitt was "wounded in sixteen places. He was shot, tomahawked and speared."

Soon the ball from one of the traders' rifles found its mark. An Indian fell from his pony to the ground. "When the painted demons saw one of their number shot down by us, they left us for a time," wrote Bryan. The lull gave the traders time to regroup, corral their wagons and build a breastwork with harnesses and saddles.

The traders had barely finished the job when the Indians returned. They made charge after charge at the small circle of four wagons: a makeshift fort on the plains. Fortunately for the traders, they were carrying a good supply of powder and bullets in their wagons.

The Indians continued their attacks into the night. But they withdrew about two hours after dark when the moon went down. Then there was a strange quiet over the plains. For a minute or two not a man spoke. But soon they began to talk quietly. All of them realized they had to decide on a course of action.

Bryan remembered, "It was apparent to everyone that but two alternatives were before us. Should we resolve to die where we were or endeavor to escape in the gloom that surrounded us? It was a desperate situation, but our little band looked the matter square in the face, and after a council of war had been held, we resolved to save ourselves, if possible. In order to do so, it was necessary to leave our wagons, together with a large amount of silver coin in them, as we were unable to carry all of the latter in our flight. We packed up as much of it as we could carry, and bidding our wagons and hard-earned wealth a reluctant farewell, we stepped out into the darkness like spectres, and hurried away from the scene of death."

Bryan continued, "We knew that five hundred miles lay between us and the first settlement; but we were young, life was sweet, and we knew that there were loved ones at home who would look for our return with anxious hearts."

Just where their makeshift camp was located or how much silver was left behind is unknown. Bryan makes no reference to any attempt to recover the silver left behind in the wagons. One could assume that the Indians overran the camp the following morning and carried off the silver, among other things left behind. If they didn't, some of the silver may today be buried along the Santa Fe Trail.

Regardless of what happened to the silver, the traders on that night in 1828 knew the Indians would discover they were gone and probably head east thinking the white men would take the most direct route toward Missouri. Thus the traders headed north as rapidly as they could walk. Stopping only for brief rests, they walked all the next day and part of the next night until they reached the Arkansas River. By then the men were growing weak. They had eaten nothing but some prickly pears.

On the bank of the Arkansas River the traders slept. At daybreak, gambling that they were out of hearing of the Indians, they shot a buffalo and an antelope. "We ate without salt or bread, but no meal ever did or ever has tasted better to me than that one. Oh! but it was a feast for us all," Bryan wrote.

The traders then decided on their next course of action. Soon they decided to lighten their loads by burying most of the silver coins they carried. Each man, however, would keep a few. Reconnoitering a nearby island in the middle of the Arkansas River, they decided to bury their silver between two cottonwood trees on the island. Bryan wrote that the silver amounted to more than $10,000. Another account, however, said it was closer to $6,000. Although Bryan made no mention of the fact in his recollections, the island was known by some persons in 1828 as Chouteau's Island. It is located about five miles southwest of present-day Lakin in Kearny County, Kansas.

In an effort to avoid well-established trails closely watched by Indians, the traders continued north for three or four days until they reached a small stream, presumably the Pawnee River. They followed the stream eastward for ten days until they came onto the Santa Fe Trail, probably somewhere near present-day Larned, Kansas. They then followed the nearby Arkansas River to near the site of Great Bend, Kansas, and continued east on the trail until they reached Cow Creek, not many miles north of where Hutchinson, Kansas, stands today. When they reached that point they were completely exhausted from living only on buffalo meat. Some of the men simply could not travel any further.

Independence, Missouri, was still two hundred miles to the east. At Cow Creek the five strongest men were sent ahead to get help. The remaining fifteen traders would get along as best they could.

"I was one of the five selected to go ahead," wrote Bryan. "I shall never forget the terrible suffering we endured. We had no blankets to sleep under, and it was getting late in the fall. Some of us were barefoot, and our feet were so sore we left stains of blood in every footstep. Deafness seized upon us so greatly, occasioned by our weak condition, we could not hear the report of a gun a few feet distant. Two of our men laid down their guns, saying they could carry them no farther, and would die if they did not get some water.

"We left them, and went in search of some. After following a dry branch several miles, we found a puddle of muddy water, from which we got half a bucket full. Although muddy, it was life for us, and we guarded it with jealous eyes. We returned to our comrades about daylight, and the water so refreshed them, they were able to resume the journey," wrote Bryan.

Bryan and the four other men resumed their weary line of march east, averaging about twenty miles a day. Bryan later recalled that they "subsisted for eleven days on one turkey, a coon, a crow and some elm bark, with an occasional bunch of wild grapes."

After crossing the Missouri border into Jackson County, they discovered a cabin near the Big Blue River fifteen miles from Independence. "The occupants of the cabin were women, seemingly very poor, but they offered to share with us a pot of pumpkin they were boiling. . . . They jumped upon the bed while we greedily devoured the pumpkin, having to refuse some salt meat, as our teeth were so sore from long abstinence from salt. . . . We had not tasted bread or salt for thirty-two days. . . . In a short time two men came to the house, and took three of our party home with them," wrote Bryan.

Soon after daybreak the next morning the settlers brought horses and took Bryan and the four other traders to Independence. "Some one had gone on before, to notify the people of our safety, and when we arrived, they were having regimental muster, and the most intense excitement prevailed. All business was suspended, and the whole town flocked around, to hear the story of our remarkable adventures, and to render us assistance. We were half naked, footsore, haggard, and presented such a pitiful picture, the greatest sympathy was aroused in our behalf. We told the story of our comrades who had been left behind and without delay, seven men, with fifteen horses, started out to rescue them," wrote Bryan.

Within a matter of days the rescue party found all fifteen men. According to Bryan, the rescuers arrived "just in time to save them from death by starvation and exhaustion. Two were found about one hundred miles from Independence, and the balance were scattered along a further distance of fifty miles, no more than two being found together." The traders had retained sense enough to travel together in pairs.

As for Milt Bryan, he spent several days at the home of Charles

Owens, then county clerk of Jackson County. After regaining some strength, he bought a horse and started for his mother's home in Boone County taking with him $200 in Mexican silver and a check on a St. Louis bank for $500. That was all of his trading profit he had been able to carry.

When Bryan got to Franklin on the Missouri River near present-day Boonville, Missouri, he informed Captain Means's family of the man's death. It was a painful task for Bryan. He then completed the journey to his mother's home where he remained all winter. His feet were so sore he could hardly use them during the winter.

After suffering such agony, one might expect that Milt Bryan had had his fill of adventure on the Santa Fe Trail. Such was not the case. By spring he was determined to return to Santa Fe and, in the process, recover the buried silver. Bryan joined a new trading caravan of nearly forty wagons and about seventy men. The caravan captain was Charles Bent, who would later control much of the trade on the southern plains from what became known as Bent's Fort in what is today eastern Colorado.

"We left Fort Leavenworth about the 10th of May, and soon were out on the lonesome plains, seeing nothing alive but vast herds of buffalo and wild horses," recalled Bryan. "Many of the soldiers had never seen any buffalo before, and took delight in slaughtering them. At Walnut Creek we halted to secure a cannon which had been thrown in there two years before, and succeeded in fishing it out. With a sein [e] made of brush and grapevine, we caught more fine fish than we could dispose of; and one day a great deal of excitement was produced by a band of Indians running an enormous herd of buffalo onto us. The soldiers fired at them [the buffalo] by platoons, killing scores of them. We always travelled in two lines, and formed a hollow square at night, in which all slept, except those on guard. Frequently some one would discover a rattlesnake or a horned frog in bed with him, and it did not take him long to get up."

The soldiers mentioned by Bryan were under the command of Brevet Major Bennet Riley, for whom Fort Riley, Kansas, was later named. In response to demands by Santa Fe traders for protection, President Andrew Jackson, who took office March 4, 1829, directed that four companies of soldiers escort the spring caravan as far west as the Arkansas River, then the border between Mexico and the United States. Riley had 200 soldiers of the Sixth Infantry in his command. The U.S. Army had no mounted units in 1829.

The traders' caravan with its foot-soldier escort reached the Arkansas River near Chouteau's Island on July 10, 1829. There, near the

Two pages from Milton Bryan's gold field record book covering August through early September of 1853 and listing the dollar value of gold discovered on the Salmon River in what is today Idaho. At the bottom of the right hand page Bryan has written: "Taken out all together $2161.80." *Photo by author*

international border, Brevet Major Riley set up summer camp. The following day, Bryan and a companion from the journey the year before went out with a squad of soldiers to recover the buried silver.

"It was a few miles further up the Arkansas River, and when we came to the memorable spot, we found the money safe on the island, where we had left it. The water had washed the earth away, and the silver was exposed to the view of any one who might have passed along. We placed the money in sacks, and left it with [Bvt.] Maj. Riley," wrote Bryan.

Bryan and his companion rejoined Captain Bent's caravan and started for Santa Fe. "We had not travelled far when our advance guard met some Indians. They turned, and when in two hundred yards of us, one man, Samuel Lamme, was killed, his body being completely filled with arrows. His head was cut off, and all his clothes stripped from his body. We had a cannon, but the Spaniard who drove it had it tied up in such a manner that it could not be utilized for some time; but when it was turned upon them, the Indians fled in dismay.

"The soldiers, hearing the firing, came to our assistance. The next morning the hills were covered with fully two thousand Indians, who had evidently gathered there for the purpose of annihilating us. The coming of the soldiers was indeed fortunate, for when the cowards saw them, they disappeared. Captain [Bvt. Maj.] Riley accompanied us for a few days, and seeing no more Indians, he returned to his camp," Bryan wrote.

Arriving safely in Santa Fe, Bryan and the other traders turned a profit and by early fall had returned to Major Riley's camp. There Bryan picked up the money entrusted to the army's care and, with the military escort and caravan, returned to Fort Leavenworth.

"We reached Fort Leavenworth late in the season, and from that point we all scattered. I received my share of the money, and bade my companions adieu, many of whom I have never seen since," recalled Bryan in 1885.

Bryan married in 1833 and settled down near St. Joseph, Missouri. Gold fever attracted him to California in 1852. He left St. Joseph and traveled to New York where he took a ship around Cape Horn to San Francisco. He spent time looking for gold in California but apparently had little luck. He then went north into central Idaho where, according to his gold-field record book, he panned $2,161.80 in gold along the Salmon River between July 25 and September 8, 1853. He returned to St. Joseph before winter.

With the opening of Kansas Territory in 1854, Bryan crossed the Missouri River and helped to settle the Doniphan County town of Wathena, which he named for a nearby Kickapoo Indian chief. An undated newspaper clipping, among several owned by Bryan's descendants, tells the story of a cornfield planted by Chief Wathena. Milt Bryan "agreed to pay him $1 a row for 20 rows of corn." When the chief came to be paid, Bryan handed him a $20 gold piece. The old chief looked at it carefully, turned it over in his hand and then walked over to Bryan and laid it down at his feet and walked off. He had never seen one before, and the corn was paid for in 25-cent pieces, as the chief would accept nothing else.

Milt Bryan lived the final years of his eventful life in the Wathena, Kansas, area. His roots in America were deep. He was a great-nephew of Daniel Boone's wife, Rebecca Bryan. He was a great-nephew of James Wilson of Pennsylvania, one of the signers of the Declaration of Independence and later a U.S. Supreme Court justice. And Bryan's grandfather, Dr. Thomas Bryan, served as a surgeon in the Revolutionary War. Milton E. Bryan died at Wathena, Kansas, March 27, 1892, about three months after his eighty-fifth birthday.

The Massacre on Walnut Creek

The June sun was already high in the Kansas sky when the two wagon trains rolled slowly out of Fort Leavenworth, their oxen soon striking the dusty military road that would lead them toward the Southwest. The date was June 27, 1864. Jerome Elmore Crow, a lean wiry old speculator, a native of Illinois, owned the lead wagon train. It consisted of twenty-one wagons and twenty-four men. James Riggs was wagon master. The other train was owned by Richard F. Barret. It consisted of nine wagons and ten men. John Hiles was its wagon master. Both trains were under contract with Stewart, Stemmans & Co., government contractors at Leavenworth, to carry sacks of flour and wagon bows to Fort Union, New Mexico, more than seven hundred miles away.

The freighters were concerned about the journey. Hundreds of Kiowa, Comanche and Arapahoe Indians, dissatisfied with their treaties, land allotments and with the government rations and goods supplied them, had left their reservations and had been raiding over a wide area of the plains for more than a year. Freighting was almost at a standstill. Prices of goods had skyrocketed in Colorado and New Mexico, with flour selling at $45 a sack.

Both wagon trains had been refused a military escort to Fort Union. The teamsters also had been refused military weapons for their protection. The army assured the freighters that treaties existed between the government and the Indians and therefore no danger should be expected. But Crow, Hiles and a few of the other teamsters were old hands at freighting across the plains. They knew better, unlike several boys in their teens who had signed on to make their first trip west.

After much discussion with government officials, the freighters agreed to make the trip only after the government provided an idemnifying bond against loss that might be caused by the Indians. But even so the freighters had reservations about making the journey. Only one teamster was armed. He was Albert Gentry, who had a smoothbore muzzle-loading shotgun.

Slowly the two wagon trains inched their way across Kansas. They averaged about ten miles a day. The smaller train remained a few miles behind the large train as they followed the military road from Fort Leavenworth to a crossing on the Kansas River west of Topeka. From there they pushed southwest to near the tiny settlement of Wilmington in Wabaunsee County where the military road joined the Santa Fe Trail.

On the night of July 17, 1864, twenty-one days after leaving Fort Leavenworth, Jerome Crow's wagons corralled for the night near the big bend of the Arkansas River, about seven miles below where Walnut Creek empties into the Arkansas River. Before darkness the smaller of the two wagon trains under John Hiles's command caught up with the first train. Both corralled together and spent an uneventful night under the stars. The freighters felt safer in numbers, even though only one man was armed. Then too, they were only about seven miles from a newly established military camp on Walnut Creek, a stream they planned to cross the next morning.

The freighters were up well before daylight. After breakfast their yoked oxen were hooked to the wagons, the few horses they had were saddled and camp was broken. James L. Riggs, Crow's wagonmaster, was given charge of both trains. Slowly, as the sun peeked over the eastern horizon, the wagons formed a long column of perhaps half a mile in length.

Shortly before ten o'clock in the morning, Riggs, riding at the head of the column, spotted Walnut Creek ahead. He could make out the faint outlines of the military camp, stage station and the "ranch." The ranch, not a real ranch by today's meaning of the word, was a general store of sorts where persons traveling the Santa Fe Trail could buy supplies and perhaps get a meal. But the ranch, established in 1855 and operated in 1864 by Charles Rath, was deserted. Riggs was unaware that Rath had gone to Fort Larned, about thirty-two miles to the southwest, because of recent Indian troubles. Near the ranch was a station of the Kansas Stage Company. There were a handful of men at the station.

Between the stage station and the ranch was the newly established

A photograph of a nineteenth-century painting by Henry Worrall, Kansas artist, of Fort Zarah, first called Camp Dunlap. Located on the Santa Fe Trail, the military post was being constructed in July 1864 when Indians attacked the wagon train within sight of soldiers at the post. *Courtesy Kansas State Historical Society*

military post, hardly a month old. Just about three weeks earlier, forty-five to fifty-five soldiers (one account says there were eighty-five soldiers) of the Fifteenth Kansas Cavalry Volunteers, Company H, under the command of Captain Oscar F. Dunlap, a printer by trade from Topeka, were ordered to establish the camp at the Walnut Creek crossing. The soldiers called it Camp Dunlap. It would later be known as Fort Zarah.

Dunlap and his men, however, were not professional soldiers. The professionals were in the East on the Potomac front. The Civil War was still very real. The second war of the 1860s, the Indian wars on the plains, was being fought almost entirely by volunteer troops.

Wagon master James Riggs may have felt relieved at the sight of the military camp, but if he felt any joy it was short-lived as the two trains moved closer to Walnut Creek. At about ten o'clock that morning, as the first wagon reached a spot about a mile and a half from Walnut Creek, Riggs saw about one hundred and twenty-five Indians on horseback approaching the head of the train. The Indians divided into two bodies, about half of them going on one side and the other half on the opposite side of the train. They appeared to be friendly, shook hands and asked for different things. Riggs gave tobacco to several of them and talked with one of them for about five minutes. When the Indians got about halfway down the train, they commenced firing on the teamsters.

What followed was nightmare for the freighters. Most of the Indians were armed with bows and arrows. A few carried spears. Some had rifles. As the fighting began, the head of the train was free of Indians. At the first sign of trouble Riggs and Crow made their escape on horseback toward Camp Dunlap. Albert Gentry, the only teamster with a gun, was walking beside his wagon. An Indian shot him in the leg with a rifle ball. Although wounded, Gentry got into his wagon, seized his shotgun and fired at the Indian. Both horse and rider were knocked to the ground. The fallen Indian appeared to be a chief.

The sound of the shotgun and the sight of the fallen Indian caused confusion among some of the Indians. Four of them seized their wounded brother, wrapped him in a blanket and rode off. The Indian's horse was lying on the ground. The animal was dead. Whether the Indian survived his wounds is unknown. One account says he died.

As Gentry backed away carrying his empty shotgun, the Indians did not follow. But many teamsters gathered around Gentry and fled toward the safety of Camp Dunlap. Meantime, an Indian sent a rifle ball across the abdomen of teamster James Brockman. As other Indians then tried to surround Brockman, he brought his bullwhip into action and "laid about him so fiercely with his novel weapon that he beat the Indians off." At that moment another commotion drew the Indians farther down the train and Brockman escaped with Gentry and the others.

Watching the Indian attack from Camp Dunlap was Henry Tisdale, assistant superintendent of the Kansas Stage Company. Tisdale had arrived at the post from Topeka earlier in the morning and learned that Indians had been seen around the camp during the night. From the safety of the post Tisdale watched the Indians attack the wagon trains. He also watched as Captain Oscar Dunlap ordered his soldiers to mount their horses.

"They counted off as fast as on parade and filled their cartridge-boxes. The captain ordered one-half of them out in the direction of the Indians. After going about halfway he wheeled them to the right, returning them to camp. The captain dismounted near where I stood, and asked a soldier to take his horse, he sitting down on a hardtack box perfectly exhausted by fright and nervousness, making a very pitiful and disgusting appearance. . . . The men were brave enough. One sergeant requested the captain to let him take a part of the company and attack the Indians. The captain would not allow it," recalled Tisdale.

Although there are several accounts claiming that Captain Dunlap was later "cashiered for cowardice and unsoldierly conduct," no such official record can be found. The Kansas Adjutant General's Report says that Dunlap resigned a year later on June 10, 1865. And in his account of the massacre, Dunlap claimed there were anywhere from 800 to 1,000 Indians, not 125, in the attack. Dunlap wrote, "I proceeded with my company at once to the scene of action, where we arrived soon after the Indians had left the ground."

Another conflicting account of what happened was written by Reeder M. Fish, a former officer under Dunlap, who was actually at Fort Larned when the massacre occurred. In a letter written three days later, Fish reported that "Capt. Dunlap, with his company, rushed to the assistance of the train, but soon discovered a large body of Indians, 300 or more, proceeding from the woods of Walnut Creek, with the intention of cutting him off from his fortifications, which compelled him to fall back."

Fish noted that the Indians who attacked the wagon train were "boys, undoubtedly sent to attack the train for the purpose of drawing the troops out, while the braves cut them off from their fort, and destroy the company."

Whether this was actually the case is unknown as is the length of the Indian attack. The Indians, however, appear to have taken their time in plundering the wagons. They took away all the wagon sheets and the teamsters' personal belongings. In filing a claim for compensation from the government for personal items lost in the raid, one teamster listed the following: "3 coats, each valued at $10; 4 shirts, each valued at $3; 3 pair pants, each valued at $5; 2 vests, each valued at $5; 2 pair drawers, each valued at $2.50; 1 blanket valued at $7.00; 2 buffalo robes, at $15 each; 1 satchel valued at $5.00; 10 pounds of tobacco, each pound valued at $1.00; 1 handkerchief valued at $1.00 and 400 pounds of bacon, at 25 cents per pound."

Jerome Crow later reported that the Indians destroyed all 132 sacks of government flour "by ripping open the sacks and throwing the flour on the ground, and carrying off the sacks. They also took away some of the flour."

It was apparently early afternoon before Captain Dunlap and several teamsters moved out of Camp Dunlap to the besieged wagons. What they found was not a pretty sight. Ten men were dead. John Hiles, who had spent a decade on the plains as a freighter, recalled that he found eight of the dead men. "All of them had been shot with arrows, and all except two, who were Negroes, had been scalped."

But two teamsters found lying in the trampled prairie grass near the wagons were not dead. Although scalped, fourteen-year-old Robert McGee of Easton, Kansas, and sixteen-year-old Allen W. Edwards, a native of Iowa, were still alive. Vividly, Edwards later recalled what happened:

"At the time of the attack I had become tired of riding and was walking along side my oxen. I had nothing with which to defend myself except a buffalo skinner's knife, and so I was easy pickings for the half dozen Indians who swarmed about me. I was knocked senseless for the time by the onslaught. When I gained consciousness, as nearly as I can

This turn-of-the-century drawing by Carl Bolmar, a Kansas artist, shows a freighter's wagon train crossing the plains. The train in this drawing is similar to those attacked by Indians near the big bend of the Arkansas River in July 1864. *Courtesy Kansas State Historical Society*

recall, I was lying close to a tree, with arrows sticking in me on both sides, near my abdomen, also an arrow in one of my arms and several bullets in other parts of my body. I was weak from the loss of blood, and suffering mightily. Sure thought I was going to croak. I have a sort of hazy recollection of watching the Indians scalping the dead and dying.

"Then they came to me; seemed to hesitate, deliberating probably whether they had best skedaddle, or wait and get my scalp. Then one of them stooped down and grabbing my hair cut a piece of scalp off the back of my head. They evidently thought I was dead," recalled Edwards, who lived to be an old man.

As for fourteen-year-old Robert McGee, he was knocked down by the force of a tomahawk. An Indian had shot two arrows through his body, pinning him to the ground. McGee received fourteen other wounds before he too was scalped.

The almost lifeless forms of Edwards and McGee were carried by some soldiers and teamsters to nearby Walnut Creek where their wounds were cleaned. Edwards was delirious. McGee asked someone to shoot him and relieve him of the agony he was suffering. But no one did. That night when the moon came up McGee and Edwards were loaded into a wagon and taken under an armed escort to Fort Larned, thirty-two miles to the southwest. There army surgeon H. H. Clark treated the wounded and scalped men.

Back at Walnut Creek soldiers and teamsters had dug a large grave not too far from the stream. The following day the eight white teamsters were "silently laid away," according to one account, while the two black teamsters were buried in a separate grave nearby. The dead men were William Weddell, Perry Beabee and his son from Brownsville, Nebraska; James Lassel, Robert Lucas and Lewis Sampson from Clay County, Missouri; Talbot O. Edwards from Des Moines County, Iowa; Enos Gardner, residence unknown; and Perry and Charles, the Negroes (no last names reported) from Leavenworth, Kansas.

For more than a century the story of the massacre on Walnut Creek was just another page of forgotten frontier history. In April of 1973, however, Wendolin Herrman, a farmer east of Great Bend, Kansas, was inspecting the swollen Walnut Creek that flows across the land he was farming. With Herrman were two sons. Excessive rains had caused Walnut Creek, normally about ten feet wide, to spread to a width of about 150 feet in spots. Portions of the bank had crumbled when the water level returned to normal. At one of these cave-ins, the Herrmans discovered two bones about a foot or two below the surface of the ground. They began digging. When parts of human skeletons were uncovered, the Herrmans called the Barton County sheriff. The bones appeared old, and Thomas Witty, state archaeologist from the Kansas State Historical Society at Topeka, was called to the scene.

Witty supervised the removal of ten human skeletons, eight in one grave and two in another. Metal arrowheads were embedded in some of the bones. Each of the bodies had been placed in the ground with their feet pointing east, the Christian burial pattern. Today there is no question that these remains were those of the victims of the massacre on Walnut Creek in 1864.

A Ride for Life

On a November day in 1864, about four months after the massacre near Camp Dunlap on Walnut Creek, a light wagon carrying two army officers rattled over the log bridge that spanned Walnut Creek and hit the Santa Fe Trail toward the southwest. Captain Henry Booth of the Eleventh Kansas Cavalry, one of the men in the wagon, was under orders to inspect the military posts along the Santa Fe Trail. Booth, twenty-six years old, was chief of cavalry and inspecting officer of the military district of the upper Arkansas, a district that extended from the Missouri River westward to the foothills of the Rocky Mountains.

Booth had just finished an inspection of Fort Zarah on Walnut Creek. Now, with a Lieutenant Hallowell of the Ninth Wisconsin, Booth was heading for Fort Larned, about thirty-two miles to the southwest. A few days earlier, Booth and Hallowell had left Fort Riley, Kansas, with a cavalry escort of one hundred soldiers. Between Fort Riley and Fort Zarah (the recently renamed Camp Dunlap) the escort had remained with the light wagon carrying Booth and Hallowell. The escort was for protection from Indians. But the night before, while sitting around the campfire, the commander of Fort Zarah, Captain Theodore M. Conkey, said to Booth, "Captain, it won't require more than half an hour in the morning to inspect the papers and finish up what you have to do. Why don't you start your escort out very early, so it won't be obliged to trot after your wagon or you to poke along with it?"

Well aware that only four months earlier ten teamsters had been killed by Indians within sight of the post and that there had been other incidents involving Indians nearby, Booth asked, "What about the Indians?"

"There hasn't been an Indian seen around here for over ten days," said Captain Conkey, assuring Booth there was no danger.

Booth thought for a moment and then gave orders for the escort to move out early the next morning. He said that he and Lieutenant Hallowell would catch up to them.

Early the next morning the cavalry escort left Fort Zarah as Captain Booth and Lieutenant Hallowell began the task of finishing their inspection. But their work took almost three hours, not thirty minutes. By then the cavalry escort was several miles away.

As Booth and Hallowell climbed into the wagon, said goodbye to Captain Conkey and left Fort Zarah, neither officer appeared concerned about the distance between them and their escort. And after all, Captain Conkey had assured them there was no danger.

The morning was bright and clear. A stiff breeze was blowing in from the northwest as the wagon hit the Santa Fe Trail. The ride, however, was rough. The trail was frozen hard in places. The wagon kept hitting ruts cut up by the heavy wagons that had traversed the trail earlier in wet weather. Lieutenant Hallowell was driving the wagon. Captain Booth sat to his left cracking a bullwhip over the heads of the two army mules pulling the wagon.

The wagon belonged to Captain Booth. He had decided to use his own wagon on the trip in place of a large and lumbering army wagon. And before leaving Fort Riley, Booth had a set of bows fitted to his wagon. Over the bows was thrown a white army wagon sheet, drawn up behind with a cord. In the wagon they carried two gripsacks containing their dress uniforms, their sabers, a box of crackers, some cheese, meat and sardines and a bottle of "anti-snake bite medicine."

As the wagon picked up speed, Hallowell started to sing. Booth joined in. It was a bright morning. The crisp air made both men feel good. But soon Hallowell observed, "The buffalo are grazing a long way from the road today."

"Yes," replied Booth, adding, "It may be because our escort came through here and frightened them off."

The wagon had traveled about five miles from Fort Zarah when Booth, looking south toward the Arkansas River, noticed something that appeared to be a flock of turkeys. As the wagon moved closer, however, it became evident that it was a body of horsemen.

Booth pointed toward the horsemen. Hallowell knew what they were.

"Indians," he yelled.

A photo of Henry Booth as he appeared several years after he and another army officer had their hair-raising escape from Indians on the Kansas Plains. Booth went on to serve in the Kansas legislature. He died in 1898. *Courtesy Kansas State Historical Society*

Within moments Booth was cracking the bullwhip on the backs of the two mules as Hallowell was turning the wagon around and starting back toward Fort Zarah.

Booth, keeping his eyes on the Indians, saw them emerge from a ravine with their horses at full gallop. Some of the Indians slipped off their buffalo robes and began pulling arrows from their quivers. Others drew up their spears in readiness as they headed toward the wagon. It appeared that one or two Indians had rifles.

"I'll do the driving, you do the shooting," yelled Hallowell, slipping to the floor of the wagon in front of the seat where the sideboards offered some protection.

Booth crawled to the back of the wagon under the canvas, pulled out one of the revolvers—between them they had three—and looked toward the charging horsemen. Booth counted twenty-eight Indians, and they were gaining on the wagon.

Hallowell, attempting to get more speed out of the mules, cracked the bullwhip even harder on the backs of the animals. He couldn't see the Indians and he yelled at Booth, "How far are they off?"

Before Booth could answer, two of the rapidly approaching Indians fired their rifles. They were single-shot weapons. The bullets whistled through the wagon sheet between Booth and Hallowell.

As the shots were fired, the Indians began yelling and divided into two groups, one going on each side of the wagon. And as they moved parallel to the wagon both groups fired a volley of arrows toward the wagon.

"Captain, I'm hit!" yelled Hallowell. Turning around, Booth saw an arrow sticking in Hallowell's head above his right ear.

"Does it hurt?" yelled Booth, amazed that Hallowell was alive and still driving the team.

"Not much," came Hallowell's reply as he plied the bullwhip to the mules.

Booth crawled forward in the wagon and pulled the arrow out of Hallowell's head. The wound was superficial.

The Indians had passed the wagon and were now circling back for another charge. The attack came and more arrows shot into the wagon. Hallowell was hit again by an arrow over his left ear. And again Booth pulled it out. Hallowell said it didn't hurt much.

Booth crawled to the back of the wagon and looked out. The Indians were all around the wagon. Booth got off two shots before an arrow struck him on his right elbow. He yelled and lost his grip on the weapon he was holding. The revolver fell to the ground and bounced a couple of times.

Just then the wagon hit a rut in the trail and Booth almost fell to the ground himself, but he held on and pulled himself back inside the wagon.

At that moment Hallowell yelled, "Off to the right." Booth looked in that direction and saw an Indian about to send an arrow toward Hallowell. Booth rushed to the front of the wagon, pulled his other revolver and fired. The Indian fell to the ground, bouncing as he hit.

Booth crawled to the rear of the wagon again. Another Indian moving up on the right was about to shoot an arrow at him. Booth stuck his revolver through a hole in the wagon sheet and took aim. But the Indian, seeing the barrel of the weapon, slid over on the offside of his galloping pony.

The pony moved closer to the wagon. Booth could almost reach out and touch the animal. But all he could see of the Indian was one arm around the pony's neck and part of the Indian's leg over the back of the pony. Booth pulled the revolver back into the wagon. As he did so, the Indian peered over the back of the pony.

Booth again took aim. Again the Indian ducked.

Twice this happened. But the third time Booth did not pull his revolver completely inside the wagon sheet. And when the Indian peered over the back of his pony, Booth fired. He hit the Indian in the upper chest. The Indian grabbed at his body and fell to the ground with a thud.

Some of the Indians slowed the chase, but others did not. Hallowell yelled at Booth, "Off to the right again." Booth looked. Another Indian was aiming an arrow at Hallowell. Booth, realizing his weapon was empty, yelled at Hallowell to use his whip.

Hallowell whacked his bullwhip toward the Indian. The knot at the end of the whip struck the Indian in the face. Grabbing for his eye, the Indian dropped his bow and arrow and moved away from the wagon, screaming in pain.

Other Indians were now charging the wagon from the other side. And a moment later another volley of arrows were sent toward the wagon that was weaving back and forth on the trail. One of the arrows found its mark.

Hallowell was hit in the left shoulder. Booth made his way to the front of the wagon and after two attempts pulled the arrow from Hallowell's shoulder. But Hallowell was still able to drive the wagon.

Just then Booth saw another Indian taking aim at Hallowell with his bow and arrow not ten feet from the wagon. But Booth's revolver was empty. He did the only thing he could do. He raised the unloaded weapon, pointed it toward the Indian and shouted "Bang" as loud as he could. Down the Indian ducked on the opposite side of his pony and away from the wagon Booth rode.

Booth crawled to the rear of the wagon to reload the revolver, but before he could do so, Hallowell yelled, "To the left."

Booth saw another Indian aiming an arrow at Hallowell. Booth rose in the wagon, grabbed a wagon bow for balance, pointed the revolver at the Indian and yelled "Bang."

But the Indian had evidently noticed the first failure. He grinned and took aim. Booth knew what he had to do. He seized the revolver by the muzzle and with all the force he could muster hurled it at the Indian. It struck him in the ribs. The Indian dropped his bow and arrow and pulled away from the wagon.

Booth and Hallowell had one revolver left. It was empty. Before Booth could reload it, Hallowell was hit again. An arrow passed through the fleshy part of his right thumb.

By then the Indians were changing their tactics. They tried to force the mules and the wagon off the trail into a large stand of tall sunflowers that had grown along the trail during the previous summer. Now their dry stalks stood as thick as a cane-brake. If the wagon got caught in the stalks, it would be impossible for the mules to keep their pace.

One Indian was riding close to the off mule throwing his spear at the animal and then jerking it back with the thong, one end of which was fastened to the Indian's wrist.

Realizing the consequences should the Indian succeed, Booth stepped out on the footboard of the wagon. Holding on to a bow, he kicked the mule as Hallowell pulled on the reins to maintain control. They succeeded in keeping the wagon out of the sunflowers. And before pulling himself back inside the wagon, Booth hurled his revolver—the last one they had—at the Indian with the spear. It missed its mark but struck the Indian's pony causing the animal to turn and race across the prairie away from the wagon.

Booth and Hallowell were now unarmed. They did, however, have two sabers in the wagon. And these were thrown at the Indians along with the scabbards as the Indians attempted to spear the mules. Fortunately, the Indians had run out of arrows.

By now the wagon had traveled about four miles. There was still about one mile to go to reach Fort Zarah. As Booth's eyes scanned the contents of the wagon for possible projectiles, he spotted the two grip-sacks containing their dress uniforms and other personal belongings. He grabbed the grips and threw them out the back of the wagon as the Indians prepared for another charge. The grips hit the ground with dull thuds, one of them breaking open.

When the pursuing Indians saw the grips they stopped, dismounted and poured the contents on the ground. Booth smiled as he watched one Indian pull out a sash and wind it around his head. The Indians now had other things to amuse them.

The ride ended minutes later as the wagon rumbled across the bridge at Walnut Creek into the safety of Fort Zarah. Captain Conkey and others came running out of their tents and dugouts and surrounded the wagon. After hearing what had happened, Captain Conkey took ninety cavalrymen and gave chase. By then most of the Indians had scattered.

As for Booth and Hallowell, a surgeon treated their wounds. To Booth's surprise, the doctor found an arrowhead in his shoulder. Booth, in the excitement, hadn't realized he'd been hit. Twenty-two arrows were pulled from the wagon bed.

Both Booth and Hallowell recovered. What eventually happened to Hallowell is unknown. As for Booth, he was mustered out of the army late in 1865 at Fort Leavenworth and moved to Manhattan, Kansas. There he went into the hardware and implement business down the street from where my great-grandfather owned and operated a mercantile company. Later Booth became recorder at the United States Land Office at Larned, Kansas, where he built the first house in that community. Booth served in the Kansas Legislature and was speaker of the Kansas House from 1889 to 1890. He died near Larned at the age of about sixty years in 1898.

The Crazy Bet of F. X. Aubry

Darkness still covered the village of Santa Fe as the black man awakened his master. Francis Xavier Aubry, twenty-four, a small man with black piercing eyes, quickly dressed his one-hundred-pound frame and ate a hearty breakfast. Then he walked outside. To the east, over the rim of the Sangre de Cristo Mountains, Aubry detected the first faint glow of dawn. He liked to watch the sunrise over the mountains, but on this morning he had no time to spare.

Nearby at the Plaza, men were waiting, men who doubted that the little man—he stood only five feet two inches tall—could ride horseback from Santa Fe to Independence, Missouri, in only six days. Yet Aubry said he could and even bet $1,000 he could.

Little Aubry's servant had saddled a fast horse. The saddlebags had been filled with food and a canteen of fresh water. The horse had been taken to the Plaza. It was there, minutes later, that the little man with a black goatee and long black hair that touched the lobes of his ears greeted the waiting group of men.

Some have said Kit Carson was among those waiting. Carson had returned to Santa Fe a few days earlier after delivering government dispatches to Washington. Though he was well under six feet in height, Carson towered over Aubry as did most of the other men in the group. But unlike Aubry they had been up most of the night in the cantina, drinking and talking and wagering their money on whether the little guy with the sad face would make it.

Some of them shook Aubry's hand and wished him good luck.

Some patted him on the back and told him not to hurry. Others just watched as Aubry swung into the saddle, waved goodbye and rode out of Santa Fe at a fast gallop.

That was on the morning of September 12, 1848.

What little Aubry was setting out to prove was nothing new. Since leaving his home in Canada at the age of eighteen, he had been obsessed with the desire to do things better than other men. Aubry—his name is sometimes spelled Aubrey—was a French Canadian who had left his poverty-stricken home in Masknonge, Quebec, six years earlier. He had struck it rich as a freighter hauling goods from Independence to Santa Fe, and he had already broken one record riding horseback from Santa Fe to Missouri in eight days and ten hours, something it generally took horsemen two to three weeks to accomplish. It took the military mail thirty days to make the same trip.

Now at the age of twenty-four the little guy had bet $1,000 that he could make the 800-mile ride to Independence in six days. To do so, he'd have to average 133⅓ miles each twenty-four hours. This seemed impossible to Aubry's acquaintances in Santa Fe and therefore they bet against it. It was, they thought, easy money, but they may not have considered Aubry's weight. At one hundred pounds he was a light load for any horse.

When Aubry left Santa Fe that September morning, he had fresh horses positioned along the route as he had done before. The little guy rode like the wind through the sleepy village of San Miguel and sped on to Rio Gallinas, now the site of Las Vegas, New Mexico, where fresh horses were waiting.

Riding one horse and leading two others, Aubry turned toward Point of Rocks. Riding all night, eating and sleeping in the saddle, he stopped only at his relay points to change horses. By the dawn of the second day he had strapped himself to the saddle to prevent falling off while dozing in the saddle.

He passed a wagon train bound for Santa Fe without stopping for the news as was the custom. Nor did he stop hours later as he sped past a Mexican packtrain. At his next relay point he waited only long enough for his man to stir the coals around a pot of coffee and to saddle a fresh mount, a yellow mare, a Spanish dun named Dolly. She was Aubry's favorite horse.

"I'd kill every horse on the Santa Fe trail before I'd lose that $1,000 bet," he reportedly told his man, "but it's not the money I care about. I'm riding to prove that I can get more out of a horse and last longer than any other man in the West."

Aubry's man did not have time to answer. Dolly was saddled and

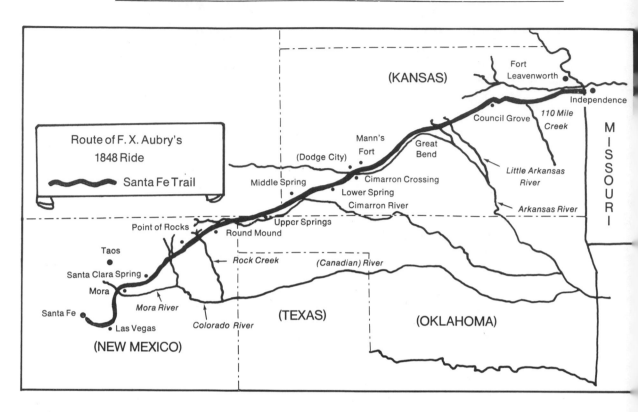

ready. Aubry gulped more coffee and jumped onto the mare with a roasted buffalo rib in his hand.

"Adios," yelled Aubry as he galloped off. As the man watched Aubry disappear, he wondered if the little man would make it.

The hours seemed like days as Aubry galloped toward Point of Rocks. Leaving the high country behind, Aubry did not spare Dolly and she didn't seem to mind. The autumn chill was in the air. Soon clouds hid the sun and it began to drizzle, but Aubry didn't stop nor slow his pace.

Pushing on, Aubry began to look for his fresh horses and their keeper. Soon he saw the camp, but as he pulled up to the remains of a campfire he found no horses, only a dead man with a scalped head. Indians had surprised his man.

Aubry had no choice. He spurred Dolly on. During the next twenty-six hours Aubry covered nearly two hundred miles. Dolly did not fail him. The yellow mare set what undoubtedly was a record for one horse. But how long could she last?

Little Aubry did not find out. When he met a wagon train he got a fresh horse from the wagon master who promised to take Dolly back to

This drawing of F. X. Aubry appeared in *Les Canadiens de L'Ouest* published in 1878. *Courtesy Kansas State Historical Society*

Santa Fe. Aubry rode on toward the Arkansas River. He was nearing his halfway mark.

Above a ford on the Cimarron River southeast of modern Ulysses, Kansas, Aubry found three fresh horses hidden in a patch of timber. They had been left there by one of his men. Mounting one horse and leading the others, Aubry headed east. He did not spare horseflesh now, but after ten miles the first horse gave out. Another ten miles and the second horse wore down. And not quite another ten miles the third horse stumbled exhausted and fell dead. Aubry had driven the horses too hard.

Hiding his saddle and blanket in some tall grass, Aubry, silver-plated bridle in hand, set out on foot running and walking. The hours passed. Ten miles. Fifteen miles. After more than twenty miles he reached the crossing on the Arkansas River that was to become known as "Aubry's Crossing." He staggered across and fell to the ground exhausted.

Catching his breath after several minutes, the little man got to his feet and walked a mile or so to Fort Mann, west of present-day Dodge City, Kansas. There he asked to see a friend. But Aubry's friend, he was told, was out hunting buffalo. Aubry said he would wait and curled up in a corner and slept.

When the friend returned two hours later, Aubry got up, conducted his business, borrowed a horse and galloped off past Pawnee Rock and on to Council Grove where new horses were waiting. Aubry paused long enough for coffee to boil. Then, tying himself on a fresh horse, he left

A drawing that shows a portion of Independence, Missouri, a few years after F. X. Aubry's ride. This engraving appeared in *United States Illustrated* published in 1854. *Courtesy Kansas State Historical Society*

Council Grove in a swinging gallop. Independence was still 150 miles away. It took little Aubry twenty-four hours to travel that distance and most of it was in rain.

It was about ten o'clock on the night of September 17, 1848, when down the street from the Merchants Hotel in Independence (it was then sometimes called the Noland House), a horse and rider, half running, half staggering, were seen approaching. As Aubry and his horse reached the front of the brightly lit hotel a man in the doorway yelled, "Aubry's here!" Men rushed out of the bar to lift the motionless rider from his blood-soaked saddle. Aubry was alive but weak. He had made the ride from Santa Fe in five days and sixteen hours and had won his bet, with eight hours to spare.

Inside the hotel Aubry could only whisper, but everyone listened as he ordered food. He bolted some ham, eggs and coffee. Then he was helped to bed. Aubry told the proprietor to wake him in three hours. The proprietor waited six.

When little Aubry was awakened, he was angry. "I like to take my food and rest in broken doses," he said, as he put on fresh clothes and left the hotel.

With only six hours' rest Aubry headed for St. Louis to make arrangements to send his third wagon train of the season through to Santa Fe. Aubry was determined to prove to other traders that he could take three wagon trains—not the usual two—from Independence to Santa Fe in one season. Most traders doubted if it could be done because of the winter weather, but Aubry said he could do it. And it had been his determination to do so that led to his record-breaking rides.

Aubry's desire to do things better than other men probably developed in his youth. Aubrey, who was born in Canada on December 4, 1824, had to interrupt his schooling at the age of thirteen because of his father's financial reverses. The family lost their small farm and moved to the town of Three Rivers.

Determined to do better than his father, Aubry left Canada at the age of eighteen. He traveled to St. Louis where, in 1842, he became a clerk in the general store of Lamoureaux and Blanchard, both French Canadians. Aubry sold goods consigned to Independence, then the jumping-off spot for the West. As a clerk he heard stories about life on the plains, as told by bullwhackers, trappers, rivermen and traders. Soon he felt his job was dull. It had no excitement. He soon believed it had no future.

Aubry quit his job in St. Louis. With his savings of $400 plus credit for an equal amount, he bought a wagon and filled it with new merchandise. On May 9, 1846, Aubry set out from Independence for Santa Fe, joining the wagon train of W. S. "John" McKnight, an experienced trader.

The trip to Santa Fe took more than two months. The train averaged about fifteen miles a day. But during that time little Aubry learned much. McKnight taught him how to survive on the plains, how to read Indian signs, how to follow landmarks and where to find water.

Once in Santa Fe Aubry sold his goods for a handsome profit receiving $50,000 to $60,000 in gold and silver. Then Aubry returned to

This photograph, taken during the 1890s, shows an old Indian house adjacent to the San Miguel Church in Santa Fe. This house was standing at the time F. X. Aubry made his unbelievable horseback ride from Santa Fe to Independence, Missouri. *Courtesy Kansas State Historical Society*

St. Louis in late August to pay his creditors. At twenty-two years of age, Aubry was a successful trader.

His success, however, only whetted his appetite. The following summer he led two of his own wagon trains to Santa Fe. He was becoming wealthy, but by the following winter Aubry was restless. He was impatient for success.

Aubry remained in Santa Fe spending much time talking with other traders. Although friendly, they made Aubry feel uneasy. He was still little Aubry and he was not treated as an equal. Meantime a large number of volunteer troops who had served in the Mexican War were discharged in New Mexico. Most were destitute of many articles of clothing. Stores were bare.

It was then that Aubry announced he would make three trips from Independence to Santa Fe that year, not the usual two. He would supply the goods that were needed.

Three days before Christmas, 1847, Aubry left Santa Fe for Independence with five horsemen, several mules and his black servant. An early start from Independence was a must if he was going to bring three trains through that season.

A few miles outside Santa Fe, Mexican bandits attacked Aubry's party and stole his mules. Determined not to turn back, little Aubry spurred his horse on. So did the others in his party, but they gradually dropped out. They couldn't keep up with Aubry and returned to Santa Fe.

Fourteen days later, on January 5, 1848, Aubry arrived at Independence. He organized a wagon train and bought merchandise. On March 16 Aubry and his train set out for New Mexico. It was the earliest anyone had ever left for Santa Fe with such a large train. Many persons predicted he would not make it. But Aubry did. He reached Santa Fe with the first merchandise that spring and it was quickly gobbled up. Little Aubry added to his wealth, and traders began to envy the little guy. They showed him new respect.

Aubry immediately prepared to leave for Independence to organize a second train. He knew his success depended on how fast he could get back to Missouri. He decided to go alone.

Sending four men ahead with relay horses, Aubry left Santa Fe on May 19. Shortly before dawn on May 28 he reached Independence. He made the journey in eight days and ten hours, a record for one man at the time. But he killed three horses and two mules, went for three days without food, slept only five hours on the whole trip and walked at least forty miles of the way. Still he averaged almost one hundred miles a day.

This second ride gained Aubry much attention, but he did not stop to enjoy it. He quickly organized another wagon train, bought goods and started for Santa Fe. He reached there in early August. There was still time to bring a third wagon train through. And it was then, as little Aubry was preparing to return to Independence by horseback that he heard others discussing his ride.

"I can do even better," boasted Aubry, betting one thousand dollars that he could make the ride in six days.

As related, Aubry proved he could. Commenting on his record ride, a St. Louis newspaper reported that "besides breaking down six horses and walking 20 miles on foot, he made the trip, traveling time only counted, in about four days and a half." Aubry averaged about thirteen miles an hour.

When Alexander Majors, the overland freighter, heard of Aubry's ride, he said, "Perhaps not one man in a million could have lived to finish such a ride." And years later, when William F. "Buffalo Bill" Cody was asked about Aubry's ride, he described the little man as superhuman. "Fifteen miles an hour on horseback will in a short time shake any man all to pieces," said Cody, whose story of riding 296 miles without stopping to rest as a Pony Express rider is detailed later.

Aubry's record has not been broken.

The little guy with the steel nerve received many honors for his ride. A new fast steamboat on the Missouri River was named for him. Later, an army post near present-day Syracuse, Kansas, was named in his honor.

During the three years that followed his most famous ride Aubry continued to send wagon trains to Santa Fe. His wealth increased. Then in 1852 the California gold rush drew him to the Pacific. He led ten wagons loaded with goods, a herd of 3,500 sheep and more than 100 surplus mules and horses to California. The following year he gathered 14,000 sheep and drove them to the booming California market. On his return trip to Santa Fe, Aubry pioneered a new route across the deserts and mountains, a route that a St. Louis newspaper described as "the best route which has yet been discovered for a railroad to the Pacific."

In a letter to a friend at St. Louis, Aubry wrote, "I am willing to travel in search of railroad routes, at my own expense, but am not sure that I shall live to see a road built."

Aubry did not.

When he returned to Santa Fe on August 18, 1854, he stopped at the cantina run by the Mercure brothers on the south side of the Plaza. Across the street, sitting on a tree-shaded plaza, was a Colonel Weightman who formerly edited a newspaper at Albuquerque. Seeing Aubry ride up, Weightman walked across the street and into the cantina where Aubry had gone to have a drink.

Inside the two men shook hands. Aubry invited Weightman to have a drink but the Colonel declined. The two men then began to talk about Aubry's journey to California. Soon Aubry began to discuss *Amigo del País,* the newspaper that Weightman had edited. Aubry asked Weightman what had happened to the newspaper.

"Amigo del País died for lack of support," replied Weightman.

"Well," said Aubry, "any such lying paper ought not to live."

At this Weightman asked what Aubry was referring to.

"Last fall you asked me for information about my trip and I gave it to you and you afterwards abused me," asserted Aubry.

"That's not so!" yelled Weightman.

Aubry brought his little fist down on the counter with much force and barked, "I say it is so!"

Weightman jumped down off the counter where he had been sitting and picked up a tumbler about one-third full of whiskey. He pitched the contents into Aubry's face.

What happened next was described by Henry Mercure:

"Weightman stepped back while Aubry was taking his pistol from his belt, a shot went off in the ceiling. Weightman walked up to Aubry. The two men seized hold of one another. I jumped over the counter and took hold of Weightman and my brother took hold of Aubry. Then I saw a knife in Weightman's hand covered with blood. I told him to let go and he said that Aubry was hurt. We parted them. Aubry fell in Henry Cuniffe's arms. Weightman went off."

Little Aubry died in the cantina about ten minutes later.

Weightman was arrested and tried, but a jury acquitted him saying he had acted in self-defense.

Aubry was buried in the Catholic cemetery in Santa Fe. A simple tombstone marked the grave in late August, 1854, but today there is no trace of that stone in the Rosaria Cemetery. No one knows for sure which grave is Aubry's. Time has eroded much, but so long as men have horses the story of Francis Xavier Aubry's ride of 1848 will live.

Windwagons and Samuel Peppard

When Samuel Peppard and his crew set sail in their windwagon in May, 1860, people at Oskaloosa in northeast Kansas, shook their heads. They called the windwagon "Peppard's Folly." Surely! they said, that strange-looking contraption would never reach the Rocky Mountains.

Would it?

And who was this character named Peppard?

Samuel Peppard was a millwright by trade. He was born in Wayne County, Ohio, in 1833. During the early 1850s he moved to central Iowa where he lived until 1856. Then, at the age of twenty-three, Peppard moved to Kansas, settling at Oskaloosa in Jefferson County. There Peppard established a saw and grist mill on a branch of the Grasshopper, now called the Delaware River.

After gold was discovered in 1858 at Cherry Creek in far western ·Kansas Territory—near present-day Denver—life became rather dull in Oskaloosa. And a drought the summer of 1859 made things even worse; why try to eke out a meager living from the parched soil when you could be striking it rich in the Kansas gold fields.

The call was "Pike's Peak or Bust."

Samuel Peppard and a few of his friends began to feel the gold fever. They talked about going to the Rockies. Peppard suggested they use a windwagon for transportation. At first his friends laughed, but the more they thought about it the better the idea sounded.

The idea of a windwagon—a wagon with sails pushed along by the wind—was not new. On the plains the thought of such transportation may have passed through the mind of Captain Meriwether Lewis when he and William Clark crossed the plains early in the nineteenth century. One of Lewis's boats, which was being transported on wheels, was blown along by the wind, the boat's sails being set. And by the 1840s, several writers who had crossed the plains had drawn an analogy between the winds of the ocean and the winds of the plains. Why not a sailing vessel on the plains. The winds are plentiful. Captain J. C. Frémont, who crossed central Nebraska during the summer of 1842, observed, "The place is celebrated for winds . . . they are terrible."

Just who first had the idea to use wind energy for locomotion on the plains is unknown. But one of the first men in the West to do more than think about such transportation was a fellow named Thomas who lived at Independence, Missouri, in 1846. His first name is unknown.

A Liberty, Missouri, newspaper reported in October, 1846, that "Mr. Thomas" was "building a wagon to run across the prairies to Bent's Fort, to be propelled by the wind." With masts and sails, Thomas said he expected his windwagon to run at fifteen miles an hour, and he added that he planned to "blaze the way" before the year's end.

But Thomas didn't meet his deadline. In April 1847, about six months later, an Independence newspaper reported that Thomas was still working on his windwagon and hoped to make an experimental trip on the plains with his "wind ship" very soon. Nowhere, however, can I find an account of such a trip during the late 1840s. It appears that Thomas did not raise sufficient money to construct his windwagon until about 1853. It was then that his windwagon was built at Westport, Missouri. Thomas supposedly sailed it southwest of there for about 100 miles over the Santa Fe Trail before returning to Westport.

Thomas then decided to raise funds to build an even larger windwagon. He succeeded but wrecked the windwagon on a trial run near Westport. Thomas's supporters pulled out from his scheme but Thomas continued to work on his dream of having a fleet of windwagons traversing the Santa Fe Trail with freight and the mail until about 1859. After that date I can find no reference to "Windwagon Thomas" in old newspapers and documents of that period.

In April 1860, the *Rocky Mountain News* in Denver reported the arrival there of three men in a "combined wind wagon and hand car." The newspaper reported the trip from eastern Kansas was made in twenty days, "thus equalling the speed of horse teams, with but a tithe part of the expense." But who these three men were is unknown. The newspaper failed to mention their names.

About the time the trio arrived in Denver, Samuel Peppard was nearing the completion of his windwagon at Oskaloosa, Kansas. With the aid of a few friends, he had started construction early in 1860. By early May of that year the windwagon was finished. It attracted much attention. A Topeka newspaper reporter, after inspecting the windwagon, reported:

> It is made of rough lumber and shaped like a skiff. It is eight feet long from prow to stern and three feet across amidships, and two feet deep. The bed was placed on a running gear with axles six feet apart, the wheels all the same size and about as large as the front wheels of a buggy.
>
> A ten foot mast was fastened to the front axle, and came up through the bottom of the wagon box, and to this two sails were rigged; the larger eleven feet by eight, the other seven by five. They were both to be worked by a rope through a pulley at the top of the mast. If the wind was high the smaller was to be used and if it was low, the larger was to be employed. The wagon had a brake and a rudder for steering. The hounds, instead of having a tongue attached, came up over the top of the bed and were welded together. A bar was fastened here and extended backward three feet. There was a seat placed at the end of the bar for the captain and he steered by pushing the bar to the right or to the left.
>
> The craft rigged out weighed 350 pounds, carried a crew of four men, a cargo of 500 pounds, a camping outfit and provisions serving as ballast.

On May 9, 1860, Samuel Peppard had the windwagon towed about a mile south of Oskaloosa. There, on a level stretch of ground, Peppard climbed aboard. He raised the large sail for the first test run of his windwagon. There was a good stiff breeze. When it caught the large sail the craft stuck its nose down near the ground and came near capsizing. But Peppard slacked the sail and set out again with the large sheet reefed and the smaller sail full against the wind.

Away the windwagon went. It traveled so fast, in fact, that the boxing in the wheels began to heat. Then the windwagon went over a little knoll of earth. It leaped about thirty feet into the air and came down with a crash.

The windwagon didn't move. It was damaged. But the damage was not serious and Peppard was not discouraged. He was learning how to handle his windwagon. Within a day or two the windwagon was repaired and Peppard, Steve Randall, J. T. Forbes and Gid Coldon then set sail for the Kansas gold fields. They carried with them 400 pounds of provisions, including a camping outfit, guns and ammunition.

From Oskaloosa, the travelers headed northwest until they reached

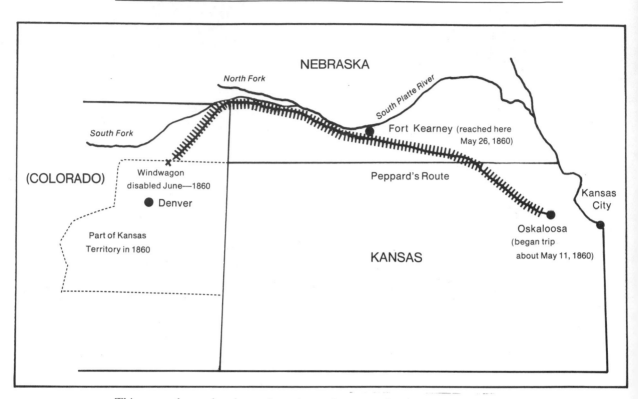

This map, drawn by the author, shows the approximate route believed followed by Samuel Peppard on his windwagon journey to the Kansas gold fields in 1860.

the Oregon Trail near the Little Blue River southwest of present-day Marysville, Kansas. At times the deep ruts in the trail helped the windwagon's travel. But most of the time Peppard found the best sailing on the open prairie parallel to the actual trail ruts. There was more room for maneuverability.

"Our best time was two miles in four minutes," recalled Peppard. "We could not run faster than that rate as the boxing would have heated. One day we went fifty miles in three hours, and in doing so, passed 625 teams. There were, you know, a great many people enroute to the gold fields in those days. . . . If we went ninety miles a day it was considered a good day's travel."

While there is little doubt that Peppard's windwagon did, at times, speed across the prairie, Peppard and his crew spent much time waiting for the wind. Of more than four weeks on the trail, the wind was favorable for travel only nine days.

"Many amusing incidents happened," wrote Peppard, "and we had no little fun joking the teamsters as we flew by them." But when the wind would drop off and the windwagon would roll to a stop, many a teamster joked of the "windless wagon."

The most humorous incident of Peppard's journey occurred five days after the windwagon left Oskaloosa. Peppard recalled:

It was about noon and we were traveling along probably at about ten or twelve miles an hour. The wind was blowing about 25 miles an hour but having been well shaken up by a rough stretch of the prairie, I had put on the brake and reefed my sail, so that we were journeying leisurely.

A cloud of dust attracted our attention in the southeast and we decided to stop and wait. We thought it was a band of Indians ... who would do us harm if we allowed them to overtake us. When we had finished our meal and smoked a pipeful apiece, the band of Indians had approached to within a mile of where we had stopped. Strange to say they had not yet seen us. I cannot account for this unless it was because we were in a depression of the prairie and were not noticed. We were thoroughly covered with dust and this served to make us the same color as the road.

Nor [sic] caring to have them approach too near, I let the brake partially off and again resumed our journey. When we came out of the low place, and I spread the sail, we could plainly see each Indian rise in his saddle with a start of surprise. As quick as a flash, each mustang was put into a gallop and the band ... was bearing down upon us. I knew that we could outrun them with ease and so I gave myself no alarm.

The wagon was just getting under way when snap went a bolt that held the brake. The brake was useless and the wind had risen until it was blowing thirty miles an hour. To give ourselves up to the wind with no means of checking our speed would be madness. To allow the Indians to catch us ... might result in our being personally molested. Time was precious. I again reefed the sail and bidding my companions to follow my example, I jumped to the ground and seized a wheel. The wagon stopped. I seized a halter or rope that we had picked up on the road, to bind the broken brake. It would serve the purpose. If the delay was not too long we could yet escape.

As quick as my hands would let me I made secure the brake and we were ready to start. The Indians were upon us, but fortunately, through suspicion and superstition, they had slackened their speed and were within one hundreds yards of us, advancing cautiously. This allowed me to give sail to the wind slowly and thus not wreck the wagon. A fresh look of surprise upon the faces of the Indians greeted our eyes as the wagon began to move and gradually increase in speed.

If the Indians had been curious at the appearance of the vehicle, they were now astonished at seeing it move. Just as they put their horses into a canter I released the brake and gave the full sail to the wind. Quick as a flash the little craft shot into the road and we were off at a pace of about thirty miles an hour.

The Indians, as it turned out, were not hostile. It soon became evident to Peppard and the others aboard the windwagon that the race was one of rivalry. The Indians were racing the windwagon. The swiftest Indian was riding a little gray mare. "She clearly outclassed the others and as she gradually drew away from them the race resolved itself into one with her alone. For about a mile we had a race that was exciting. The Indian leaned far over the mare and patted her neck. Again and again he called her name and urged her to catch the 'White man.' The mare was fleet but the race was ours," said Peppard.

But then the wind became stronger and Peppard was obliged to reef the sail to keep from being carried into the air. Soon he saw that the Indian's mare was weakening. In order not to outdistance the brave, Peppard applied the brake to slacken the windwagon's speed. Seeing this the Indian smiled. Peppard and his crew waved at the Indian, who was heard to say, "White man fly like bird!" The Indian turned back to rejoin his friends and the windwagon continued on its journey toward the Kansas gold fields.

Peppard appears to have followed the Oregon Trail to the Platte River and Fort Kearney in what is today south central Nebraska. On May 26, about fifteen days after leaving Oskaloosa, a correspondent for *Leslie's Illustrated* magazine was at Fort Kearney. Although he did not identify Peppard by name, he described what undoubtedly was Peppard's windwagon.

"The ship hove in sight about eight o'clock in the morning with a fresh breeze from east, northeast; it was running down in a westerly direction for the fort, under full sail, across the green prairie. The guard, astonished at such a sight, reported the matter to the officer on duty, and we all turned out to view the phenomenon. Gallantly she sailed, and at a distance on the far stretching level prairie, not unlike a ship at sea," wrote the correspondent.

He noted that the windwagon was "a very light built wagon, the body rounded in front, something in shape like a boat, to overcome the resistence [*sic*] of the air. The wheels are remarkably light, large and slender and the whole vehicle strongly built.

"Two masts, somewhat raked, carry large square sails, rigged like ship sails with halyards, braces, etc., etc. In front is a large coach lamp

This drawing appeared in *Leslie's Illustrated* magazine on July 7, 1860. It supposedly illustrates the departure of a windwagon from Fort Kearney, Nebraska Territory, on May 26, 1860. It is believed that an Eastern artist drew the illustration after receiving a written report from the magazine's correspondent in the West. Because the artist did not see the windwagon, the accuracy of the illustration is questioned by some. But the windwagon in question was undoubtedly Samuel Peppard's. *Author's collection*

to travel by night when the wind is favorable; and it is steered by a helm attached to the fore wheels. A crank and band wheels allow it to be propelled by hand when wind and tide are against them."

Peppard and his crew did not remain long at Fort Kearney. The captain of the windwagon, according to the correspondent for *Leslie's Illustrated,* gave "fabulous accounts" of the windwagon's speed, "asserting she had made 40 miles per hour." But the journalist was skeptical. He wrote that such a speed was "impossible as at one-half that rate of going she would have been torn to pieces." But the unidentifed correspondent added in his report to the magazine, "I timed her going two miles and with the moderate breeze at the time, she made it in little less than 14 minutes (about 8 miles an hour)."

As Peppard's windwagon was pushed from the fort, its departure was observed by the journalist, who later wrote, "Getting clear of the fort, she again caught the breeze, and went off at a dashing rate towards Pike's Peak. Stampeding all of the animals on the road, scattering the horses and mules, of the old fashioned sort of traveler ... to the right and left. And followed by the curses, both loud and deep, of the incommoded Pike's Peakers against 'that ere darn windwagon.' "

Peppard's windwagon followed the Platte River to near present-day North Platte, Nebraska. There the windwagon turned southwest following the south fork of the Platte. Crossing what is today the Colorado border near modern Julesburg, Colorado, the windwagon headed in a southwesterly direction passing near the site of where Sterling, Colorado, stands today.

The windwagon made good time as it blew on to a point not many miles southwest of present Fort Morgan, Colorado. Then the natural force that provided life to Peppard's windwagon intervened. About 50 miles north-northeast of Denver, Peppard and his crew spotted a dust devil approaching. They had encountered several on their journey. This time, as before, they prepared to lower the sail until the whirlwind was upon them.

"It required quick action and I made a mistake in my hurry that put the sail wagon past recall. The ropes that held the sail caught in the pulley. I gave it a jerk and it broke, leaving no means of lowering the sail. In an instant the whirlwind struck the wagon and carried it about twenty feet into the air. When the wagon came down it struck on the hind wheels and they broke down under the weight. By what seemed a miracle, none of us was hurt," recalled Peppard.

"By the time we had gathered ourselves together we were sur-rounded by travelers who extended us invitations for a free ride for the

This windwagon, perhaps inspired by stories of Samuel Peppard's adventures, was constructed in Logan County, Kansas, around the turn of the century. The men are unidentified, and the adventures of this particular windwagon are unknown. *Courtesy Kansas State Historical Society*

remainder of the journey. A baggage train was not far behind and we cast our lot with it," he said.

Thus ended a journey of more than 500 miles for Samuel Peppard, his crew and windwagon. What happened to the windwagon is unknown. It apparently was left on the plains to the elements. Peppard remained in the Rocky Mountains. So far as is known, he never found any gold, nor is there any record of Peppard ever sailing the plains again in a windwagon.

Less than two years later Peppard enlisted in Company C of the Second Colorado Volunteers and served the Union cause for more than three years. After the Civil War he returned to Oskaloosa, married, settled down and fathered thirteen children. In 1916, at the age of eighty-two, Samuel Peppard died. He is buried in Pleasant View Cemetery at Oskaloosa, Kansas.

Bill Cody and the Pony Express

It was about midday when the rider from the east came galloping into Red Buttes, just west of present-day Casper, Wyoming. The rider reined to a fast stop in front of a small log building, jumped from his horse and yanked the mochila (Spanish for knapsack) containing the mail from his saddle. He handed it to a tall and somewhat slight boy of fifteen years standing beside another horse. Without a word the boy threw the mochila over the stripped-down saddle on his horse, pulled his 100-pound frame atop the animal and rode off toward Three Crossings, seventy-six miles to the west.

The year was 1860. It was summer, and the boy was William Frederick Cody, Pony Express rider, who later became know as "Buffalo Bill." But young Cody had not yet been given the nickname. He would earn it nearly a decade later in Kansas where he would kill buffalo to supply workers building the Kansas Pacific Railroad with fresh meat.

The teenager who rode out of Red Buttes on that summer day in 1860 was no greenhorn. Three years earlier Cody had left his home near Leavenworth, Kansas, to take a job as messenger between wagon trains on the trail to Utah. In a short time he became a seasoned rider. From the experienced plainsmen he met, young Cody soon learned how to hunt buffalo, to fight Indians and to survive the elements on the open plains.

Bill Cody became a Pony Express rider at Julesburg in what is today northeastern Colorado, soon after the Pony Express began operation on April 3, 1860. The backers of the Pony Express, Russell, Majors

An artist's conception of a Pony Express rider crossing the plains. *Courtesy Kansas State Historical Society*

and Waddell, succeeded in cutting in half the twenty or more days it took the mail to reach California by stagecoach over the southern route via El Paso. The first westbound mail reached Sacramento in nine days and twenty-two hours.

But about two months after becoming a rider, Cody's mother became ill. Young Bill returned to Leavenworth and stayed with her until she recovered. He then rejoined the Pony Express at Red Buttes earning about fifty dollars a month plus board and room.

When Bill Cody left Red Buttes that summer day in 1860, he followed the trail southwest along the North Platte River near the northern edge of the Laramie Mountains. Soon he came to where the trail crossed the North Platte. In the spring the river was sometimes a half-mile wide as melting snow rushed downward from the mountains. But now it was summer and the flow was less. The water was not very deep as he urged his horse into the stream.

He had little difficulty crossing. Once on the other side he spurred his animal and galloped off. He had to average about fifteen miles an hour to maintain the established Pony Express schedule of ten days between St. Joseph, Missouri, and Sacramento, California.

Twelve miles from Red Buttes was Willow Springs. It was Cody's first stop to change horses. He made the switch in less than a minute—two minutes were allotted for changing horses—and hurried on toward

Horse Creek Station, fourteen miles away. The country was rough with low hills and buttes and some rolling plains. Most of the seventy-six miles between Red Buttes and Three Crossings were lonely. The country was unsettled. But young Cody didn't mind. He loved the thrill of racing across the open country carrying the mail including letters and telegraphic dispatches costing $5 a half ounce. The fact that his run from Red Buttes to Three Crossings was considered one of the most dangerous of the 1,838-mile Pony Express route was something he had accepted.

The cool dry mountain air brushed past young Cody's face as he galloped toward Horse Creek Station. There he paused only long enough to drink a dipper of cool water from a bucket and to throw his mochila on a fresh horse. Then off he went toward the next relay station, Sweetwater, twelve miles to the west. But Sweetwater Station had been abandoned a few weeks earlier for the summer months. Pony Express officials felt there was no need to man the station during the months of good weather. Therefore young Cody kept riding.

He passed near Independence Rock, a massive granite monolith, rising 193 feet out of the almost flat countryside. Hundreds of passing travelers had inscribed their names on the landmark that can still be viewed today. But Cody had no time to stop. He gave the huge landmark only a passing glance as he hurried by.

The mochila, under young Cody's weight, clung to the saddle. It

Rosa Bonheur's portrait of William F. "Buffalo Bill" Cody painted in 1889, about 30 years after he carried the mail for the Pony Express. *Courtesy Kansas State Historical Society*

was made of heavy leather, with a hole for the saddle horn and a slit for the cantle. Weighing less than thirteen pounds, it covered the entire saddle and reached halfway to the stirrups on both sides. On each of the four corners of the mochila was a stitched cantina or box of sole leather. Three of the cantinas were for the thrown mail carried from St. Joseph to Sacramento. The fourth was for mail picked up along the way. It was not locked as were the other three cantinas.

Near Independence Rock the trail left the North Platte and entered the valley of the Sweetwater River. Cody liked this portion of the trail to Three Crossings. Not only did it suggest to him that he was getting near the end of his run, but the countryside was beautiful. It was nothing like the dull arid country along the quiet North Platte River. "A perfect Naiad of the mountains" is one 1860 description of the Sweetwater River. The sound of its rushing waters was music to the ear.

But young Cody's galloping horse drowned out much of the Sweetwater's sound until Cody entered Devil's Gate. It was a gorge about 250 yards long, 40 to 105 feet wide, and from 300 to 400 feet deep, through which the Sweetwater River runs. There the sound of the rushing water could be heard above the sound of the horse's hooves.

A few miles on the other side of Devil's Gate was Split Rock Station, operated by a French Canadian by the name of Plante (sometimes spelled Plonte). There Cody paused to drink some cool mountain water and eat a piece of buffalo jerky. After transferring the mochila to a fresh horse, he rode off toward Three Crossings, fourteen miles away.

By now Bill Cody was getting tired. He had been in the saddle for more than four hours. But another hour and he would be at Three Crossings. There, the wife of the stationkeeper would have a hot meal waiting and there would be another rider to take the mochila on its westward journey.

Three Crossings was so named because the stream that followed the bed of a rocky canyon had to be crossed three times within a space of sixty yards. The water coming down from the mountains was always icy cold. The current was usually swift, deep and treacherous. The whole bottom of the canyon was often submerged making it difficult to cross, but young Cody, moving slowly, made each crossing without incident.

As the youthful rider rode into Three Crossings Station, the rider who was to take the mail on west was nowhere in sight. As Bill jumped to the ground, the stationkeeper, a man named Moore, told young Bill the bad news; the rider (one account says his name was Charlie Miller) had been killed the night before in a drunken fight with another man. There was no one to carry the mail west to Pacific Springs, 72 miles farther west. Although there would be fresh horses waiting at the relay

William F. "Buffalo Bill" Cody as he appeared many years after he carried the mail for the Pony Express. *Courtesy Kansas State Historical Society*

stations, each about 12 miles apart, the country was rugged. The trail led across South Pass, 7,500 feet above sea level.

Without any hesitation and aware of the risks involved, young Cody told Moore he would carry the mail. He appeared anxious for the added responsibility, perhaps to prove to himself and others that he had the endurance and stamina needed to make the ride. But he was hungry. He ran inside and gulped down the hot meal that had been prepared by Mrs. Moore. Meantime her husband placed the mochila on a fresh horse and held the animal in readiness just outside the door.

Minutes later Bill Cody emerged, jumped atop the fresh horse and headed west. The next station was Ice Springs, twelve miles away, named for an area where ice, a few inches below the top soil and heavy grass, was found the year round.

A quick change of horses at Ice Springs and young Cody hurried on to Warm Springs, a dozen miles farther west. There he changed horses in less than a minute and hurried off toward Rocky Ridge Station on the Sweetwater River.

William A. "Bill" Reid, stationkeeper at Rocky Ridge, was surprised to see young Cody carrying the mochila. Cody quickly explained what had happened as he transferred the mochila to the fresh horse that was waiting. In less than two minutes he left and rode off toward Rock Creek Station, twelve miles to the southwest.

By then the sun was setting behind the southern edge of the Wind River Range to the west. There was a chill in the air. And in the dim light of dusk the desolate country had a strange almost unfriendly appearance. But young Cody pushed on. He knew he could make Rock Creek Station within an hour. And he did.

In the faint light from a small lantern hanging outside the door of the Rock Creek Station, young Cody changed horses in less than a minute and hurried on toward the Upper Sweetwater Station, sometimes called the Burnt Ranch, twelve miles farther west at South Pass.

Now South Pass is not a pass but a wide level plain slightly tilted up on edge. Travelers scarcely know they are going higher in altitude because the climb from the east is so gentle. But to young Bill Cody, who had been over the route before, South Pass was something special. Crossing it gave him the feeling of having accomplished something special because it is the Continental Divide. Many motorists who travel Wyoming State Highway 26 over South Pass experience the same feeling today.

As young Cody crossed the divide, it also meant something else. Just two miles beyond was Pacific Springs Station, where relays for both stages and the Pony Express were kept.

It was about ten o'clock at night when Cody galloped into Pacific Spring Station, a small log shanty. He was on time and gave his mochila to a fresh rider who immediately rode west. Knowing that the eastbound mail would soon arrive and that he would have to carry it back to Red Buttes, Cody paused to eat. He had no more than finished the meal when the eastbound mail arrived. Young Cody put the mochila on a fresh horse and galloped east, back toward South Pass, Three Crossings and Red Buttes.

The return trip was uneventful. Bill Cody rode all night without a formal stop for rest. He averaged about 14 miles an hour. Early the following morning Bill Cody, weary and sore, rode into Red Buttes and gave the eastbound mochila to a waiting rider. Exhausted, he went to sleep. In about 21 hours and 40 minutes, young Cody had covered 296 miles. He had exhausted more than 20 horses, but the mail had gone through on schedule.

Years later, when press agents praised the accomplishments of "Buffalo Bill" as a Pony Express rider, they claimed that his ride was the longest continuous one in the history of the Pony Express, but Cody himself never claimed it was, and the facts show that other riders did better than Cody.

What may have been the longest ride was made in 1860 by "Pony Bob" Haslam during the Paiute War in Nevada. Indians killed a rider

An early Kansas artist's conception of the Pony Express stop and Overland Mail Office at Fort Kearney, Nebraska Territory, in 1861. The station was typical of many Pony Express stations along the route. Carl Bolmar drew this picture about 1901. *Courtesy Kansas State Historical Society*

and burned one of the relay stations. Haslam supposedly carried the mail 380 miles in about 36 hours. Some contemporary writers claim, however, that Haslam took an 8-hour nap somewhere along the route. Even so, it was quite a ride.

The next longest ride supposedly was made by Jack Keetley, who reportedly rode 340 miles in 24 hours. And next comes Howard R. Egan, who is believed to have ridden 330 miles in one day.

Yet of all of these rides, Bill Cody's is perhaps best remembered because of the fame he later earned as Buffalo Bill and the publicity he received. Yet the fact that a boy of fifteen years made such a ride is a remarkable feat in itself.

On October 24, 1861, the final link in the transcontinental telegraph was completed. In a matter of hours the Pony Express became obsolete. When it died, a California newspaperman wrote what might be described as its obituary:

A fast and faithful friend has the Pony been to our far-off state. Summer and winter, storm and shine, day and night, he has traveled like a weaver's shuttle back and forth till now his work is done. Goodbye Pony! . . . You came to us with tidings that made your feet beautiful on the tops of the mountains; tidings of the world's great life, of nations rising for liberty and winning the day of battles, and nations' defeats and reverses. We have looked to you as those who wait for the morning, and how seldom did you fail us! When days were months and hours weeks, how you thrilled us out of our pain and suspense, to know the best or know the worst. You have served us well!

The Battle of Coon Creek

The 71 young Missouri recruits shivered in the cold morning air. It was May 19, 1848, but the warmth of summer had not yet arrived on the bluffs above the Missouri River at Fort Leavenworth.

The young soldiers, mounted atop cavalry horses, were boys from the backwoods of Missouri. Most of them had never been far away from home before, but on this May morning they were leaving to reinforce the decimated ranks of the Santa Fe battalion then in Chihuahua, several hundred miles to the southwest.

Lieutenant William B. Royall, their commander, looked pleased as his command saluted the flag and turned into line and began to sing "Ho, for the Rio Grande." And no wonder. All 71 men had been issued new breech-loading carbines.

The rifles could be loaded and fired five times in a minute. The load of an ounce ball emerged as a slug when fired. And for 400 yards the slug could hold up its force.

Although his men were raw recruits, most had been raised on horseback in Missouri with guns in their hands. Their new carbines were like toys.

Lieutenant Royall and his column joined a larger force of 300 Illinois infantry recruits also heading toward what is today New Mexico. After crossing the Kansas River, the soldiers and troopers pushed southwest until they hit the Santa Fe Trail. This they followed to Council Grove, then the last settlement for travelers heading west over the Santa Fe Trail.

In Council Grove Lieutenant Royall and his men were given the job of escorting Major Thomas S. Bryant, a military paymaster, to Fort Mann, a rest stop and repair station midway between Fort Leavenworth and Santa Fe. The remains of Fort Mann are about four miles west of present-day Dodge City, Kansas.

Royall and his troopers were given the added job of escorting two wagon trains consisting of 60 wagons to Santa Fe. The wagon trains were owned by two men named Burnham and Fulton.

On June 5, 1848, Royall and his men left Council Grove with the paymaster and the 60 wagons and headed southwest following the Santa Fe Trail. Travel was slow. At best the long column averaged about 15 miles a day. But the late spring weather—clear blue skies and cool breezes blowing up from the Staked Plains of Texas—made the overland travel bearable.

The journey was uneventful until west of Walnut Creek where a battalion of U.S. Army artillerymen coming from the southwest joined Royall and his recruits. The artillery battalion—64 men with two six-pound cannons—had been ordered to accompany Royall and his men on their journey.

After crossing Coon Creek on the afternoon of June 16, the soldiers and freighters made camp for the night near where the creek empties into the Arkansas River. The campsite was about eight miles northeast of modern Kinsley, Kansas.

Tandy Giddings, an old plainsman traveling with the wagon trains, walked up to Lieutenant Royall as the sun was setting and said, "You'd better double the guards tonight."

"Why?" asked the lieutenant.

"Well sir, we haven't seen a buffalo for two days, and that's a sign there are Indians around."

Lieutenant Royall took Giddings's advice and posted an extra guard that night around the 60 wagons that had been placed in a circle. Nearby the soldiers had set up their tents. But nothing happened during the night. However, at daybreak, just as everyone was about to have breakfast, the soldiers heard what sounded like wolves. There were howls from the far side of Coon Creek, then from down near the river, and finally from the uplands on the side where the soldiers had pitched their tents.

"Look out, boys, I've heard them wolves many a time," shouted Giddings. "Them's Indians howling."

Moments later an immense herd of buffalo appeared on the uplands side stampeding straight for the soldiers' camp. For a moment, the soldiers forgot Giddings's warning. Some grabbed their carbines and prepared to "get some fresh meat for breakfast."

But Giddings yelled, "Hold on, boys, the Indians are behind them buffalo." The soldiers held their fire.

The buffalo kept coming, heading straight for the camp. As they neared, for some unknown reason they veered to one side, passing the soldiers' tents and circled wagons at a safe distance. Behind them, just as Giddings had predicted, came Indians mounted on horses charging forward.

As they came into full view, others appeared from two other directions charging toward the camp of soldiers and civilians. It was a war party of about 800 Comanches and Apaches that converged upon the 71 recruits, 60 artillerymen and perhaps 70 freighters. Holding shields made from the necks of bull buffalo, the Indians merged into one charging force. The soldiers opened fire.

These Indians had fought the U.S. Army before. They were used to drawing the soldiers' fire while at a pretty safe distance. Then, before the soldiers would have time to reload their muzzle-loaders, the Indians would swoop down and lance the troopers to death. But this time things were different. The troopers had their new breech-loading carbines.

As the Indians charged in for what they thought would be the kill, the soldiers opened fire again. There was a surprised look on the Indians' faces and some fell to the ground. The Indians withdrew, but soon they attacked again. The soldiers fired again. Not understanding how the soldiers could load and fire their rifles so fast, the Indians withdrew about half a mile from the camp. The soldiers could hear them shouting and yelling at each other.

Fifteen minutes passed. The soldiers and freighters waited. Then they saw the Indians preparing to charge again. When the charge came, the Indians were spread out in a line about 100 yards wide and 8 to 10 yards deep. In front of their line was a woman, an Indian Joan of Arc, who urged them on. She was dressed in red.

This time the Indians apparently thought they could drive the soldiers back to the creek bed, where other Indians were waiting. The ground between the soldiers and the Indians was clear. The Indians charged in their new formation, shouting with unearthly yells, their lances held high in the morning sun.

At 400 yards the soldiers fired, then again at 300 yards, at 200 yards and at 100 yards. But the Indians kept coming. Then someone yelled, "Shoot their horses." Everyone dropped his carbine to the level of the horses and fired. In an instant several Indian horses fell to the ground.

They were either dead or wounded. Those Indians behind the front ranks stopped, looked at the fallen horses and their horseless comrades scrambling to their feet.

The soldiers were relieved. And a few moments later Lieutenant Royall ordered his men to mount their horses. They would give chase. The Indians turned and retreated across Coon Creek and up one of the nearby sand hills. The Indians led the troopers up one hill and down another until suddenly the soldiers saw Indians moving toward them on two sides. It was a trap. The troopers retreated to the top of the small hill they had just crossed and prepared for battle.

One of the troopers, James H. Birch, who later settled in Plattsburg, Missouri, told how one of his fellow soldiers, Smith Carter, dropped his carbine during the retreat. When he started to get off his horse to pick up his weapon, the horse threw him.

"He was forced to follow on foot, with the Indians after him. He was a man and had sense enough, when the Indians dashed over him and attempted to lance him, to drop on the ground, and only received a bruise on the shoulder from the horse's foot," recalled Birch.

Nearby was Dave Rupe of Ray County, Missouri. He had been a hunter and still kept his old Missouri rifle with him to kill deer and antelope. Seeing Carter's danger, he turned his horse. The Indian came at him with his lance.

"Instead of having on a 'U.S.' belt, Rupe had on his hunter's belt, with a large iron buckle. The Indian's lance struck the buckle and the tongue held it. Rupe seized the lance with one hand and, drawing his holster pistol, blew the Indian's head off," wrote Birch many years later.

From the top of the hill the troopers began using their carbines. The firepower stopped the Indians. One of the last shots fired hit a beautiful iron-gray horse. As the horse fell to the ground the Indian rider tumbled to the ground. The saddle and bridle plainly showed that the animal belonged to an Apache chief, who started to retreat on foot. But just as quickly he turned, ran back to his fallen horse and attemped to remove the saddle. The troopers fired and the Apache chief fell dead.

Within a few moments a strange quiet swept the battlefield. The Indians who had survived the last charge viewed the soldiers from some distance as if trying to decide what to do next. Between the two forces were dead and wounded horses, perhaps 15, and the bodies of a few Indian warriors.

Suddenly a young Indian boy rode out from the Indian ranks to where the body of the Apache chief had fallen next to his iron-gray horse. The soldiers, admiring the boy's courage, held their fire. They could have killed the boy but they did not. The boy slipped a rope around the Indian's body and slowly dragged it from the field of battle.

The boy, according to legend, was called Goyakla or "One Who Yawns," by the Apache. But years later whites knew him as Geronimo, perhaps the most able Apache warrior who ever fought U.S. forces. The fallen chief was his father.

Soon after the boy returned to the Indian lines, it was obvious the Indians had little fight left in them. By then the artillerymen had their two six-pound cannons in position and fired toward the Indians. The Indians fled. And soon the troopers returned to where the freighters' wagons were circled. Later in the day they resumed their journey down the Santa Fe Trail.

The battle of Coon Creek was history.

Part II

BURIED TREASURE ON THE PLAINS

I have remarked that the stories of treasure buried by the Moors which prevail throughout Spain are most current among the poorest people. It is thus kind nature consoles with shadows for want of substantials.

—*Washington Irving*

The Big Springs Treasure

In that half-forgotten era,
With the avarice of old,
Seeking cities he was told
Had been paved with yellow gold,
In the kingdom of Quivera—

Came the restless Coronado
To the open Kansas plain,
With his knights from sunny Spain;
In an effort that, though vain,
Thrilled with boldness and bravado.

This is how Eugene Fitch Ware, the nineteenth-century Kansas poet known as "Ironquill," begins his poem *Quivera—Kansas*. Coronado's quest is well known. Many years ago I read somewhere that the wildest of all wild-goose chases in America's history was his search for the fabled Quivera, or Seven Cities of Cibola. The treasure-seeking Spaniards wandered over more than three thousand miles of unexplored land, much of it plains, in search of the cities where streets supposedly were paved with gold. As nearly everyone knows, Coronado failed to find them.

Today there are many legends of lost mines and buried treasures along the routes believed followed by Coronado and other Spanish explorers. Countless other treasure legends exist along the many other trails used by explorers, gold miners, outlaws, freighters, settlers and others who crisscrossed the old-time plains. If you search long enough, you probably could find at least one buried treasure legend for each county in every state from Texas northward to Canada and from the Missouri westward to the Rockies. And even that is probably a conservative guess as to the number of treasure tales that exist on the plains.

Most such legends have some basis in fact. Usually there is much logic connected with treasure tales—good reasons why the treasures probably exist. While many may be the result of wishful thinking on the part of lonely old-timers now long dead, others may be true. If they are, however, then treasure hunters face the likelihood that the gold or silver or whatever have been found and quietly converted into ready cash with which to make dreams come true.

One legend that has caused many men to dream of instant wealth is laid in the rolling countryside north of Big Springs on the old Oregon Trail in eastern Kansas. The community, first settled in 1854, was named for large springs that gushed from the earth in what became known as Big Springs. The cool water from the springs was reputed to contain medicinal qualities, but whether or not it did, we will never know. The springs dried up many years ago because of nearby land cultivation that caused a shift in the earth underground.

The legend of the Big Springs treasure was born, however, in a day when the cool water from the springs was plentiful and when countless travelers stopped to fill their canteens or water barrels on the long trek west or as they were heading back east after busting on the plains. Big Spring was then the only water stop between Lawrence and Topeka.

Like so many treasure legends on the plains, this one involves a wagon train supposedly laden with gold and a band of robbers. Tradition has it that six wagons were returning east about 1860 from the Kansas gold fields in what is today Colorado. The wagons and those men with them stopped for water at Big Springs, and it was there that a spy for a band of roving outlaws became interested in the tightly covered and heavily guarded wagons. The outlaw spy supposedly overheard someone say the wagons contained gold.

After learning the wagon train planned to camp for the night on the bluffs overlooking the Kansas River, a few miles north of Big Springs, the outlaw rode away to tell the gang. About dusk, as the men with the wagon train were relaxing with their evening meal, the outlaws attacked the camp. The party with the wagon train held off the robbers until after dark when the shooting ended for the night. At the first light of dawn the robbers overran the wagons only to find the travelers gone and their wagons abandoned.

Whether the men with wagons actually had any gold is unknown. According to tradition, however, there was gold and it was too heavy for the men to carry as they escaped under cover of darkness. Old-timers later claimed that the men buried the gold nearby before fleeing. What happened to the men who fled and who they were is still a mystery, but according to the legend the gold was buried on the steep, timber-covered hills to the north, along the Kaw or Kansas River bluffs a few miles north of Big Springs.

Many persons have searched for the gold including one early settler at Big Springs, the late Otto Durrow. In 1927, Durrow, then in his seventies, said he firmly believed that the treasure existed. Many times he used a magnetic needle in the area where he believed the fight occurred, but he died without finding any treasure. So far as is known, no one has ever found it.

The Du Pratz Gold Mine

A tale of lost treasure on the plains with a different twist is that of the Du Pratz gold mine. It takes its name from a map more than two hundred years old appearing in a book written by Lee Page du Pratz, a Frenchman. He was born in 1695 and later came to America where he lived for many years in New Orleans, then the capital of all of the vast territory called Louisiana. Du Pratz did some traveling up and down the lower Mississippi River, but he didn't venture too far from New Orleans. He was very interested in the territory of Louisiana, much of it unexplored, including the area of the Arkansas River. That stream starts in what is today Colorado and flows east across much of Kansas and then dips south into present-day Oklahoma. From there it runs through Arkansas joining the Mississippi about two hundred and fifty miles above New Orleans.

During the early 1750s Du Pratz wrote a book titled *History of Louisiana,* which was published in London in 1757. On a page of that book is a map, apparently drawn by Du Pratz or at least based on his information. On the map Du Pratz laid down the proper route of the Arkansas River from where it begins in the Rocky Mountains to the point where it flows into the Mississippi. At the point where the Little Arkansas River runs into the Arkansas River, Du Pratz lettered in the words "Mine d'Or." Translated from French to English, the words mean gold mine. The spot where the gold mine is pinpointed on the map is today near the center of Wichita, Kansas.

Unfortunately, aside from placing the gold mine's location on the

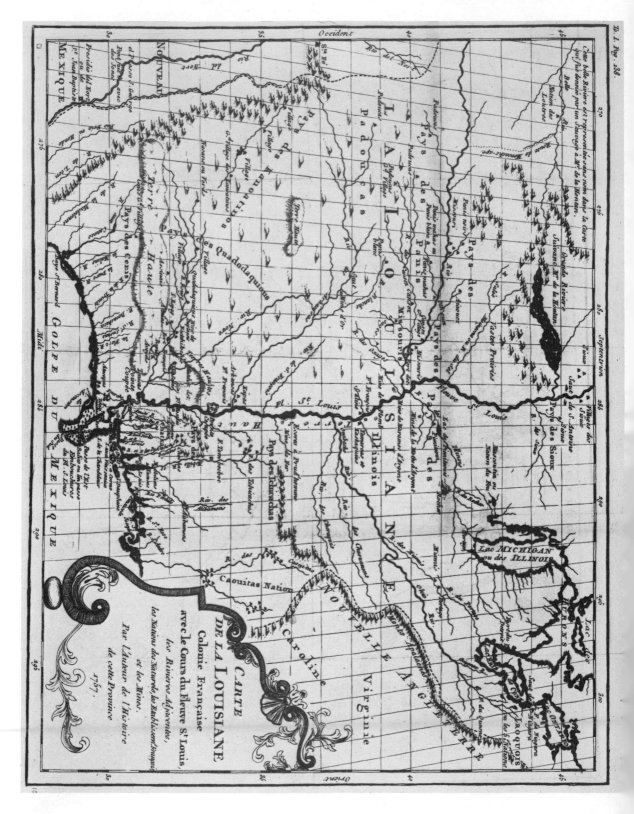

CARTE
DE LA LOUISIANE
Colonie Française
avec le Cours du Fleuve St. Louis,
les Rivieres Adjacentes,
les Nations des Naturels, les Etablissements François,
et les Mines;
Par l'Auteur de l'Histoire
de cette Province
1757.

map in his book, Du Pratz made little mention of the mine in his book. And nowhere have I been able to locate anything to suggest that a gold mine has ever been located at the junction of the Little Arkansas and Arkansas rivers. In fact, there is no record of gold having been mined anywhere in that portion of south central Kansas. There is not the slightest chance that gold ever existed in the ground there.

Since it is highly unlikely that a gold mine existed, Du Pratz's reference to a "Mine d'Or" suggests the possibility of a buried treasure. The most plausible answer to the puzzle seems to be a tale handed down through the years by persons in and around Wichita. Where and when it originated is unknown, but the late Jim Mead, a longtime resident of Wichita, wrote in 1909 that there was a tradition that long ago a party from New Mexico, descending the Arkansas River in boats, was surrounded by Indians in the night at the place where the two rivers join. After a siege of several days, all of the party were killed but one, who escaped after he had buried the party's gold and silver.

If one believes this tale to be true and the basis for Du Pratz's notation of a gold mine on his 1757 map, the treasure probably was

Jesse Chisolm, an early plainsman, who led the earliest known attempt to locate the reported treasure in 1836. *Courtesy Kansas State Historical Society*

Map of Louisiana Territory published in London in 1757 in a book written by Lee Page du Pratz titled *History of Louisiana.* It appears to be the basis for the legend of a gold mine at the junction of the Little Arkansas and Arkansas rivers in what is today Wichita, Kansas. At the point where the two rivers meet are the words "Mine d'Or." Translated from French to English, the words mean gold mine. *Courtesy Library of Congress* buried during the first half of the eighteenth century, between 1700 and 1750, and Du Pratz's source of information probably was voyageurs who had traversed the Arkansas River.

It is known that Du Pratz obtained much information about the territory of Louisiana from voyageurs who traveled the uncharted waterways to the north and west of New Orleans. Most of their information was apparently correct since Du Pratz's map is approximately correct on the location of rivers and streams, Indian villages and other prominent features. The map was a valuable aid to exploration and to the geography of the West when it was published.

The earliest known attempt to locate the treasure occurred about 1836 when Jesse Chisholm, a frontier trader, guided a party of white men up the Arkansas River in an attempt to locate the gold mine indicated on Du Pratz's map. There is no record that they found the mine, but Chisholm made his headquarters near the junction of the Little Arkansas and Arkansas rivers for many years afterwards. It should be noted that during the Civil War Chisholm operated a trading post there. After the war he blazed a wagon trail south from Kansas to the Red River. He died at Left Hand Spring near modern Geary, Oklahoma, in 1868, about the time the traders' routes across Indian Territory became the Chisholm Trail, used as a cattle highway by Texas ranchers moving their longhorns to railheads in Kansas.

Since Chisholm first sought the treasure about 1836, other men have searched for the mine or for buried treasure near the junction of the two rivers, but so far as is known no treasure has been found.

Don Antonio José Chavez's Treasure

Another treasure tale—this one without a map but with considerably more documentation than the Du Pratz gold mine legend—involves a fortune in gold and specie and perhaps some silver that tradition has it was buried beside a small creek in present-day Rice County, Kansas, about 1843. That was before the territory of Kansas had been established and when the Republic of Texas claimed part of what is today southwest Kansas.

Where the road to Santa Fe crossed the creek—it was later named Jarvis Creek for a man murdered on its banks in 1846—Don Antonio José Chavez reportedly buried a treasure. Alfred T. Andreas, in his monumental 1,616-page *History of the State of Kansas,* published in Chicago in 1883, provides one of the earliest descriptions of the legend that was told by old-timers in the area. Andreas wrote that the treasure consisted of "$25,000 in specie and gold," and he recounts the tale of how Chavez set out from Santa Fe in February 1843 with two wagons and five men, all Mexicans. The wagons were loaded with a small lot of furs that Chavez had obtained in trade with mountain men and perhaps Indians at Santa Fe. These he planned to sell for a nice profit when he reached Missouri. His wagons also carried the specie and gold and perhaps some silver that would be used to buy new merchandise at Independence, Missouri. He planned to carry the merchandise back to Santa Fe and sell it for a profit.

When Chavez left Santa Fe he had fifty-five head of mules. He used most of them to pull his heavily laden wagons. As the small party pushed eastward past the Great Bend of the Arkansas River, the weather became bitterly cold and a winter storm swept eastward out of the Rockies. Within a day or so all but five of Chavez's mules died from exposure. Chavez and his men barely survived in a makeshift camp established on the bank of what was to be known as Jarvis Creek. With only five mules, hardly enough power to pull one or even two of the heavy wagons, Chavez's party was stranded.

In camp Chavez and his men prepared to hold out until another wagon train would happen along. For safety, Chavez buried his treasure near the camp, not far from the little creek. How he managed to dig through the frozen earth to cache his treasure is unknown.

A day or so later the gray winter clouds began to disappear and the April sun appeared. Life began to look better to the Mexicans, especially Chavez. But without more mules the party and their cargo could go nowhere, and there had been no sign of another wagon train along the trail.

Early the next afternoon fifteen men on horseback rode into camp. They were Missourians—border ruffians—under the command of John McDaniel, who claimed to hold a commission as a captain in the Texas army. During this time the Republic of Texas was having increased difficulty with Mexico. McDaniel and his men—outside the law—were supposedly heading west to join forces with a Colonel Warfield who had been lurking along the Santa Fe Trail attacking Mexican caravans in the name of Texas, but who in truth was taking what he could get for himself and his men.

As McDaniel rode into Chavez's camp he saw that the freighters were Mexicans. Immediately he made the trader and his party captives. During the hours that followed the Mexicans were robbed. McDaniel's men divided their loot. It was then that seven of the Missourians, apparently of the opinion that they had had enough adventure on the plains, announced that they were going back to Missouri. When morning came they loaded their spoils on Chavez's five mules—part of their share of the loot—and rode east, back toward Missouri.

But McDaniel and the others remained in Chavez's camp. It appears that McDaniel believed there was more plunder to be had. Searching Chavez again he found some money hidden in his clothing, but it was a small sum. McDaniel apparently believed that a trader such as Chavez would be carrying a great deal of money with which to buy goods at Independence. Nearly all traders heading east did.

McDaniel again asked Chavez if there was any more money. Chavez refused to answer. At that, McDaniel beat him and tried to get Chavez to talk, but the old Mexican remained silent. A little later McDaniel beat the man again until finally Chavez admitted there was more money, but he refused to tell McDaniel where it was. For two days McDaniel and his remaining followers tried to get Chavez to talk. The

Mexican refused. As a last resort McDaniel decided to put a scare into Chavez. The Missourian lined up the five Mexicans in front of the old trader and one by one had them shot down in cold blood.

But the old trader refused to tell McDaniel where he had buried the treasure. McDaniel's men continued to search the area but found nothing. It was then that McDaniel lost his temper. He led Chavez to a nearby ravine that emptied into the creek. He asked the trader again where he had buried the money. Chavez refused to answer. McDaniel shot Chavez.

McDaniel and his men loaded the six bodies onto one of the wagons and pushed it into the creek. Then McDaniel and his men loaded their bloody booty on their horses and rode east, back to Missouri.

Whether one of McDaniel's men bragged about attacking Chavez's wagon train or whether one of Chavez's men survived the shooting is unknown. But not long afterwards John McDaniel was arrested in Missouri and taken to St. Louis charged with killing Chavez. While on trial, McDaniel disclosed the existence of Chavez's treasure, which he said had not been found. On that day the legend of the Chavez treasure began to grow.

McDaniel was convicted for the murders and hanged for his part in the crime. But others who had taken part in the killings escaped prosecution. During the years that followed it seems likely that they may have returned to search for the treasure.

One story told by the late M. F. Baker, an early pioneer in Rice County, described how a party of men—strangers in the neighborhood—camped on Jarvis Creek sometime during the late 1860s. They made camp on the spot where Chavez and his men had been killed. After they left, some residents of the area discovered that the straw floor of the strangers' tent site covered a deep pit. At the bottom, some of the residents claimed, was the imprint of a large iron kettle. Had the treasure been buried in a kettle? Others who saw the pit said there was nothing but shadows at the bottom, however.

Over the years other men, excited upon hearing the tale, have attempted to locate the treasure but without success. Old newspaper stories and still older verbal accounts handed down by old-timers place much stock in the fact that Chavez did have a treasure. It is a matter of McDaniel's court record in St. Louis. The treasure is believed to have been buried along the banks of Jarvis Creek, just north of the present-day community of Saxmon, about four miles southeast of Lyons, Kansas. But to this day, so far as is known, the treasure of Don Antonio José Chavez has never been found.

Jesus M. Martinez's Treasure

About a decade after Chavez supposedly buried his treasure on the plains, the captain of another Mexican wagon train became the subject for still another treasure legend along the Santa Fe Trail. It began on a late summer day in 1853 when Jesus M. Martinez's wagon train came to a halt on the sun-scorched plains just west of present-day Dodge City, Kansas. Martinez was captain of the train, described in one account as a small man with gentle eyes. He ordered his men to put their wagons in a circle and prepare to camp for the night. Soon the wagons were drawn into a tight circle and the Mexican freighters prepared for the evening meal. The men began to relax as the heat of the day gave way to the coolness of the evening.

Martinez, an old hand at taking wagon trains back and forth along the Santa Fe Trail, posted his usual guards against the three evils of the plains—Indians, bandits and prairie fires. Indians had been seen during the day at some distance, but Martinez did not worry. Indians had never bothered his trains in the past. And those he had seen off the trail that day did not appear to be hostile. Then too his wagon train was large. There were 120 wagons and 82 men, and each man was armed. It was like a small army.

Unconcerned about Indians, Martinez checked his wagons, especially the one that carried thousands of dollars in Mexican silver. It was secure. After checking the guards, Martinez went to bed.

The camp was peaceful until early in the morning when the moon climbed high in the night sky. It was then that freighters' dogs started barking. The guards saw the shadows of Indians not too distant from camp and immediately told Martinez. Being an old plainsman and understanding Indian tactics, Martinez ordered all of his men to prepare for an attack. Trenches were dug, dirt mounds were built and guns and powder were checked. Then the men waited.

As the first faint light of dawn could be seen in the east, the Indians—yelling and shouting—charged the camp from all sides. Martinez and his men were ready. They fired their weapons and Indians fell on the moonlit plain, some dead, others wounded. The other Indians withdrew to regroup. The Mexicans waited.

It was perhaps an hour before the Indians attacked. Through the morning and into early afternoon the Indians charged the camp at regular intervals, but each time Martinez and his men fought them off. The siege continued into the second night, then a second day and a third night. For five days the battle supposedly continued. Only a handful of Mexicans were killed or wounded during this time, but many Indians died.

By the sixth night the tired freighters were running low on ammunition. The Mexicans hoped the Indians—apparently they were Cheyennes, Arapahoes and Kiowas—would soon give up and leave. But the Indians didn't. Later that night the Indians made a massive and desperate attack on the camp. The freighters' powder didn't last long and soon the Indians overran the camp.

Every Mexican was killed, according to the legend, except Jesus Martinez. Under the cover of darkness he hid from the Indians as they pillaged the wagons and then set them afire. Just where Martinez hid is not told in this tale, but he didn't move until the first rays of morning light could be seen on the eastern horizon. When he crept out from his hiding place Martinez was alone with the dead. The Indians were gone.

As the sun began climbing into the sky Martinez thought of the silver. He searched through the charred wagons. To his surprise some of the silver remained. There were 21 small bags, each containing one thousand Mexican dollars. Martinez picked up a few of the bags and moved some distance from camp. There he dug a hole on the plains. Martinez made several trips back to the camp until all the bags were in the hole. Then he carefully covered them.

During the weeks that followed Jesus Martinez made his way back to his home in Mexico. According to the legend it was there that he told his son of the silver buried on the plains. On his deathbed Martinez described the spot where he had buried it. Martinez then died.

For several years young Martinez gave little thought to what his father had told him. But as he grew older and wanted the material things of life, he decided to go north to find the treasure. He made his way to Kansas. By then Fort Dodge and the town of Dodge City had been built. It was the early 1870s. The young Mexican revealed the secret of the buried silver to two men in Dodge City, one of whom agreed to help young Martinez search for it.

The site of the wagon train massacre was located about four miles west of the town of Dodge City. Pits and dirt piles were still plainly visible in the area even early in this century. Using a sharpened wire young Martinez spent days probing the plains around the site but his patience ran out. He could not find the silver. He did, however, discover the bottle in the several saloons near the military post. He became a hard drinker and eventually returned to Mexico a broken man.

So far as is known, he never returned to Kansas. Somebody may have long since found the 21 bags of Mexican silver dollars, but there's always the chance that they are still buried on the plains west of Dodge City, Kansas, waiting for someone to uncover them.

The Dutch Oven Treasure

Still another treasure tale dating back more than a century ago when the Santa Fe Trail was America's nineteenth century superhighway, is set in modern Edwards County, Kansas, a few miles southwest of the small community of Kinsley. But aside from sketchy stories, handed down from generation to generation, there is little documentation to back up the tale.

The story began in 1851, long before Edwards County was settled. A small wagon train of emigrants were returning east from the California gold fields. They had struck it rich and were heading home, perhaps to Missouri, Indiana or Ohio, to make their dreams come true. When their lumbering wagons reached the Arkansas River a few miles south of where Offerle, Kansas, stands today, they camped for the night on the south side of the river. Their camp was on what became the Lightner Ranch. Still later the ranch was owned by a family named Taylor.

Early the following morning as the travelers were preparing to break camp, one of their party saw Indians approaching the camp on the treeless plains. Fearing the worst, the travelers forded the Arkansas River. Once on the other side they prepared to do battle. And they buried their gold in a Dutch oven under a small tree.

The worst happened. The Indians, who outnumbered the travelers, swept down on the camp, thundered across the river and killed all of the travelers except one. The lone survivor was an eight-year-old girl, who was taken captive.

What happened to the little girl is unknown. But because of later events, she apparently survived. About 1918 a woman arrived in Kinsley, the county seat of Edwards County. She hired a local taxi driver, Lee Smith, to drive her in his Maxwell south of Kinsley to the Arkansas River. On the river the woman kept looking at maps and checking a notebook she carried.

The woman knew exactly where she wanted to go and directed Smith to where the old Santa Fe Trail crossing had been located. Smith was not too thrilled with his passenger who insisted he drive his Maxwell through the sand to the riverbank. The car got stuck several times. But once there she convinced Smith to ford the river with her. Once on the other side she located several mounds of earth about seventy-five feet beyond the crossing.

Pointing to the mounds, she told Smith she believed people murdered in an Indian raid on a wagon train many years earlier were buried there.

Smith, still in the dark about what his passenger was doing, began to question her. She told him only that she lived in the East and was a relative of some person who had escaped the massacre. The woman spent some time looking over the area but, according to Smith, made no attempt to dig anywhere. Later he took her back to Kinsley and never saw her again.

So far as is known, the woman never returned to Edwards County. And no one has ever admitted finding the treasure if one existed. Old-timers say a young boy once found a gold wedding band buried in the sand near the crossing. But it is doubtful that the ring was worn by one of the women massacred. Indians usually stripped their victims of all such jewelry.

The strongest evidence that a wagon train was destroyed at the crossing was turned up many years ago by Wilbur Oliphant, who once lived and worked on the Lightner Ranch. One day he went to a sand hill close to the Santa Fe Trail crossing on the Arkansas River. As he dug a hole to bury a dead horse, he found the remains of old wagons, the iron parts including wheels, rims and frames. There is little doubt they were the remains of a destroyed wagon train. But Oliphant did not uncover a Dutch oven filled with gold.

The tale of the Dutch oven treasure remains just that—a tale.

The Nemaha River Treasure

It wasn't too many years ago that the Nemaha River two miles north of Seneca, Kansas, made a wide bend. Then some men who didn't like nature's way blasted a new channel out of the earth for the Nemaha. Today the river does not make the wide bend it once did. Instead, it runs straight north and south. But one thing didn't change and probably couldn't is the flow of the water. The Nemaha is one of the few rivers in Kansas that flow north.

Although the old riverbed is still visible, it is gradually filling in. The old riverbanks, where the bend once curved like a silver dollar, are not as easy to recognize today as they once were. Many of the landmarks including the huge trees that once lined the river's banks are gone. Many were cut down for wood. Others simply died. Man's efforts and the passing of time have changed the landscape considerably and have created problems for treasure hunters who still, from time to time, seek what has become known as the Nemaha River treasure.

In 1855, according to the legend, two young Argonauts returning to their homes in Massachusetts buried a powder can full of gold for safekeeping while they went into the small settlement of Richmond, Kansas Territory, for supplies. But before they could dig up their fortune and continue their journey east, one was killed in a fight with two ruffians and the other fled for his life and never returned.

Many persons have tried to locate the gold, but none have apparently succeeded. Jay Adriance, the longtime editor of the *Seneca Courier-Tribune,* told me in 1971 that "over the years a number of people have come to Seneca, some with detection equipment, but so far as I know no one has never found anything."

Adriance put me in touch with A. J. "Tony" Wempe, then in his eighties, whose cousin, the late C. H. Wempe, owned the land where the treasure supposedly was buried. Tony Wempe had lived in Seneca since 1892.

"I've never put much stock in that legend. Many times folks have looked for the treasure but found nothing. I believe it's just somebody's wild-haired idea. I can't believe anything else, it's just a legend," said Wempe.

Yet treasure seekers have trampled over the area about two miles north of Seneca on and off for more than fifty years. "It's mostly outsiders who come," Adriance told me. "The attitude of most folks around here is that if there was a treasure, someone has probably found it by now."

Adriance, who was editor of the Seneca newspaper from 1930 until 1970, said that over the years many of the treasure hunters would stop by the old newspaper office and ask to see an article published by the *Courier-Tribune* in its 75th anniversary issue on December 12, 1938. The article, the basis for much of the legend, was written by the late W. F. Thompson, a well-known Seneca businessman, who in 1920 moved to Topeka, Kansas, where he later died. What follows is Thompson's story:

The year was 1849. Gold was discovered in California, and among the early forty-niners who headed west to make their fortune were two young men, both twenty-three years old, from Boston. Just who they were is unknown. For nearly five years they panned for gold and gradually their patience was rewarded. They accumulated a fortune in gold, but talk of home and memories of loved ones in the East brought renewed attacks of homesickness. In the spring of 1855 they decided they had enough gold and prepared to return home.

Buying a wagon, team and supplies, the two young Argonauts joined a caravan of freighters for protection and company and slowly began the two-thousand-mile journey east. From California to Julesburg in what is today northeastern Colorado, the journey was calm except for a few scares from Indians and delays caused by large herds of buffalo crossing the trail. By the time the wagon train pulled into Julesburg the young men were more anxious than ever to reach home. Then too they didn't like the gambling and drinking going on, and they began to have suspicions about two ruffians—gamblers, hard drinkers and fellows rather handy with their guns. It appeared the ruffians suspected the two young men were carrying gold.

It was then the young Argonauts decided to go it alone the next five hundred miles to the Missouri River. With their wagon loaded lightly, they quietly left Julesburg without telling anyone. Not too many days later they reached the settlement of Richmond on the west bank of the Nemaha River. Now in 1855 Richmond was only a few months old. It was the trading center for the area, but the town consisted of only a dozen shacks. Most were used for eating houses, saloons and gambling, but one was a combination store, saloon and gambling hall.

It was late on a Saturday afternoon when the two young men in their wagon passed through Richmond, forded the Nemaha River and set up camp on the east bank. As soon as it was dark they buried their powder can filled with gold. They did not want to leave the gold unguarded in the wagon when they went for supplies.

According to the legend, they selected a site "across from a big tree which might have been an oak, elm or cottonwood." The tree was on the west bank "in direct line with the rays of light shining from the window of the saloon to the place on the east bank where they buried their gold."

Once their treasure was covered with dirt and branches, they forded the river and walked the short distance to Richmond's only store to replenish their supplies. They made their purchases and were about to leave when two men emerged from the store's back room where the saloon and gambling hall were located. They were the same two ruffians whom the young prospectors had fled from at Julesburg. The two ruffians had been drinking.

When they saw the Argonauts they tried to stop them from leaving. Fists flew and then a gun flashed, the shot reverberating inside the small frame building like a clap of thunder. One of the young men from Massachusetts fell to the floor mortally wounded.

What happened next is unclear, but the lights in the store went out. The surviving Argonaut fled. He made his way to his team and wagon, hitched them up and fled east leaving the gold buried in the ground where he believed it would be safe. By noon, two days later, he reached St. Joseph, Missouri. Why he didn't get help and return to Richmond is unknown. It may have been that he felt his life was more important than the gold. Regardless, he returned to Massachusetts.

The years passed quickly. He married his dead partner's sister, but for some unknown reason he kept putting off a return trip to Kansas to reclaim the gold. Then the Civil War broke out. He answered the call and enlisted. Before saying goodbye to his wife and two baby sons, he drew a map showing the location of the buried gold. Should he not return, he told her, his wife and sons could locate the gold.

He did not return. The man died in battle and his widow reared

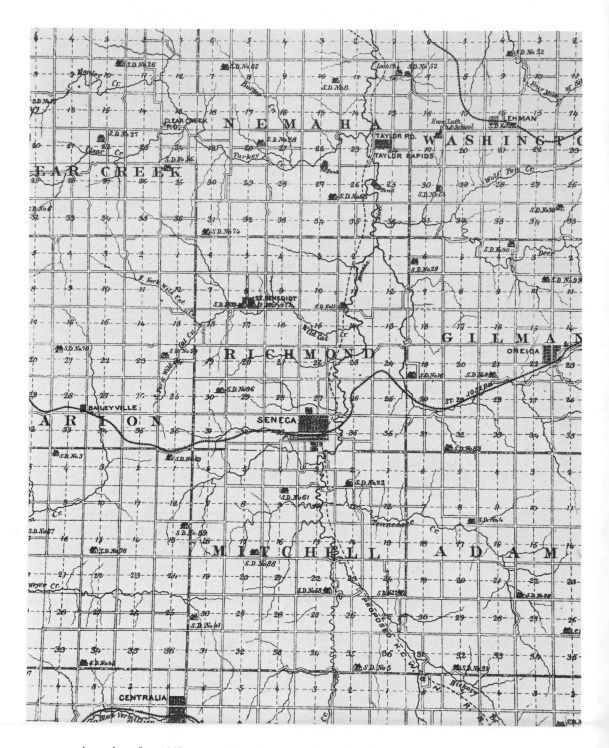

A portion of an 1887 map of Nemaha County, Kansas. The approximate location where the legendary Nemaha River Treasure supposedly was buried lay between the letters N and D in the word RICHMOND just above the town of Seneca. *Courtesy Kansas State Historical Society*

and educated his two sons. The years moved slowly. She made no effort
to recover the gold, but in 1883 the sons, grown to manhood, set out for
Kansas with their father's map to find the treasure. With the help of old
settlers, they located the site of old Richmond about two miles north of
Seneca. An abandoned well was the only visible landmark. The timber
had been cleared off and the land on both sides of the river was in
cultivation.

With bayonets they prodded the ground trying to locate the
powder can. They spent several weeks going over every foot of the
ground where they thought the gold was buried, but they did not locate
it. Tired, discouraged, with hands that were blistered, they gave up and
returned home.

The tale might end here, but it does not.

Twenty-two years later, in 1905, W. F. Thompson became involved
in the search for the treasure. On a hot, sultry afternoon in August, a
prosperous-looking old gentleman walked into Thompson's real estate
office at Seneca carrying a large leather handbag. Thompson greeted
the man thinking him a prospect.

"You are Mr. Thompson?" asked the man.

"Yes," was the reply.

"In the real estate business?"

"Yes sir," said Thompson.

"Know the country pretty well, I suppose?"

Thompson said he did.

At that point the elderly gentleman asked to speak to Thompson in
private. The door was closed and the elderly man introduced himself.
His name was William Davis Ripey. He had amassed a fortune years
before in the overland freighting business between points in Missouri
and Salt Lake City.

During that August afternoon, as W. F. Thompson later recalled,
"Mr. Ripey told me a lot of very interesting history of the early days on
the plains, some of which was entirely new to me. He told me how he
and his wife had made their wedding trip with a train of freight wagons,
camping over Sunday at a ford on the Nemaha River near a place
called Richmond."

Thompson learned that Ripey and his wife had been camped
beside the Nemaha River across from Richmond the night one of the
young Argonauts had been killed at the store. Ripey had met the two
young men earlier in the day when they were setting up their camp.
Years later he had located the two sons of the lone survivor and had
learned of their fruitless search for the lost treasure.

Ripey told Thompson that after the sons failed to find the gold, their mother had sold the map to him provided they would get a share of the treasure should Ripey find it. "The country has changed so much in nearly sixty years since I camped at the ford at Richmond, I am not sure I would be able to find the place. I believe I can trust you and I want you to help me. Will you do it?" asked Ripey.

"I assured him I would," said Thompson, "providing we first get the consent of the owner of the land. Mr. Ripey strenuously protested against any publicity." But Thompson told him how the owner of the land had posted notices in the local papers warning that all trespassers would be arrested. "This he had to do for protection of his place because it had been over-run with prospectors after the young men had given up their search many years earlier, said Thompson.

Ripey finally agreed and the two men drove north from Seneca late in the afternoon. "We left the car by the roadside and started out on foot, as near as possible along the old trail leading across a field to the ford. We located the ford but there was nothing in evidence whereby we could locate the camping site of his honeymoon trip. It was a real disappointment to the old man," said Thompson.

The two men returned the next day after getting permission from the land owner. But they found nothing. Ripey left town the next day only to return again several weeks later. He searched again without finding the gold.

"The vanishing of Richmond, removal of timber along with re-peated floods of more than half a century had changed the countenance of the earth so much that both of us were at a complete loss to find anything we could recognize. Not willing to give up, Mr. Ripey planned to return at some future time for another effort. This, age and Father Time prevented," said Thompson. Ripey died not long afterwards.

That is the story told by W. F. Thompson in 1938.

Many attempts have since been made to find the treasure, but all have apparently been unsuccessful. Yet about 1955, C. H. Wempe, who then owned the land where the gold supposedly was buried, said he had found a freshly dug hole near the river. He speculated that someone had found the gold. But Jay Adriance said many people at Seneca suspected that Wempe made up the story to discourage treasure seekers from trespassing on his property. If that was the case it did not work. They kept coming.

The only gold known to have been found in Nemaha County was located in 1917. Two gold nuggets were discovered in the craws of ducks being dressed for eating. One nugget, weighing two and one-half grains, was discovered by Mrs. G. W. Potts. The other—its weight is unknown—was found by Frank Wikoff. Both ducks came from the G. W. Potts farm near Oneida where the birds had roamed beside nearby Harris Creek.

It is doubtful that the gold found in the ducks was from the buried powder can. Even if a flood had washed the can into the river and had broken it open, it would have been impossible for the gold to have been washed into Harris Creek. That creek runs north joining the Nemaha River at a point about five miles north of Seneca. The gold would have had to wash upstream against the current of Harris Creek for several miles to the Potts farm.

It is possible the gold nuggets were lost in the creek during the 1860s when a prospector drowned. He was returning east from the gold camps near Black Hawk, Colorado, at the time.

Certainly the possibility exists that someone found the buried gold many years ago and never reported the find. And there is always the possibility that no treasure exists. Yet the legend persists. Only time and the river know the secrets of the mystery of the Nemaha River treasure, and they will not tell.

Part III

THE LAWLESS AND LAWMEN

Where law ends, there tyranny begins.

—William Pitt

The Man Who Really Tamed Abilene

Anyone acquainted with the American Wild West has heard the name "Wild Bill" Hickok. James Butler Hickok gained an exaggerated reputation on the plains during the last century, thanks in part to Colonel George Ward Nichols, who wrote an article about Hickok for *Harper's Monthly* in 1867. It helped to make Hickok a legend in his own time. When "Wild Bill" was killed at Deadwood in Dakota Territory in 1876, the Hickok legend clearly included the statement that he had killed one hundred men during his lifetime. But my good English friend, Joseph Rosa, an authority on Hickok's life, has only been able to document that "Wild Bill" killed about seven men, and in each instance, according to Rosa, Hickok was provoked.

An unduly emphasized part of the Hickok legend includes many stories about his days as marshal of Abilene. Few persons realize he served in that position only about seven months, from the middle of April until mid-December in 1871, when he lost his job because the Texas cattle trade had moved elsewhere. Yet the legend persists that it was Hickok who tamed Abilene, but the facts prove otherwise. The man who really did the taming was a tall good-looking man in his twenties, perhaps early thirties, with broad shoulders, auburn hair and a light mustache. His name was Thomas James Smith.

Tom Smith rode into Abilene on a bright and warm day in late May of 1870. He had heard that Abilene needed a marshal. The town was growing fast in a cattle boom that had been touched off by the arrival of the Union Pacific Railroad three years earlier. Soon after the

This nineteenth-century drawing supposedly shows a Texas herd of long-horns owned by a Colonel Wheeler being driven toward Abilene, Kansas. *Courtesy Kansas State Historical Society*

Marshal Tom Smith of Abilene. This photo was taken during the early 1870s. *Courtesy Kansas State Historical Society*

railroad had arrived, Joseph G. McCoy of Springfield, Illinois, had built cattle pens and established Abilene as a market and shipping center Texas longhorns, worth $2 to $4 a head in Texas, brought $20 to $40 in Abilene. This was reason enough for Texas cattlemen to make the long trail drive overland to the railroad at Abilene, a journey of four hundred to six hundred miles over what became known as the Chisholm Trail.

Almost overnight Abilene's log and mud huts had given way to frame buildings on both sides of the railroad tracks. By May 1870 when Tom Smith arrived, two Abilenes had emerged. North of the Kansas Pacific tracks was "Kansas Abilene" and south of the tracks was "Texian Abilene"—the hotels, saloons, cattle pens and the houses of pleasure. The main thoroughfare in the "Texian" area was Texas Street.

Tom Smith rode to the office of Mayor Theodore C. Henry and applied for the job of marshal. Some persons including T. C. Henry have claimed that Smith was the celebrated "Bear River" Tom Smith who more than a year earlier led a riot at Bear River, or Bear Town, Wyoming Territory, in November 1868. A story in the Utah *Desert News* December 24, 1868, however, observed that "Tom Smith, the leader of

T. C. Henry, mayor of Abilene, the man who hired Tom Smith as marshal. *Courtesy Kansas State Historical Society*

the riot was sent to the Salt Lake Penitentiary" raising doubts that the Abilene Tom Smith was in fact "Bear River" Tom Smith. T. C. Henry claimed that Smith had been born in New York about 1849, where he supposedly served as a policeman for a short time. Henry added that Smith later served as town marshal of Kit Carson, Colorado, before coming to Abilene.

Regardless of Smith's background, the two men talked. Henry then told Smith he would discuss the job possibility with the town's trustees. Henry did, but two days later the trustees rejected Tom Smith's application, saying they did not know him well enough to put the town in his charge. The truth was that T. C. Henry had another plan in operation. Several Abilene men had tried to bring law and order to their town. All had failed. By May 1870, the town was wide open. Texas cowboys did what they pleased. Ordinances passed by the town's trustees could not be enforced. Seeking outside help, Henry had contacted the chief of police at St. Louis, who had suggested two former soldiers as marshals. Henry had already asked the men to come to Abilene.

They arrived one afternoon soon after Tom Smith had left Abilene to go to Colorado Territory. The soldiers spent the afternoon and evening looking over Texas Street. The Texans, however, had learned they were coming and had provided "special deviltries" to discourage them. The two former soldiers reportedly left Abilene on the midnight train without saying goodbye to Mayor Henry.

Delighted by the turn of events, some Texas cowboys decided to tear down a small stone jail that was nearing completion on Texas

Street. The jail was rebuilt, under a day-and-night guard, in time to house a Negro cook from a cattle camp. While drunk, the cook had shot out some streetlamps.

The Texas cowboys resented the indignity. They chased the guards away, shot the lock off the jail door and released their cook. Before riding out of Abilene, they ordered all business houses to close. Then, to the Rebel yell, the cowboys rode down Texas Street, buried a few shots in some of the buildings and headed for their camp outside town.

The residents of Abilene were mad. They had been openly defied again by the Texans. A few of the braver citizens armed themselves with pistols and rifles, got their buggies and saddle horses and went after the Texans. The townsfolk arrested a few Texans but the ringleader and the cook were not found. The citizens of Abilene had lost another round. Mayor Henry was under pressure to act.

The town's trustees held an urgent meeting. They agreed to offer Tom Smith the marshal's job at $150 a month plus $2 for every arrest he made. Mayor Henry telegraphed Smith, locating him at Ellis, Kansas, on the road to Denver. Smith returned to Abilene.

It was the morning of June 4, 1870, when Tom Smith arrived back in Abilene. Mayor Henry immediately made a clean breast of everything. Henry told Smith to look around Texas Street. If he still wanted the job, to come back and they would "do a little figuring."

Smith returned to Henry's office late that afternoon. Standing in the office doorway, Smith said he had looked around. "I haven't seen

A nineteenth-century Eastern artist's idea of life in an early Abilene saloon.
Courtesy Kansas State Historical Society

"DANCE-HOUSE."

anything much different from what I expected," he said.

"You mean you will take the marshal's job? Do you think you can control the town?" asked Henry.

"I think it can be done," replied Smith, whose conversation with T. C. Henry was recorded for history by Stuart Henry.

The two men discussed the lawlessness. Smith asked about an ordinance against arms being carried in Abilene. Henry said it was still in effect, but "the Texans won't disarm."

"We might as well try to take away their wives—if they had any—as their six-shooters. We posted the ordinance. They tore it down—shot bullets through it. To try to insist would bring on just the trouble we're trying to keep out of. We don't want to force impossible issues," said Henry.

Smith thought for a moment. Then he looked squarely at Henry. "Post up the ordinance again ordering every person to disarm on coming to town and staying disarmed while here," said Smith in his quiet but firm voice.

Mayor Henry looked at Smith with surprise. Was Tom Smith insane?

"You . . . don't . . . think . . . that . . . necessary?" asked Henry, somewhat bewildered.

Smith looked Henry squarely in the eyes and replied, "Nobody can handle this town if the cowboys go armed. When they drink, they think only of shooting. If they have nothing to shoot with, their drinking and gambling won't hurt much."

Mayor Henry thought for a moment and said, "All right. You can have new copies of the ordinance from the printer tonight for posting. You can have anything you want if you're sure you control the trump suit."

Henry turned, stepped inside his office and found a Bible.

"I guess there's nothing to do now but swear you in," said Henry, standing in the doorway of his office with Smith standing just outside. Tom Smith raised his right hand, put his left hand on the Bible and the mayor pronounced the formal words.

"This is a grave moment for me as well as you," said Henry. "I'm giving the town over to you. But I'm betting on you—that's all."

Mayor Henry pinned the silver badge on Smith and they shook hands. Smith turned, swung himself atop his horse and rode off in the direction of Texas Street.

The citizens of Abilene awoke the next morning to find the ordinance against carrying weapons posted all over town. Smith had not only tacked them up on buildings along Texas Street, but he had convinced the town's hotel proprietors that it was financially in their interest to help enforce the ordinance. They cooperated and posted a notice that read: ALL FIREARMS ARE EXPECTED TO BE DEPOSITED WITH THE PROPRIETOR.

Employing the same logic, Smith convinced the storekeepers and saloonkeepers to do the same. As one Abilene resident later remembered, "These proprietors, one after another, agreed to keep charge of the firearms of their customers and even invite such action. They saw in it an advantage in holding trade. Texans would deal where their weapons could be claimed."

It was not long before Tom Smith had his first showdown. It was with a cowboy called Big Hank, who was very obnoxious and constantly boasted that no one could disarm him. Wearing his revolver, Big Hank approached Smith and asked him if he was the man "who proposed to run the town."

Smith replied quietly that he was the marshal and that he would try to maintain order and enforce the law.

"What are you going to do about that gun ordinance?" asked Big Hank.

"See that it is obeyed," said Smith, adding, "I must trouble you to hand me yours."

"To hell I will," said Big Hank.

Smith again asked for Big Hank's weapon and was met with profanity and abuse.

In a flash Tom Smith sprang forward and struck Big Hank with his fist, grabbing the cowboy's pistol. Smith then ordered Big Hank out of town.

As Mayor T. C. Henry later recalled, "The news of this encounter ... was heralded over a radius of many miles. The unique punishment employed was wholly new to cowboy warfare, and every phase of the combat was debated. In a camp on a branch of Chapman Creek a wager was laid by a big burly brute that he could go to town and defy the surrender of his gun. Promptly next morning, a Sunday, Wyoming Frank was on hand to fulfill his boast."

But Wyoming Frank had to wait. As he grew impatient waiting for Marshal Smith to appear on Texas Street, he went into one of the saloons and began drinking. When the marshal had not arrived by midmorning, Wyoming Frank began to brag that the marshal had probably heard that he was in town and "had lighted out."

It was late morning when Tom Smith came slowly down the middle of Texas Street. Wyoming Frank went to meet him. Like Big Hank the evening before, Wyoming Frank began to chaff Marshal

Smith with the idea of involving him in a quarrel, an excuse for resisting the demand he knew would be made.

Smith told Wyoming Frank to surrender his pistol. Frank refused. Smith looked squarely at Wyoming Frank with his gray eyes and began to walk toward the cowboy. Frank began backing away and a few moments later Smith had backed Frank into a large saloon where a crowd gathered around them.

To Smith's courteous but firm demand for the cowboy's weapon, Frank exploded with "an insulting oath and vile epithet."

Without warning Smith rushed Frank and with a terrific blow sent the cowboy to the floor. Then, standing over the stunned cowboy, Marshal Smith said, "I give you five minutes to get out of this town, and don't you ever again let me set eyes on you."

A moment after Frank left, the saloon proprietor stepped from behind the bar and told Smith, "That was the nerviest act I ever saw. You did your duty, and that coward got what he deserved. Here is my gun. I reckon I'll not need it so long as you're marshal of this town."

In the words of Mayor Henry, "That was a signal. Everyone pushed forward offering Smith pistols and overwhelming him with a profusion of compliments, expressions of admiration and so forth. He quietly thanked them and said, 'Hand your guns to the bartender to keep until you want to go out to camp.' From that moment Tom Smith was master. The cowboys, as a tribute to his marvelous nerve and gentlemanly self-command, were his allies and loyal friends.

"No guns thereafter were openly worn on the streets of Abilene, nor was Smith ever again publicly affronted," wrote Henry. "Of course, there were drunkenness and quarreling; dens of iniquity flourished and some murders even occurred; but his tact, courage and good judgment were always adequate to minimize consequences, and without resistance. . . . In a short time he ruled practically without oversight."

Unlike his predecessors, Tom Smith rode on horseback while on duty and used his fists to enforce law and order. Although armed, his weapons were never visible, even when he was riding his beautiful iron-gray horse described as from "Kentucky thoroughbred stock." The animal was called Silverheels. "A cowboy on a pony might have a start of a quarter of a mile or more, but the marshal soon would overtake him," recalled Almon C. Nixon, an early day resident of Abilene.

In his recollections of Smith, Nixon remembered the evening when "a Mexican cowboy loped up and down Texas Street crying 'ca-rach-o! ca-rach-o!' Smith stepped out from a doorway and caught the Mexican's leg in one hand and the horn of the saddle in the other and threw both pony and rider on their side in the street."

An early photograph of Abilene showing the Merchants Hotel. *Courtesy Kansas State Historical Society*

In early August, 1870, two months after Tom Smith became marshal, the town's trustees increased his salary to $225 a month. It was their way of expressing their appreciation of his work. Tom Smith had tamed Abilene.

The tale of Tom Smith might end here, but it did not. By mid-October, 1870, most of the Texas cowboys who had trailed herds of longhorns to Abilene during the summer and early fall had returned south. And the annual exodus of the gamblers, prostitutes and other undesirables was nearly complete. Abilene grew quiet.

On Sunday, October 23, 1870, Andrew McConnell, a Scotsman living in a dugout on Chapman Creek, about ten miles northeast of Abilene, went deer hunting. When he returned home he found several cows belonging to his neighbor, John Shea, grazing on his unfenced land. McConnell was enraged. The animals had been eating his corn. Shea was on hand, trying to drive the animals back onto his land. The two men had words and McConnell shot Shea through the heart.

McConnell's friend Moses Miles, also a Scotsman, had come over from his nearby claim about then and was a witness to the argument. The killing was reported to the authorities and McConnell and Miles testified that McConnell killed Shea in self-defense. McConnell was not charged. But within a few days other neighbors presented evidence contradicting McConnell and Miles. A warrant for the arrest of McConnell was given to Joseph Cramer, Dickinson County sheriff, at Abilene.

Sheriff Cramer and Deputy J. H. McDonald went to McConnell's dugout, only to be driven off by McConnell and Miles. What happened next is unclear, but on November 2, 1870, Deputy McDonald and Marshal Tom Smith rode out of Abilene to arrest McConnell. Why Sheriff Cramer was not on hand is unknown.

There are several conflicting accounts of what happened next, but it is known that as Smith and McDonald neared McConnell's dugout McConnell and Miles were working in a nearby field. They dropped their tools and ran to the dugout when they saw the lawmen approaching. When McDonald and Smith reached the dugout, Smith said he had a warrant for McConnell's arrest. Without warning McConnell aimed his rifle at Smith and shot him through the right lung. Smith returned the fire wounding the Scotsman. The two men, being close together, grappled.

Meantime, Deputy McDonald and Miles exchanged shots. McDonald, perhaps believing that he had met his match, is reported to have turned and fled on foot leaving Smith to try to subdue McConnell. Marshal Smith, probably thinking that McDonald had Miles in hand, failed to see or hear Miles approach. Miles struck Smith on the head with a gun and then did the same with an ax.

Fleeing the homestead, Deputy McDonald looked back in time to see Smith attacked. He ran to a nearby claim, borrowed a pony and rode back to Abilene for help. Soon a posse returned to McConnell's claim. Marshal Tom Smith's body lay on the ground not far from the dugout. He was dead. McConnell and Miles were gone. They had fled on horseback.

By nightfall the two killers had reached Junction City and started up the Republican River Valley toward Clay Center, Kansas. The posse was in pursuit. The outlaws were arrested a few days later at a farmhouse fifteen miles northwest of Clay Center. C. C. Kuney, Abilene police magistrate, and James Gainsford, a butcher, are credited with capturing McConnell and Miles. They offered no resistance.

Feelings were so strong against the two Scotsmen in Abilene that the district court later granted them a change of venue to Riley County in Manhattan, just northeast of Junction City. There both McConnell and Miles were found guilty. Miles was sentenced to sixteen years, McConnell twelve years, in the Kansas State Penitentiary at Lansing, just south of Leavenworth.

Two days after Smith's death, funeral services were held in Abilene's Baptist Church at 10:30 in the morning. All businesses in town closed. After the service the procession moved toward Abilene's cemetery. Stuart Henry, who witnessed the funeral, recalled it vividly:

"Behind the hearse, banked with branches and flowers, walked the dead marshal's iron-gray horse, Silverheels, saddled and bridled as he had left it. Tom's pearl-handled brace of revolvers, presented to him by the community, hung in their holsters from the pommel. Crape [*sic*] fluttered from hats, arms, bosoms. All proceeded on foot to do their highest and humblest honors to their revered protector.

"The file of people wound through Texas Street where the marshal had patroled in such local prominence. Then across the railroad track the line trailed through the north or civilian part of the straggling village. Finally the concourse mounted the gentle slope of the hill on whose breast, upraised to the sky, spread the small prairie grass cemetery.

"The residents seemed much like dumb, animated monuments. No music. Not a voice could be heard . . . and the coffin was lowered. The first hopeless clods fell dully upon it. Flowers and sprigs dropped into the forlorn cavity. Women wept. Men stirred and batted their eyelids hard to hide emotions."

Smith's grave was simple. It cost two dollars. It was marked with a plain ornamented board for the headstone. A small picket fence was placed around the grave, but as the months and years passed, coarse weeds covered the grave. The fence collapsed and the headstone disappeared.

In 1904, J. B. Edwards, an Abilene resident, decided to do something about the memory of Smith. He obtained a new cemetery lot in a more prominent part of Abilene's cemetery, had the metal casket placed in a new grave and had a large boulder shipped up from Oklahoma and placed as a monument over the new grave. Edwards then had a bronze plate attached to the boulder. The plate reads:

THOMAS J. SMITH

MARSHAL OF ABILENE, 1870

DIED A MARTYR TO DUTY NOV.

2, 1870

A FEARLESS HERO OF

FRONTIER DAYS

WHO IN COWBOY CHAOS

ESTABLISHED THE SUPREMACY

OF LAW

On Memorial Day, May 30, 1904, thirty-four years after his death, the monument was unveiled and the early settlers made certain that history would not forget Tom Smith, the man who tamed Abilene.

The Collapse of the Dalton Gang

The fifth day of October 1892 dawned bright and clear over southeast Kansas. It was a promising day for the five men camped on Onion Creek, about three miles south of Coffeyville, Kansas. After breakfast they broke camp, saddled their horses and rode across a plowed field to a road that led to Coffeyville. The riders—Grat, Bob and Emmett Dalton, Bill Powers and Dick Broadwell—talked and laughed as they rode along. They may have been laughing at themselves, for Emmett was wearing a beard, Bob had a black mustache and goatee while Grat had a mustache and whiskers. All of them were false.

The Daltons were wearing them because they were going into their hometown and they didn't want to be recognized. As for Bill Powers and Dick Broadwell, they were not known in Coffeyville, so they made no attempt to hide their features.

The horsemen did not ride fast. The banks were not yet open. The riders wanted to arrive in the town plaza at about the time the banks opened.

Presently they came to the town limits and the road became Eighth Street. The five riders spurred their mounts and trotted along. A man and his wife saw the riders and thought they were a United States marshal and his posse coming up from Indian Territory.

The riders turned down Maple Street with Grat, Bob and Emmett riding abreast in the lead and Broadwell and Powers riding to the rear. Passing a lumber company, the riders turned down an alley that would lead them to the plaza. Soon they stopped, dismounted and hitched

The Condon Bank at Coffeyville, Kansas, one of the two banks the Dalton gang attempted to rob on October 5, 1892. *Courtesy Western History Collection, University of Oklahoma Library*

"Death Alley" at Coffeyville where the Dalton gang tied their horses before robbing two banks; it was also the place where some of the gang and the Coffeyville city marshal died. *Courtesy Kansas State Historical Society*

their horses to the back fence on the property of Police Judge Charles Munn. The banks were just a short distance away to the east.

The five men, thus far not recognized by anyone, walked toward the plaza. It was already crowded for a Wednesday morning. People were walking, others moving by on horseback and in buggies conducting business.

The outlaws, carrying Winchesters under their arms, entered the plaza and Alex McKenna, a storekeeper, glanced at the men. Even with their disguises he recognized one of them as a Dalton. A moment later he spread the alarm as did Charles Gump, a drayman, who had been nearby.

By then the outlaws had split up. With guns in ready, Grat Dalton, Dick Broadwell and Bill Powers had entered the Condon Bank while Bob and Emmett Dalton had crossed the plaza, entering the First National Bank. There Bert S. Ayres, bookkeeper, played a delaying game with the two outlaws biding for time. Finally Bob and Emmett forced the bankers to turn over about $23,000 in gold and bank notes. As the two gunmen were preparing to leave, the sound of gunshots filled the plaza outside.

At the Condon & Co. bank, Grat Dalton's party had forced Charles M. Ball, cashier, to turn over all the money except that in the inner vault. When Grat demanded the inner vault be opened, Ball said it was automatic, that it would not open until about 9:45 a.m. Grat said they would wait, not realizing it was a delaying tactic.

As they waited, a volley of bullets shattered the windows. The townsmen had been given enough time to seize arms and organize their forces. Dick Broadwell and Bill Powers fired back. The bankers and two customers dropped to the floor. Another volley of bullets hit the bank and a moment later Dick Broadwell was struck in the shoulder. He could not use his shooting arm.

Grat Dalton knew it was time to leave. He asked if there was a back door. He was told there was none. Grat then ordered the cashier, Charles Ball, and the bank's co-owner, C. T. Carpenter, to carry the loot outside. As they started to do so, another volley of bullets struck the outside of the building. The cashier and banker dropped the money and ran for cover.

Taking only the currency, the outlaws—Grat Dalton, Bill Powers and Dick Broadwell—ran through the door onto the plaza. Not twenty steps away Grat Dalton was hit. Staggering, Grat made it across Walnut Street and down the alley to near where the horses had been tied. Just then Charles T. Connelly, Coffeyville city marshal, started toward Grat. A bullet from Grat's gun dropped Connelly.

Meantime Bill Powers and Dick Broadwell had been wounded. Broadwell fell to the ground not far from Grat. Powers, although wounded, finally made it to a horse and went riding off. About then Bob and Emmett Dalton reached the spot where they had left their horses. Fleeing out the back door of the First National Bank, they ran down the alley north to Eighth Street to reach the spot where they had left their horses.

Emmett Dalton tossed a money sack across the saddle of his horse and mounted. As he did, shots rang out, one bullet hitting his right arm, the other lodging in his groin.

The front doors of the Condon Bank in Coffeyville showing bullet holes. *Courtesy Kansas State Historical Society*

About the same moment, Bob Dalton was struck down.

Emmett, still in the saddle, rode to where Bob lay. As Emmett stretched down a hand to pull Bob into the saddle, Carey Seaman, a Coffeyville barber, fired both barrels of his shotgun at Emmett. The youngest Dalton fell.

Moments later jubilant townspeople rushed into the smoke-filled alley, apparently intent on lynching any of the outlaws still alive. But David Steward Elliott, publisher of the *Coffeyville Journal,* kept the crowd under control.

Word spread that all the outlaws except Emmett Dalton had been killed. Emmett, just over twenty-one years old, had been taken to a nearby drugstore where Dr. W. H. Wells and two colleagues patched his sixteen wounds. Later, Emmett was moved to the Farmers' Home Hotel.

The battle claimed the lives of eight men; the outlaws Grat and Bob Dalton, Dick Broadwell and Bill Powers, and four Coffeyville residents, Marshal Connelly, Lucius M. Baldwin, George B. Cubine and Charles Brown. Three other townsmen were wounded.

For nearly two hours after the fight the bodies of Grat and Bob Dalton and Dick Broadwell lay in what became known as "Death Alley." When the body of Bill Powers was found on the edge of town, where it had fallen from his horse, it was brought back. All four bodies were propped up and photographs were taken. Afterward the bodies were thrown into the little city jail. The next afternoon the outlaws were buried in black-varnished coffins made of wood.

All but about $22 of the robbery money was recovered. The robbers had taken about $25,000. By nightfall the word had spread across the plains and from New York to San Francisco that "the Dalton gang is no more."

The four dead members of the Dalton gang in the Coffeyville city jail. *Courtesy Kansas State Historical Society*

Coffeyville residents including an unidentified lawman *(center)* hold up the bodies of Bob Dalton *(left)* and Grat Dalton *(right)* in order that a Coffeyville photographer could make this photo a few hours after the shootout. *Courtesy Kansas State Historical Society*

About five months after the raid Emmett Dalton went on trial at nearby Independence, Kansas. He pleaded guilty to murdering one of the four Coffeyville citizens and was sentenced to life in prison at the Kansas State Penitentiary at Lansing.

The story of the Daltons might end here, but it does not. After fourteen and one-half years in prison, Emmett Dalton was pardoned by E. W. Hoch, governor of Kansas, in 1907. Emmett's childhood sweetheart, Julia Johnson, had waited for him. They were married and settled in Tulsa, Oklahoma, where Emmett was employed as a special police officer. He supposedly was a good one.

About 1918 Emmett and Julia Dalton moved to California where Emmett was determined to enter the new motion picture industry. With a former Coffeyville photographer, John Tackett, the reformed Emmett Dalton helped produce a western film called *Beyond the Law*, the supposedly true story of the Dalton gang. Emmett was the star. But it was a bad movie. He did not become a famous movie star, but in the years that followed he did well as a building contractor.

In 1931, when Emmett Dalton was sixty years old, he and his wife, Julia, returned to Coffeyville. A. B. Macdonald, longtime reporter with the *Kansas City Star,* spent much time with the former outlaw, walking about the plaza, retracing the route taken by the Dalton gang thirty-nine years before. Then they drove out to Elmwood Cemetery, first to the grave of Frank Dalton, then to the graves of Grat and Bob Dalton and Bill Powers.

After a time Emmett Dalton moved away from the graves and told Macdonald, "I challenge the world to produce the history of an outlaw who ever got anything out of it except that," pointing to the graves, "or else huddled in a prison cell. . . . The biggest fool on earth is the one who thinks that he can beat the law, that crime can be made to pay. It never paid and never will, and that's the one big lesson of the Coffeyville raid."

On July 13, 1937, Emmett Dalton, sixty-six, died peacefully in Hollywood, far from the scene of the Dalton gang exploits that produced as much fiction as fact. Even before they were stopped at Coffeyville the Daltons had become legendary characters much like Jesse and Frank James, the Youngers and other outlaws of the Old West.

Some writers have suggested that the Dalton boys turned outlaw because of their upbringing. This is possible. Their father, Lewis Dalton, came west to Missouri during the late 1840s. Writer Harold Preece, author of perhaps the best study of the Daltons—*The Dalton Gang: End of an Outlaw Era*—described the father as a "roaming, shiftless, 6-foot ex-Kentuckian" who loved fast horses. By 1850 Lewis Dalton was trading horses and running a small saloon at Westport, now Kansas City. It was there on the Kansas-Missouri border that he met prim Adeline Younger whose home was Independence, Missouri. She was fifteen and he was thirty-six.

In March 1851, they were married at Independence. For a time Lewis Dalton continued to run his saloon at Westport. Eventually it became too much for his wife. She made him swear off drinking and sell the saloon. The Dalton family then moved to near Belton in Cass County, Missouri, in 1866. There Mrs. Dalton's parents provided the

An autographed photo from Emmett
Dalton to Kansan Jay E. House now
in the collections of the Kansas State
Historical Society in Topeka.

*To my good friend
Mr Jay E. House
Sincerely.
Emmett Dalton*

couple with land. Lewis Dalton, however, would have nothing to do
with farming. Leaving that task to his wife, he said goodbye and joined
a circus as a barker, horse trading in his spare time.

During the years that followed, Adeline Dalton did the best she
could. Friends and relatives harvested the family's meager crops. Lewis
Dalton returned home only a few times each year with even fewer
dollars in his pockets for the family. He usually stayed around only long
enough to give his wife another baby.

In all there were fifteen Dalton children. Ten were boys and three
were girls. Two died in infancy.

The first five boys—Charles, Ben, Littleton, Henry and Simon—
turned out well. All except Simon grew to manhood. He died at the age
of fourteen.

It was Adeline Dalton's second batch of boys that produced the
future outlaws. First was Grattan, born near Lawrence, Kansas, in 1861.
He was named for a dead Irish statesman. Then came Bill—William
Marion Dalton—in 1863. He supposedly was the smartest of the second
batch, a con artist. He was the worst of the five. Next was Frank who
learned to cuss at an early age. Fourth was Bob—Robert Renick
Dalton—who was a cautious young man. Finally there was Emmett, the
youngest, named for an Irishman who had been hung on the gallows in
England.

"Em," as his brothers and friends called Emmett, idolized his older
brother Bob. Emmett, like Grat, could fight well with his fists and he

had some ability as a con artist like brother Bill. Three of the four boys including Emmett were to take part in the Coffeyville raid. The fifth brother, Bill, would later make a name for himself as a wanted Oklahoma outlaw, dying a violent death.

In 1882 Lewis Dalton, after one of his frequent visits to Indian Territory, returned to Missouri and moved his family to what is today northeastern Oklahoma. Although Adeline protested, the family "squatted" on land near Vinita. There the Daltons lived until 1886 when they moved to Coffeyville for a short time. Coffeyville became the hometown of the Dalton boys.

In 1884 Frank Dalton became a deputy United States marshal riding out of Fort Smith, Arkansas, for Judge Isaac Parker, known as the "hanging judge." Brother Grat went along as Frank's posseman. But being lawmen did not pay well. Frank Dalton received more experience than he did money. For every outlaw he caught he was paid two dollars and the money sometimes took months reaching him. Posseman Grat Dalton received even less.

Frank Dalton's career as a peace officer came to an abrupt end in 1887. While trying to capture a band of whiskey runners in Indian Territory near the Arkansas line, he was killed. His brother Grat was promoted to Frank's job as deputy U.S. marshal. Grat then hired Bob Dalton as posseman. Soon afterward Emmett Dalton joined his older brothers.

The three Daltons did not take law enforcement as seriously as had Frank. Whenever possible Grat and Bob used their badges to take what they could. On the side they stole horses and sold them across the line north around Baxter Springs, Kansas. At other times one of the brothers would slip bottles of whiskey into the wagons of squatters coming into Indian Territory where liquor was not allowed. Then the Daltons would stop the wagons and, as U.S. marshals, impose a fine on the squatters, a fine they never reported.

In December 1888, the first of a series of events occurred that was to lead to the formation of their outlaw gang. Bob Dalton shot and killed Charlie Montgomery, a young man at Coffeyville, who had run off with Bob Dalton's girl friend, his cousin Minnie.

A few months later Bob Dalton mistakenly shot the son of a Claremore, Indian Territory, man, Alex Cochran. The incident further discredited the Daltons as lawmen and by the spring of 1890, Grat had lost his deputy U.S. marshal's badge.

During the months that followed the Dalton boys concentrated on stealing horses. One day they took several ponies belonging to a Cherokee Indian and set out for Columbus, Kansas, northwest of Baxter

Frank Dalton, 28, deputy U.S. marshal. He was killed in the line of duty on November 27, 1887, in Indian Territory near the Arkansas border. *Courtesy Western History Collections, University of Oklahoma Library*

Springs, to sell the animals. They never did. The Indian who owned the ponies had followed with a posse overtaking the Daltons at Baxter Springs. The Daltons fled and that day became wanted men.

They went on to train robberies and gun battles throughout the West, reaching the end of the trail October 5, 1892, with the shootout at Coffeyville. They bore out Emmett's statement that "the biggest fool on earth is the one who thinks he can beat the law."

The Shootout in Perry Tuttle's Dance Hall

The horse's hooves made clopping noises on the baked earth that summer day in 1871 when Arthur Delaney arrived in Newton, Kansas. Delaney was a heavy-set, yet rather fine-looking man in his late twenties, but he had the reputation of being arrogant and hot tempered. That may have been one reason why he got into trouble with the law in Missouri, a state he had just left. And his trouble with the law was probably the reason he was using the name Mike McCluskie.

Delaney—I will call him McCluskie in this tale—was among the speculators, gamblers, prostitutes and small-time criminals who were flocking to Newton that summer. By trade, McCluskie was a gambler, but he also had a slight reputation as a gunman. And by July 1871, when the first train arrived in Newton over the newly laid tracks, McCluskie was working as a night policeman in the town, which then consisted of a handful of hurriedly erected frame buildings, a few tents and fifteen hundred residents.

Gamblers appear to have put up the money for township officials to hire McCluskie as a lawman. His job was to maintain law and order in the tough district called Hide Park. Located on the southeast edge of town, Hide Park consisted of two large dance halls, one owned by Ed Krum, the other by Perry Tuttle. The buildings stood about thirty yards apart.

Surrounding the dance halls were smaller buildings where the ladies of the night did a thriving business after the Texas cowboys had their fill of dancing, drinking and gambling on poker, monte, faro and other games.

The town of Newton had been born a few months earlier in anticipation of the Santa Fe Railroad. The line laid tracks southwest from Emporia, Kansas, in an effort to intercept the Texas cattle trade, which was then centered on the Kansas Pacific line in Abilene to the north.

From what is known, Mike McCluskie had only one friend, young Jim Riley, about eighteen years old. Where Riley came from is unknown. He appears to have drifted into Newton one day without a nickel to his name. It was then that McCluskie befriended the boy, gave him food and a place to sleep. Riley was ever faithful to McCluskie.

On Friday, August 11, 1871, residents of Newton went to the polls to vote on a bond proposal. Hired as a special policeman at the polls was a Texas gambler called William Bailey. His real name was William Baylor. Bailey, as I will call him, had supposedly killed two or three men in Texas. He was domineering and abusive. That election day was no exception.

Bailey drank heavily during the morning hours. When he began to badger election officials during the afternoon, Mike McCluskie intervened. He removed Bailey from the area where the election officials were working.

One eyewitness recalled that McCluskie pulled Bailey outside to the street and damned him "from high heaven to the deepest pit of Hell, and figuratively speaking, turned him wrong-side out for the crows to pick. All Newton stood aghast at such eloquence, such righteous indignation."

The remainder of the afternoon was peaceful at the polls, but that night Bailey and McCluskie happened to meet in front of the Red Front Saloon where a large election night crowd had gathered. Bailey was still drunk.

When Bailey demanded that McCluskie set up the drinks for the crowd, McCluskie refused. Bailey cussed McCluskie and struck him with his fists. Then Bailey, apparently thinking twice about what he had just done, began to back away. It was too late. In a flash McCluskie pulled his six-gun and fired twice at Bailey. The first shot missed its mark and lodged in the door of a nearby store. But the second shot struck Bailey in the right side lodging below his heart.

A few men in the crowd carried Bailey to the nearby Santa Fe Hotel where Gaston Boyd, the town's only reputable doctor, tried to save Bailey's life. He failed. The Texas gambler died at eight o'clock the next morning. He was buried in Newton's boot hill, located somewhere south of what is today First Street and Slate Creek in southeast Newton.

When McCluskie was told of Bailey's death by young Jim Riley, McCluskie left town. He wanted things to cool off even though he believed he would not be arrested for the killing. Most townspeople felt the shooting was justified.

But a small group of Texas cowboys felt differently. They had liked Bailey. He was one of their kind. He was a Texan. And as they drank in one of the saloons, they quietly swore to avenge Bailey's death.

The leader of the Texans was Hugh Anderson, who with his father and brother had brought a large herd of longhorns up the trail to Newton. Young Anderson was a reckless fellow who is said to have been involved in at least two gunfights in his home state. He was from Bell County, Texas.

The Texans agreed to keep their feelings to themselves and to wait for McCluskie to return. It was then, they said, they would even the score.

The next Saturday night McCluskie slipped back into Newton and made his way to Perry Tuttle's dance hall in Hide Park. There, sitting at a corner table, he drank and gambled and laughed. Everyone was friendly, and McCluskie must have felt that all was forgotten about his killing of Bailey.

The Texans had not forgotten. Some of Hugh Anderson's friends, drinking at the bar, had seen McCluskie enter. One of them hurried to tell Anderson while the others walked over to McCluskie's table. One of them sat down and began talking with McCluskie. The others stood nearby smiling and joking as if nothing had happened.

It was a few minutes later when Hugh Anderson entered the saloon. McCluskie apparently did not see him until the big Texan, his six-shooter in hand, walked up to McCluskie's table.

Everyone moved back from the table.

"You are a cowardly son-of-a-bitch! I'll blow the top of your head off," asserted Anderson, according to one eyewitness.

Without another word Anderson fired his gun at McCluskie.

The bullet hit McCluskie in the neck. He looked at Anderson. His expression was one of total surprise. As he tried to stand up, he pulled his six-gun, pointed it at Anderson and pulled the trigger. The cartridge didn't go off.

Bleeding profusely, McCluskie fell to the floor. Anderson fired another shot into McCluskie's motionless body.

All of this happened in a matter of seconds.

There are conflicting accounts of what happened next, but it is

known that at about the time McCluskie fell to the floor his young
friend Jim Riley was entering the saloon. He apparently had heard that
Mike was back in town.

Suffering from a bad case of tuberculosis, young Riley had the
reputation of being quiet. For a moment he stood silently watching the
Texans from the doorway. He saw his friend Mike McCluskie lying in a
pool of blood on the floor. One wonders what went through his mind.

Then, as if by some mysterious command, Riley turned and locked
the saloon door. He pulled his gun and began firing. It was as though
hate and revenge controlled his soul.

The dance hall filled with gunsmoke and death. People screamed.

How many men were hit by Riley's bullets or how many might
have been shot by other participants in the shooting is not reported. But
when the smoke cleared and townsmen forced the saloon door open, two
men lay dead on the dance hall floor. Four others, including Anderson
and McCluskie, were wounded. And before too many days passed the
death toll would climb to five. Three of the wounded would die.

In the confusion that followed, Jim Riley escaped and fled Newton.

The gunfight had occurred early on Sunday morning, August 20,
1871. A few hours later, after the hot Kansas sun had climbed high in
the sky, an inquest was held. A warrant was issued for Anderson's arrest
after it was learned that Mike McCluskie had died of his wounds.

Anderson, severely wounded, had been taken to the back room of a
nearby store. His father was soon on the scene and almost immediately
began to look for ways to get better medical care for his son. Then too,
the father was concerned about the townspeople. There appeared to be
a strong possibility that McCluskie's followers might try "ornamenting
the neighboring telegraph poles," as one newspaper reported, with
young Anderson and the other Texans who had taken part in the gunfight.

Sunday afternoon Anderson's father appealed to a handful of Newton's leading citizens for help. They wanted no more trouble in their
town. They agreed to help and plans were made to sneak Anderson out
of Newton on the passenger train scheduled to leave at four o'clock the
next morning.

Two hours before the train's scheduled departure, a small number
of persons including some of Anderson's friends went to the back door of
the store where he lay wounded. Carrying him on a litter, the men
moved north of town until they struck the cattle trail. Following the
trail a short distance they approached the town from a different direction. They headed directly for the train station. Near the station a
conductor had arranged to have a passenger car left on a siding with its

doors open. Anderson was gently lifted aboard the train and locked in the closet of the car.

Shortly before four o'clock in the morning the railroad car was added to the eastbound train. Town constable Harry Nevill went through the train as he usually did every morning before it left. He did not find anything unusual and the train left on schedule. Once outside Newton the wounded Anderson was removed from the closet by his father and friends.

The train reached Kansas City early that evening where Anderson was given immediate medical treatment. He remained in Kansas City for some time recuperating. Later he returned to Texas. Badly crippled, Anderson died a few years later.

What happened to young Jim Riley remains a mystery to this day. Some say he was killed in New Mexico or Arizona a few years after the shooting at Newton. Another account suggests that he died from tuberculosis in Colorado.

As for Riley's friend Mike McCluskie—Arthur Delaney—he was buried in Newton's boot hill. A few years later his body was removed by relatives and buried in either Kansas City or St. Louis.

The town of Newton did not remain wild very long. Early in 1872 its citizens formed a law and order committee and gave every outlaw twelve hours to get out of town. They all left. One shoddy character, sick in bed, was carried to the train on a cot to make his exit before the deadline.

The summer of 1872 saw the end of the cattle trade in Newton. By fall, it had moved on to Wichita, about twenty-five miles to the south. With the cattle trade went the trouble. The pioneers who settled Newton are gone now as are all of the original buildings in Hide Park, but it was not too many years ago that a few old-timers talked of that night in late August of 1871 when the shootout in Perry Tuttle's dance hall took the lives of five men at Newton.

Who Murdered Belle Starr?

"**S**he was shot in the back; four buckshot took effect, three in the center of the neck and one in the back. She was knocked from her horse and her slayer climbed the fence and shot her a second time with a heavy charge of turkey shot as she lay on her back in the mud, the charge taking effect in the face, neck and one arm. Belle spoke one or two words, gasped and died. Neighbors gathered and the body was carried to the mountain home, a mile away."

This description of the murder of outlaw Belle Starr was written by Samuel W. Harman and included in his exceedingly rare little book *Hell on the Border* published at Fort Smith, Arkansas, in 1898.

Whether Harman's details of Belle Starr's violent death are factual is unknown. It may have been based on dime novels or sensational newspaper accounts that undoubtedly enhanced the legend of Belle Starr. But there is no doubt today that she was an extraordinary woman, perhaps in the class of Calamity Jane and Cattle Kate Watson. And, as Harman observed in his book, "there is something awful to contemplate in the thought of a woman dying 'with her boots on.' "

Belle Starr was born Myra Belle Shirley on a farm near Carthage, Missouri, in 1848. Border troubles during the late 1850s forced the family to move to Texas where, in 1866, Belle met Cole Younger. He may have fathered her first child. But the romance was short-lived. She soon joined another outlaw, Jim Reed, and journeyed to California. There Belle gave Reed a son.

In 1869 Belle and Jim returned to Texas where they made their

Belle Starr, sidesaddle, was a striking figure atop a horse. *Courtesy Western History Collections, University of Oklahoma Library.*

Nana Devena posed for this picture shortly before her death in the 1930s. Was she the killer of Belle Starr? *Courtesy Leroy Towns*

living robbing and rustling in the area around Dallas. Dressed in velvet skirts and plumed hats and riding her mare, Venus, Belle became known as the "Bandit Queen."

But tragedy stuck in 1874. Belle's husband was killed by a member of his own gang. Belle left her children with her mother and traveled north into Indian Territory or what is today eastern Oklahoma. There, in the Sans Bois Mountains, she led her own gang of cattle rustlers and horse thieves and eventually began living with a Cherokee Indian named Sam Starr.

The law caught up with Sam and Belle. Both were indicted on a charge of horse theft. Belle has the dubious honor of being the first female ever tried for a major crime in "Hanging Judge" Isaac Parker's Arkansas court. After five months in the federal prison in Detroit, Belle and Sam returned to Indian Territory and resumed their not so honorable profession.

Tragedy struck again in 1886. Sam Starr was killed in a gunfight. But Belle wasted no time. She soon took up with a young Creek Indian named Jim July. But history seemed to repeat itself. Within two years the law caught up with Jim and he was ordered to Fort Smith to face larceny charges.

Belle Starr decided to go part of the way with Jim but turned back before reaching Fort Smith. While on her way home, she was shot and killed. That was on February 3, 1889. It was her forty-third birthday.

One writer claims Jim July was the murderer. Another says she was killed by her enraged son, Ed Reed. Still another says it was E. A. Watson. Even the name Jim Middleton, brother of a former lover, has been mentioned. But no one was ever convicted for the murder and for decades the speculation has continued.

Another name was added to the list in the summer of 1970. LeRoy Towns, then editor of *Midway*, the Sunday magazine of the *Topeka Capital-Journal*, was working at his desk when a man asked to see him. The visitor was A. J. Robinson, then seventy-two years old, of Topeka, Kansas. He said he had a story to tell. Towns listened.

Robinson said he had gone to visit his grandmother in Oklahoma about 1911 or 1912. At the time he was about twelve years old.

"We went one day to visit my grandmother. I think it was Sunday morning or afternoon. We were just sitting around talking and she was telling us about the hard times she had in the Indian Territory," he added. "Then her face lit up and she said, 'I've got something to tell all of you . . . I killed Belle Starr.'"

Robinson told Towns he decided to tell the story because he was the only person alive who then knew it, and he didn't want the story

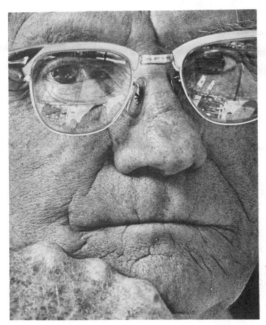

This photograph of A. J. Robinson was taken in 1970 when he said his grandmother killed Belle Starr. *Courtesy of Leroy Towns*

lost. Robinson added that his grandmother swore all those present to secrecy—Robinson, his mother and father and an aunt named Lucinda.

Why secrecy? Robinson said it may have been because of the family reputation or because then, early in this century, revenge by one of the infamous Youngers might have been possible. He wasn't sure.

Regardless, Robinson then related that his grandmother was named Nana (perhaps Nannie) Devena. At the time he heard her story she was a middle-aged widow who weighed about ninety-five pounds. Her skin was dark and leathery, the result of much outdoor living, and she was fond of smoking wood chips in a crusty corncob pipe.

He said Mrs. Devena was born in the 1840s in South Carolina. Her maiden name is unknown. She was proud of her French blood. Sometime before 1880 she and her husband moved west to Indian Territory and set up housekeeping on the Canadian River near Eufaula, in what is today eastern Oklahoma. By 1889 there were five children—one being Robinson's mother, Rene—and Mrs. Devena, then in her thirties, was a widow.

Belle Starr, he added, was her neighbor.

The events leading to Belle Starr's death, according to Robinson, began when "Grandmother sent her boys over to hoe cotton for a neighbor named Jim. The family needed the money. But other neighbors—I don't recall their name—didn't like Jim, and so they didn't like the kids helping him in the field."

Legends list many guns, many men, and many assassins in Belle Starr's stormy life. She was the legendary "bandit queen." *Courtesy Western History Collections, University of Oklahoma Library*

The neighbors, said Robinson, first warned Mrs. Devena not to let her sons hoe Jim's cotton. She glowered, gritted her teeth and told them to go to hell. But then one night Mrs. Devena's milk cows were turned loose.

"She would hear them being turned out, and would go down to put them back in," said Robinson, adding, "That went on for several nights." And once, he said, she caught her villainous neighbors stealing corn from her crib. She set a bear trap, returned the next morning to find one of the neighbor boys caught and in pain."

The feud grew hotter with the passing of weeks. The neighbors put out stronger warnings, hinting "something might happen if you don't stop being friendly with Jim."

One night it did.

As Mrs. Devena went to the corral, she was struck, thrown to the ground and beaten. Her screams brought a daughter from the house, but not before Mrs. Devena had recognized her attacker as one of the neighbor boys.

"As she told us that day," remembered Robinson, "she went back up to the house, took down the old muzzle-loader from its hook and loaded it. Then she went down to the road and waited."

Mrs. Devena saw her attacker trot off to the nearby town on horseback. Then she hunkered down at the side of the road to wait. How long she waited is not recorded. But later she saw a horse and rider coming from the direction of town. She strained to make out the rider in the growing dimness. The rider was wearing a wide-brimmed hat. Certainly, it must be the guilty neighbor. A few yards closer and she pulled the trigger.

"A little while after that they found Belle dead at the exact spot she [Mrs. Devena] shot the rider out of the saddle," said Robinson.

That is A. J. Robinson's story.

Is it true?

It seems possible that in the darkness Mrs. Devena might have killed Belle Starr by mistake. She did wear hats like men and in the darkness her silhouette could have been mistaken for that of a young man, the neighbor boy she undoubtedly intended to kill.

And what about "Jim," the man Mrs. Devena's sons hoed cotton for. Was he Jim July, Belle's lover?

These and many other questions remain unanswered. Robinson's story has simply added one more name to the list of people who might have killed Belle Starr. Today, her remains still lie buried in a wooden casket in a grave in Eufaula, Oklahoma. As for Mrs. Devena, she died in the 1930s and was buried in Sand Springs, Oklahoma. At her death, she was nearly one hundred years old.

The Bloody Benders

As newspapermen learned many years ago it is the unusual, the bizarre and odd events in man's history that make news. There is a certain fascination with such stories, especially when they involve other human beings. For more than a century this element of human nature has been found in the tale of the four Benders. Where they came from is unknown, but they arrived in southeast Kansas during the winter of 1871. They bought two tracts of land about six miles north and two miles east of Cherryvale, and built a house and small barn.

Old man Bender was about sixty years old. His wife was also about sixty. The young man, John Bender, was about twenty-five. Many persons in the neighborhood described him as a half-wit. The fourth member of the Bender family was Kate, believed to be in her early twenties. She was different from the others. She was sociable. Standing about five feet six inches, holding herself proudly erect, her brown eyes and flashing auburn hair made her something of a looker in the eyes of some young men around Cherryvale.

The Bender house was about one hundred yards off the Osage Mission trail. Over the front door hung a crudely painted sign that read "Groceries." About one hundred feet north of the house was a sod and stone barn, walled on three sides. East of the barn was a combination orchard and garden. It was there that old man Bender planted about fifty fruit trees. Between the barn and the house the Benders dug a well. That was the Bender place.

The family lived quietly. Ma and Pa Bender were not friendly to

110 ·

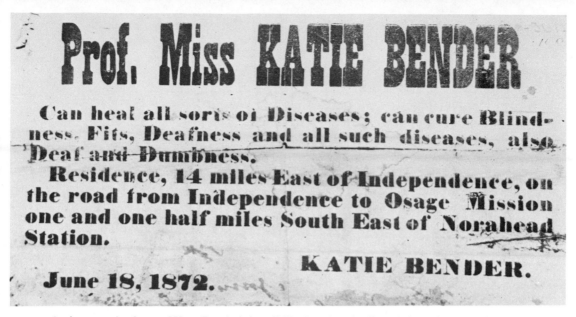

A photograph of one of Kate Bender's handbills that she distributed throughout southeast Kansas in June of 1872. *Courtesy Kansas State Historical Society*

neighbors. Neither was young John, but he and Kate sometimes went to Sunday school at nearby Harmony Grove School. And at one point during early 1872 Kate Bender began working as a waitress in the dining room of the small hotel in Cherryvale. But then she soon realized it was more profitable to give lectures on spiritualism and to conduct séances. She claimed to have a gift for seeing and hearing what others could not. One story says she claimed to have contact with a blood-thirsty Indian chief in the spirit world who helped her cure all sorts of diseases plus deaf and dumbness.

In June 1872 Kate Bender had a notice printed to advertise her so-called "powers." She then distributed copies over much of the area. The notice read:

PROF. MISS KATIE BENDER

Can heal all sorts of Diseases; can cure Blindness, Fits, Deafness and all such diseases, also Deaf and Dumbness.
Residence, 14 miles East of Independence, on the road from Independence to Osage Mission one and one-half miles South East of Morehead Station.

KATIE BENDER

June 18, 1872

About the time her advertisement was printed, strangers traveling over the Osage Mission Trail began to vanish. And in the nine months that followed, eleven persons including a man and his five-year-old daughter disappeared. In some instances, even the victims' horses and wagons vanished.

At first local residents were not too concerned. Southeast Kansas was a newly settled area and violence was not uncommon. But gradually as letters of inquiry into the missing persons began arriving in the area, the residents became concerned. The Benders, however, were not suspected as being involved. They were considered just another immigrant family struggling to make a living on the prairie.

A series of events, however, began to change the neighbors' opinions of the Benders. One day a neighboring farmer rode to the Bender store to change a one-hundred-dollar bill. Only after the Benders learned that he lived nearby did old man Bender move away from the front door—sledgehammer in hand—to let the farmer pass.

Another time, Father Paul Ponziglione, a missionary among the Osage Indians, stopped at the Bender store late one hot and humid summer night as a storm threatened. He went inside, sat down to rest and to buy his evening meal. But soon he became apprehensive. He was frightened, but tried not to show it. He did not trust the Benders.

When lightning lit up the countryside and a big roll of thunder shook the small house, Father Ponziglione jumped to his feet. On the pretext of looking after his horse, he ran out the front door, jumped on his horse and rode off in the rain as fast as he could. He escaped none too soon. He undoubtedly had been marked as another victim by the Benders.

Then there is the story told about an eccentric old woman named Hesler who lived in the neighborhood. She carried a shotgun for a companion and was fascinated by spiritualism. One night she went to see Kate Bender. As she later recalled, when the sun went down the Benders began to act queer. They drew pictures of men on the walls of the house and stuck knives into them as Kate told the old woman about the spirits.

Kate then remarked that the spirits often commanded her to kill. Suddenly, a strange expression came over Kate's face. Her lips drew back and her nose twitched. She crouched in her chair, leaned forward toward old lady Hesler and whispered, "And the spirits command me to kill you—kill you—now."

At that, the old lady jumped to her feet, turned and ran through the open front door, and, so the story goes, did not stop until she was safely behind the locked doors of her home not far away.

While such tales about the Benders did cause their neighbors to wonder about "those folks who had that store out on the prairie," it was the disappearance of Dr. William H. York, a prominent Kansas politician, that finally focused suspicion on the Benders.

In March of 1873, York was returning to his home at Independence, Kansas, after visiting his brother, Colonel A. M. York, at Fort Scott. The hour was late when Dr. York stopped at the Benders to water his horse and buy his evening meal. He never left the Benders' store alive.

When Colonel York, also a prominent politician and member of the Kansas legislature, learned his brother was missing, he set out with a posse to search. Soon, Colonel York traced his missing brother to the Bender place. There the trail ended. He talked with Kate and young John Bender who cheerfully acknowledged that Dr. York had indeed stopped there. Kate described how he watered his horse, made a small purchase at their store and then, said Kate, he had ridden on.

Whether Colonel York became suspicious of the Benders is unknown. He thanked them for the information and with his posse rode away. But his visit had frightened the Benders. And fearing he might have become suspicious, the Benders left and vanished. That was in late April 1873.

Several days later, in early May, Silas Tale passed the Bender store and noticed it looked deserted. The few animals near the barn were thin, as though starving. Tale reported what he had seen to L. F. Dick, the township trustee, who with some other men, went to the Bender store to investigate.

During the hours that followed the scene was not pleasant. Dr. York's body was found in a shallow grave in the orchard. His head was crushed. His throat had been slit. And soon other graves were uncovered in the area of the Bender garden and orchard.

As news of the discoveries spread throughout southeast Kansas, the Bender store became a center of curiosity. Men, women and children, from miles around, came to view the scene of the killings. Going in opposite directions were bands of armed men searching for the Benders. The only clue found was a wagon, team and a small dog—all apparently belonging to the Benders—on the southern edge of Thayer, Kansas, about ten miles north of the Bender store. The railroad ticket agent at Thayer said he remembered selling two men and two women tickets to Humboldt, Kansas, several miles farther north. But that was several days earlier, he said. The Benders had vanished.

What happened to the four Benders is still a mystery. Facts are few. Theories are plentiful. Over the years, the human weakness of wanting to share in the notoriety that the Benders received, has spurred the fabrication of tales by many individuals. Such stories have few, if any, facts to back them up. And even when all the stories that have been

This photo was taken on May 9, 1873, by Julius Ploetz, a photographer from Independence, Kansas. It shows the location of seven graves that contained eight bodies in what had been the Benders' garden and orchard. *Courtesy Kansas State Historical Society*

recorded have been gathered together—the old newspaper accounts, the articles, pamphlets and books—the few facts that emerge fill only a thimble.

But for the reader who insists on an ending to every tale, he or she may pick any one of a dozen or more yarns, each reputed by their teller to be the "real story" of what happened to the Benders.

Undoubtedly, the most fantastic of these was published in the *Topeka Commonwealth* in early August of 1877, about four years after the Benders vanished. A visitor to Topeka, who identified himself as Captain Don Pieppo, walked into the *Commonwealth* office one morning and announced that he knew what had happened to the Benders. He said he had commanded a small ship sailing from Mexico to Galveston, Texas, in April 1873, when a terrible storm blew in from the northwest.

Suddenly, he said, he heard voices from the heavens. Then his ship was rocked as something became entangled in the mast. A moment later a large object fell to the deck of the ship. It was a gondola from a large balloon.

Captain Pieppo then told how he found two men and two women in the gondola. But the fall, he said, had killed all but the younger of the two men. And he was near death. Immediately, the captain said, he took the young man below deck. It was there that the youth identified himself as John Bender. He told how he and the others had fled Kansas in the balloon. He told how Kate had discovered a boiling spring of gas near their Kansas home, how old man Bender had built the balloon in which the family had fled. But after floating south across Indian Territory and Texas, they had lost control of the balloon, and it had fallen on Captain Pieppo's ship during the storm.

The reward poster distributed by Kansas Governor Thomas A. Osborn in 1873. No one ever claimed the reward. *Courtesy Kansas State Historical Society*

GOVERNOR'S PROCLAMATION.

$2,000 REWARD

State of Kansas, Executive Department.

WHEREAS, several atrocious murders have been recently committed in Labette County, Kansas, under circumstances which fasten, beyond doubt, the commissions of these crimes upon a family known as the "Bender family," consisting of

JOHN BENDER, about 60 years of age, five feet eight or nine inches in height, German, speaks but little English, dark complexion, no whiskers, and sparely built;

MRS. BENDER, about 50 years of age, rather heavy set, blue eyes, brown hair, German, speaks broken English;

JOHN BENDER, Jr., alias John Gebardt, five feet eight or nine inches in height, slightly built, gray eyes with brownish tint, brown hair, light moustache, no whiskers, about 27 years of age, speaks English with German accent;

KATE BENDER, about 24 years of age, dark hair and eyes, good looking, well formed, rather bold in appearance, fluent talker, speaks good English with very little German accent:

AND WHEREAS, said persons are at large and fugitives from justice, now therefore, I, Thomas A. Osborn, Governor of the State of Kansas, in pursuance of law, do hereby offer a REWARD OF FIVE HUNDRED DOLLARS for the apprehension and delivery to the Sheriff of Labette County, Kansas, of each of the persons above named.

In Testimony Whereof, I have hereunto subscribed my name, and caused the Great Seal of the State to be affixed.

[L. S.]   Done at Topeka, this 17th day of May, 1873.

THOMAS A. OSBORN,
Governor.

By the Governor:
W. H. SMALLWOOD,
Secretary of State.

Captain Pieppo related how young John Bender died a few hours later. Then, said the Captain, his own ship was sent to the bottom of the Gulf of Mexico as a result of the storm. And with it went the bodies of the Benders.

Several other unbelievable stories were told during the years following the Benders' disappearance. A few persons claimed to be one of the Benders, but none were able to prove it. But looking back over the years since the Benders vanished, and sifting through the evidence that is available, the most logical explanation of their disappearance seems to involve a posse. Even this story has several variations. In each case, however, there is a posse of men who caught and killed the Benders and disposed of their bodies. In one version, the Benders were tracked into Indian Territory, now Oklahoma, near the Grand River, some thirty

The Bender store in May 1873, just after the Bender family vanished. The photo was taken by G. R. Gamble, a photographer from nearby Parsons, Kansas. The persons in front are sightseers. *Courtesy Kansas State Historical Society*

miles south of the Kansas border near Cherryvale. There the Benders supposedly were shot and buried in unmarked graves.

Another version relates how a posse led by Colonel York returned a few hours after their first visit, got the Benders to confess, then killed them and took their bodies away and buried them. One version of this story says the bodies were buried near Thayer, Kansas. In 1906 a Dr. James A. De Moss of Thayer claimed he knew the exact spot where the Benders' remains lay, and the names of "eight living men" who had been members of a posse that lynched the killers. But Dr. De Moss, so far as I can learn, never disclosed the location.

In 1967, the *Houston Post,* in a copyrighted story, reported that it had located a statement by Charles M. Coe, a former Kansan, who claimed to have been a member of the posse that killed the Benders. Coe had dictated a statement on the matter to Dr. William Hiram McDaniel of Gainesville, Texas. In it, Coe claimed he had been a member of the posse of citizens that went to the Bender store, took them captive and made them confess. Then, he said, the Benders were lynched, their bodies weighted and thrown into the Verdigris River northwest of the Bender store.

Perhaps this is the true end of the Bender story, but the chances are just as good it is not. There are still too many unanswered questions and the evidence is too sketchy. Probably the best ending to the Bender story—at least for now—is the one provided by the Kansas State Historical Society. On the society's historical marker, near the original Bender homesite, they have simply concluded: "The end of the Benders is not known. The earth seemed to swallow them, as it had their victims."

William Clarke Quantrill: Was He a Madman?

On August 21, 1863, William Clarke Quantrill and a force of nearly 300 men rode into Lawrence, Kansas. When they left about four hours later, nearly 150 Lawrence men were dead and more than two dozen others were wounded. Most of the business district and many homes were left in flames.

Only the gravestones at Oak Hill and Pioneer cemeteries stand as vivid reminders today of the events that occurred that August morning more than a century ago. Of course, there is a plaque or two on downtown buildings commemorating those who died, but no one is alive who was in Lawrence that summer day.

Quantrill's attack on Lawrence came during the Civil War when emotions ruled over logic. Writers favoring the South called the attack a "raid" pointing out that 200 Confederate men had been killed by Union forces in Missouri during the 15 days before the attack. But writers with Northern sympathies labeled it a "massacre" and called Quantrill a "madman."

Was Quantrill a madman? Was he simply a soldier doing his duty as he saw it? Or was Quantrill something else?

Many persons on both sides of the action later recorded recollections of what happened that day. And with other bits and pieces uncovered in old documents, letters and reminiscences, it is possible today to have a better understanding of William Clarke Quantrill. But answers to the questions above are hazy.

He was born on July 31, 1837, in Canal Dover, Ohio, the oldest of eight children. His father was a school principal.

Young Quantrill, a slender boy of medium height with blue eyes and yellow-brown hair, was bright and active. He enjoyed hunting and fishing and was a good marksman by the age of fifteen. He soon graduated from his father's school and began a career as a teacher under his father.

But young Quantrill left home soon after his father died in 1854. He eventually found a job teaching school in Mendota, Illinois. After a year, however, he returned home. Still in his late teens, he was restless.

After three Ohio friends came to Kansas Territory in 1857 and entered a claim on land on the Marais des Cygnes River near the present boundary of Franklin and Miami counties, Quantrill joined them.

He wrote many letters home to his mother. The early letters suggest that Quantrill had strong Northern sympathies. In one letter he said he believed all Democrats were rascals and all Missourians should be shot.

By the spring of 1859 Quantrill had left his Ohio friends. Some accounts suggest that he fled because of trouble with the law—horse stealing—and that he took the name Charley Hart, but the facts are hazy. It is known that Quantrill joined a wagon train bound for Salt Lake City. He was hired by Henry Chiles, a young wagon boss working for the firm of Russell, Majors and Waddell, then one of the leading freighting firms in the West.

Travel across the plains was slow. It gave Quantrill a chance to have long talks with the freighters, most of whom were from Missouri. His political views apparently began to change.

At Fort Laramie the freighters heard rumors that gold had been discovered to the south near Pike's Peak. One account says Quantrill wanted to quit bullwhacking and go in search of gold, but whether he actually did is unknown. It is known that by July 1859 he was at Lawrence, Kansas Territory.

By the fall of 1859 Quantrill was again teaching school, this time at Stanton near Ottawa, K.T., about twenty miles south of Lawrence. After teaching a normal six-month term, he returned to the Lawrence area where he lived a few miles outside of town.

Quantrill soon fell in with a group of Southern sympathizers who lived nearby. The group kept in close contact with proslavery leaders in Missouri about thirty miles to the east. By late summer in 1860 Quantrill had joined these border ruffians in trips to Missouri to return runaway slaves found around Lawrence. But when Quantrill ventured into Lawrence, he would give the impression he was against slavery.

In December 1860, Quantrill joined five abolitionists from Law-

William Clarke Quantrill dressed in a Confederate officer's uniform. *Courtesy Kansas State Historical Society*

rence who planned to steal slaves from Morgan Walker, who lived near Blue Springs just inside Missouri. Once across the border in Missouri Quantrill informed Walker's son of the plan.

When Quantrill and the abolitionists entered Walker's home on the night of December 10, 1860, the Missourians were waiting.

One abolitionist was killed, two were wounded and two escaped to Lawrence. Quantrill was jailed but soon released. He spent the winter in Jackson County, Missouri.

When Fort Sumter was fired on and the nation plunged into civil war the following spring, Quantrill headed south and joined Confederate General McCulloch's forces. He fought in the Battle of Wilson Creek and perhaps others. Then late in 1861 he returned to Jackson County in Missouri where he soon became a leader of a group of farmers who had banded together to protect their property from bands of Kansas Jayhawkers.

After one band of Jayhawkers lead by Charles "Doc" Jennison raided Dayton and Columbus, Missouri, early in 1862, Quantrill and his men attacked Aubrey, Kansas.

Within two months the Union army issued Special Order No. 2 declaring that the guerrillas were not Confederate soldiers but outlaws. Orders were given to kill them on the spot if captured.

The order strengthened Quantrill's hand. Southerners didn't like it. More Missourians joined Quantrill and soon they controlled all movement in Jackson County, just across the border from Kansas.

In August 1862, Quantrill and his men attacked Union forces at Independence, Missouri, and captured the town. Within days Quantrill and his men were rewarded for their actions and sworn into Confederate service. Quantrill was given the rank of captain.

A few weeks later, on September 6, 1862, Quantrill and some of his men raided Olathe, Kansas, killing and looting. They took every wagon in town to carry away their loot. And when they ran out of wagons, Quantrill ordered some of his men to steal more wagons from farmers outside of town. They did. Quantrill did not burn Olathe but did leave six townsmen dead.

As word of Quantrill's raid spread, troops from Leavenworth gave chase and caught up with him in Cass County, Missouri. It was a running battle that lasted several days. Two guerrillas were killed but Quantrill and the others escaped. They quickly disbanded and scattered in all directions.

By early October, however, Quantrill and a few of his men were together again this time killing fifteen Union soldiers guarding a wagon train in Johnson County, Kansas, not far from Olathe. Quantrill then surrounded what is today Shawnee, Kansas, killing, looting and burning.

The next month, November of 1862, saw Quantrill and his men wintering with the Confederate army in Arkansas. But they returned to Jackson County in the spring of 1863 and began their attacks anew.

Brig. Gen. Thomas Ewing, Jr., commanding Union forces along the border, began to arrest the mothers, wives and sisters of the better known members of Quantrill's band. And by early August of 1863, Ewing had ordered them sent south out of Missouri.

This infuriated Quantrill and his men.

In retaliation Quantrill decided to raid Lawrence, the abolitionist headquarters from where many of the Jayhawker raids into Missouri originated. He supposedly sent spies to Lawrence where a few Southern sympathizers still remained. And Quantrill himself is believed to have traveled as far west as Eudora, a town eight miles east of Lawrence, about two weeks before the raid.

The afternoon before the raid Quantrill and about 300 men entered Kansas at Aubrey where 200 Union soldiers were stationed.

William H. Gregg, a Quantrill lieutenant, later recalled: "We marched by them in full view not only half a mile away. Quantrill's order was : 'Make no attack unless fired upon.' The Federals did not fire and we did not."

Quantrill and his men entered the southern part of Lawrence at about 5 a.m. the following morning. They rode north on Massachusetts, the main street.

"We went there to kill and I don't deny it," recalled Gregg early in this century. He added that the purpose of the raid was to attack Lawrence and, if possible, capture General Jim Lane, an early U.S. senator and prominent political leader. Lane, however, fled and was not captured. But at least 143 Lawrence men were killed that August morn-

An Eastern artist's conception of Quantrill's raid. The illustration appeared in *Harper's,* September 5, 1863. *Courtesy Kansas Historical Society*

his illustration, from *Harper's Weekly,* September 19, 1863, depicts e ruins of Lawrence after Quan-ll's raid. *Courtesy Kansas State Histor-al Society*

This early photograph of the business district at Lawrence, Kansas, was taken either in the late spring or summer of 1864, not quite a year after Quantrill burned much of the town. The black fire scars may still be seen on the sides of the rebuilt stone buildings on the left and right sides of the wide street. This photograph looks north. Just beyond the trees at the end of the street is the Kansas River. *Courtesy Kansas State Historical Society*

ing and many others wounded. But not every man found in Lawrence
was killed. An Illinois newspaperman, staying at the Eldridge Hotel,
waved a white flag from the hotel balcony. Then he asked Quantrill
why he had come to Lawrence.

"Plunder," Quantrill replied.

The newspaperman, as he later wrote, replied, "We are defenseless
and at your mercy, the house is surrendered, but we demand protection
for the inmates."

Quantrill gave them protection but not before robbing them. He
then moved the guests outside and put a torch to the hotel. The guests—
now prisoners—were taken to the City Hotel where Quantrill made his
headquarters.

The newspaperman and several other men survived the raid as did
Lane, who hid in a cornfield behind his house.

At about 9 a.m. that humid Friday morning Quantrill and his
men—many of them drunk—rode south out of Lawrence toward the
Wakarusa River carrying much loot and leaving death, destruction and
much pain behind them.

Lawrence buried its dead and began the task of rebuilding. Kansans generally blamed the whole state of Missouri for Quantrill's raid.
And General Ewing issued Special Order No. 11 on August 25. All
persons living in Jackson, Bates and Cass counties and those living more
than a mile from military posts in part of Vernon County had 15 days
to leave.

Quantrill and his men continued to fight hit-and-run battles in
Jackson County, but by early October they were heading south to
winter in Texas. En route they attacked Union troops at Baxter Springs,
Kansas, killing 79 and wounding others.

In Texas Quantrill refused to obey Confederate authorities to the
disgust of many regular officers. And soon many of his own men refused
to take his orders. Many left, and by the spring of 1864 Quantrill
controlled only about 100 men.

Quantrill and his dwindling force returned to Jackson County,
Missouri, in early May of 1864. They attacked Union forces at Lamar,
Missouri, but Quantrill lost 30 men in the raid.

Through the summer of 1864 the guerrillas continued their hit-
and-run attacks. Several thousand Union troops took to the field to stop
them, but Quantrill and his men frequently dressed in Union uniforms
to escape detection.

After Confederate General Price was defeated at Westport, now
part of Kansas City, Quantrill and a handful of his men left Missouri
for Kentucky wearing Union uniforms. There they committed several
crimes.

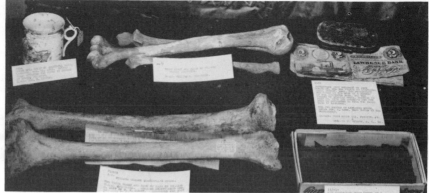

A photograph showing relics from Quantrill's raid on Lawrence, including *(lower left)* two tibia bones and *(upper center)* three arm bones that supposedly belonged to Quantrill. (See text for details on bones.) *Courtesy Kansas State Historical Society*

On May 10, 1865, Quantrill and his men were surprised by a force of Union guerrillas led by Edward Terrill. Quantrill was shot in the back. Wounded seriously, Quantrill was taken to a Louisville hospital where doctors operated. But Quantrill died on the evening of June 6, 1865, about a month after he had been shot.

Quantrill was twenty-seven years old.

The story of William Clarke Quantrill might end here, but it doesn't. He was buried in a Catholic cemetery at Louisville, Kentucky, but in 1887, at his mother's direction, his remains were dug up with the intent to rebury them at Dover, Ohio, near his birthplace.

While some of Quantrill's bones may have been reburied there, others apparently were not. Late in 1887 the Kansas State Historical Society at Topeka was given two thigh bones, supposedly Quantrill's, by W. W. Scott, a newspaper editor from Canal Dover, Ohio. Scott had arranged for Quantrill's remains to be dug up.

Later, after Scott's death, William E. Connelley, secretary of the society and author of a biography of Quantrill, purchased shin bones and arm bones that reportedly were Quantrill's. The seller was Scott's wife. Scott had been a close friend of Quantrill's mother.

These bones are still held today by the Kansas State Historical Society at Topeka, but, according to society officials, the shin bones and arm bones are those belonging to a youth of about seventeen years old. It is highly doubtful they were Quantrill's. Officials of the society speculate that they might have washed into Quantrill's Louisville grave before it was opened in 1887.

As for Quantrill's skull, it apparently remained in the hands of Mrs. Scott until around the turn of the century when a fraternity in Ohio somehow obtained it. The skull was actually used as part of an initiation ceremony until the early 1940s when the fraternity was disbanded. The skull reappeared again in 1972 and is today in the hands of the Canal Dover Historical Society in Ohio.

William Clarke Quantrill has been dead for more than a century, yet he remains a legend. Perhaps it is human nature that evil is remembered longer in time than good, and that more people remember Quantrill than those persons he and his men killed.

The Tale Texans Don't Like to Tell

About eight miles southwest of Osawatomie, Kansas, near the Linn and Miami county lines, is a little hill. It is located close to Middle Creek. A few old-timers still refer to the mound as "Battle Hill." Historians say it was the scene of a "little skirmish" in 1856.

Historically the "skirmish" wasn't very important, but what happened and who it happened to is a story worth repeating.

Kansas Territory was only about two years old in the spring of 1856. The vast territory that stretched from the Missouri River westward to the Rockies was up for grabs. Northerners, especially New Englanders, were trying to populate the territory in hopes of making Kansas a free state. But proslavery forces from Missouri and elsewhere in the South had the same goal in mind to make it a slave state.

The northeastern portion of Kansas Territory, the area just west and northwest of Kansas City, was filled with turmoil, violence and death. But until the spring of 1856, Bourbon County—south of Kansas City along the eastern border of the territory—had been generally peaceful. The county was south of the trouble spots.

Things began to change in Bourbon County one warm spring day in 1856 when a group of about thirty South Carolinians rode into the little town of Fort Scott, then the largest community in the county.

At first the South Carolinians acted like gentlemen. They were friendly and soon learned who the Free Staters were in the county. Once this was done the visitors' attitude changed. They began a campaign of intimidation against the Free Staters.

The "gentlemen" drove off the Free Staters' livestock, fired bullets into their cabins in the middle of the night and even escorted many antislavery men and their families out of the county. By late July 1856 nearly all the population of Bourbon County favored slavery, or at least said they did.

On a hot morning in early August of that year a group of men on horseback rode into Fort Scott from the south. They announced they were Texas Rangers out to get John Brown, the abolitionist, who was then living at Osawatomie, K. T., to the north. Each "Ranger" was well armed and mounted. And these "Rangers" wore spurs, according to most accounts, "as big as tin plates." Their saddles were "Texian," resting on large saddle blankets with a Lone Star in the corner.

The Rangers set up their headquarters at Fort Scott. For a day or so most of them did little except whittle on wood with their big bowie knives, make bullets or talk about what they were going to do to John Brown once they found him.

But their leader, a man identified as Captain William Barnes, was busier. He was enlisting the aid of the South Carolinians headed by G. W. Jones to help "go after John Brown."

About three days later a traveler passing through Fort Scott on his way south warned the Rangers that Free State men from Linn County, just to the north, had learned of the Rangers' presence and were putting together a posse to "run them damn Texans out of Kansas." That was late one afternoon.

Immediately the Rangers posted guards, sent women and children to safety and prepared to do battle. But several hours passed without any sign of a posse. The suspense was great. And after the August sun set on the western horizon only the sound of crickets and a few frogs broke the stillness of that hot and humid August night.

The Rangers waited.

A little after midnight the sound of a shot echoed across the countryside. It came from near the ford on the Marmaton River just north of Fort Scott. Minutes later a Ranger guard, who had been posted at the crossing, came running into town yelling that the enemy was crossing the river. He said he had killed one of the attackers.

The Rangers closed ranks, checked their guns and waited to meet the enemy. They were still waiting several hours later when the first faint rays of dawn could be seen on the eastern horizon. It was then that Captain Barnes sent a small party of Rangers to scout the area by the river where the enemy had been reported.

A few minutes later they returned. All they found was a dead cow— some farmer's milk cow—that had been shot apparently while getting a drink of water in the river. The Ranger who had done the shooting took quite a ribbing, but the humor broke the tenseness that had prevailed and everyone relaxed.

Within a couple of days the Rangers decided the Free State posse had been scared off, if there really had been a posse. The Rangers decided it was time to move north and "rout out Old John Brown" at Osawatomie.

Joined by G. W. Jones, J. P. Fox and the South Carolinians, Captain Barnes and the Rangers began to move northward toward Osawatomie, two counties away. Their total force numbered about 100 men.

They made good time and at dusk reached Middle Creek in northwest Linn County. There beside the cool waters of the little stream, the Rangers and South Carolinians made camp for the night. They posted guards.

The night was uneventful, but about dawn as the Southerners were preparing breakfast, about 100 Free Staters led by Captains Samuel Anderson and S. T. Shore attacked the Rangers from atop a small hill.

The Free Staters, after discovering the camp before dawn, had captured the guards outside the camp. Historians tell us a "lively skirmish" followed with "three or four volleys exchanged."

From good defensive positions on what became known as "Battle Hill," the Free Staters soon got the best of the Rangers and the other proslavery forces on the creek bank. And as one old-timer recalled many years later, "Them Rangers skedaddled back to Fort Scott pushing on their bridle reins and with saddle blankets flying."

According to one account, the Free Staters captured 20 to 30 horses, 3 wagonloads of arms, boots and saddles. Two proslavery men were wounded and 15 taken prisoner.

As for the Texas Rangers and their return to Fort Scott, they reached the community late that night. They woke the whole town and warned everyone that "2,000 Yankees" were chasing them. The Rangers' stories so frightened everyone that the residents of Fort Scott took to the woods on that August night and hid until daylight.

The Texas Rangers—if they really were Rangers—supposedly stopped in Fort Scott only long enough to water their horses and to hurriedly pack up supplies. They left town in a cloud of dust.

One old-timer who recalled the story around the turn of the century said with a twinkle in his eyes that he heard "them Texans never stopped riding till they done got back across the Red River down there in Texas."

Thus ended the little known invasion of Kansas Territory by some alleged Texas Rangers.

Part IV

MEN, WOMEN, ANIMALS AND SNAKES

Animals are such agreeable friends;
they ask no questions, pass no criticisms.

—*George Eliot*

Old Dan the Ox and Bob Wright

It has been said that without the horse the western plains might never have been conquered. This is probably true. But it is equally true that the trusty ox made commerce on the plains possible and in turn helped to complete the settlement of the American West. Oxen were the primary source of power for thousands upon thousands of freight wagons that carried the goods of civilization across the plains.

One of the best descriptions of how oxen were used is provided by Alexander Majors in his memoirs *Seventy Years on the Frontier,* published in Chicago in 1893. He wrote: "The number of cattle necessary to draw each wagon was twelve, making six yokes or pairs, and a prudent freighter would always have from twenty to thirty head of extra oxen in case of accident to or lameness of some of the animals."

Majors, whose memoirs were produced when he was in his eighties, observed that "oxen proved to be the cheapest and most reliable teams for long trips, where they had to live upon grass. They did good daily work, gathered their own living, and if properly driven would travel 2,000 miles in a season," wrote Majors, who in 1855 joined forces with two other men to form what became the leading overland freighting firm of Majors, Russell and Waddell, headquartered at Leavenworth, Kansas.

Majors had great respect for oxen as did the men who worked with the animals on the trail each day. These teamsters knew that oxen, like many other animals, had their own distinct personalities. To do his job right, a teamster had to understand his oxen. Many became attached to their oxen if for no other reason but that they had to walk beside them across the plains to keep the trains moving. Many oxen were given names like Old Brindle, Big Joe and Old Bill. And then there was Old Dan.

In November 1862, Old Dan was part of one of Majors, Russell and Waddell's wagon trains heading east across the plains returning to Leavenworth. It was a large train with thirty or forty wagons. The travel was slow but steady, and old Dan was part of the cavayado, or extra oxen, being trailed along with the wagon train.

Mexican freighters usually drove their cavayado ahead of their trains, but most Americans drove their extra oxen to the rear of the train. And that was where Old Dan was.

Young Bob Wright, twenty-two years old, was in charge of the cavayado. Although he had been on the plains for nearly three years, he had only recently joined the freighting company, taking the job of looking after the extra oxen.

The wagon train was traveling along the Arkansas River bottom about ten miles west of where Great Bend, Kansas, stands today. It was one of those warm November days that often cause Kansans to wonder whether winter's cold chill will ever arrive.

As Bob Wright rode along atop his horse, keeping the oxen on the move, he began to feel warm. He took off his coat. It was a heavy linsey-woolsey, manufactured on a loom in Missouri, lined with a bright yellow cloth, the sleeves being lined with red. Wright turned the coat inside out to air.

But the coat was heavy and Wright didn't want to carry it. As his horse was plodding along behind the oxen, Wright spotted Old Dan. Now Dan was a big fellow with rather large horns and was so gentle that some of the teamsters had used him as a horse in crossing streams. They could ride across most streams on Dan's back easier than they could ride many a horse.

When Wright saw the big old ox, he had an idea. Why not let Old Dan carry his coat? Catching up with the animal, Wright, with a little stretching, pulled the sleeves of his coat down over Dan's horns and let the coat flap down in front.

When Wright rode around to the front of Old Dan, he laughed. Dan looked downright strange. Wright then realized that he had created a monstrosity. From the side Dan looked like an ox, but not from the front. With the yellow and red lining of the coat flapping above the animal's head, Dan was a weird sight. But the old ox didn't seem to mind the coat. He trudged along as unconcerned as ever.

Wright began to hurry old Dan along. They had fallen behind the

A photograph of Bob Wright taken a few years after his experiences with Old Dan the Ox. *Courtesy Kansas State Historical Society*

other oxen. In a short while Old Dan neared the other oxen walking slowly behind the last wagon. Wright relaxed in the saddle, more comfortable than before.

But then it happened. A young steer in the cavayado bawled out what must have been "Good grief, what's that?" in steer language. Then the steer took off like a scared jackrabbit with the other oxen—all but Old Dan that is—following close behind.

Immediately, Wright knew what had happened. His coat hanging from Old Dan's horns and flapping in the wind had caused a stampede. In a flash he moved to Old Dan, who was still walking along leisurely, and pulled the coat from the creature's horns.

Up ahead, the stampeding cattle had reached the ox-drawn wagons. The yoked oxen suddenly took to running like the loose animals, and in a matter of seconds the drivers lost control of their oxen.

Wright lost sight of what was happening as a cloud of dust engulfed the train and a thundering noise echoed across the plains. Wright prodded old Dan to move a little faster, anxious to find out what was happening.

After what seemed like hours, Wright spotted the wagon boss heading his way out of a settling cloud of dust.

"What caused the stampede of the cavayado?" demanded the man as he neared Wright and Old Dan.

"I'm not really sure," said Wright, quickly adding, "Maybe a wolf ran across in front of them."

"Well, them cussed wolves probably did cause it. I seen several this afternoon while ridin' up front in the train."

The wagon master then related to Bob Wright how seven wagons had ended up ahead in Walnut Creek, and eleven more were wrecked, scattered along the trail ahead for five miles. One man's leg was broken and another's arm, and a lot of men were bruised up. And he said the cavayado was fifteen miles ahead and still going.

As the wagon master rode away, Wright looked down at his coat, folded neatly across his saddle, and smiled. Then he looked down at Old Dan, a mute witness to his lies.

"I think that old ox gave me a sly wink, as much as to say, 'You lie out of it well, but I am ashamed of you.' " said Bob Wright many years later when he told the story.

In time, Wright left the freighting job. He settled down on a farm in Ford County, Kansas, became postmaster at Dodge City and won election five times as state representative to the state legislature at Topeka.

Prairie Dog Dave

"Dirty Face Charley," "Stink Finger Jim," "Coon Hole Johnny," "The Hoo-Doo Kid," "Shoot His Eye Out Jack" and "Hurricane Bill" are just a few of the nicknames acquired by early-day residents of the plains. And then there was "Prairie Dog Dave."

His real name was David Morrow. He was born in Washington County, New York, in 1837. He fought for the Union during the Civil War and afterwards, as a soldier, chased renegade Navajos and hostile Apaches in Arizona and New Mexico. In 1866 he was mustered out of the army at Soula, New Mexico.

Not quite two years later, in the spring of 1868, Morrow turned up in Hays City, Kansas. He was after buffalo. In that year countless buffalo or bison roamed the prairie and plains around Hays City. W. F. "Buffalo Bill" Cody and other men including Morrow earned their living hunting the shaggy monsters and supplying meat to settlers and to the work crews building the Kansas Pacific Railroad west of Hays.

The town of Hays was not quite a year old. The townsite had been laid out in June 1867. The railroad had reached Hays City the following October, not quite six months before Morrow arrived.

Dave Morrow was a good shot. He made pretty good money killing buffalo and selling the animal's meat, but from time to time the supply was greater than the demand. It was then that Morrow did odd jobs and loafed around Hays City. He enjoyed spinning "windies"—tall tales—either to impress or to scare newcomers arriving almost daily from the East.

A photograph of "Prairie Dog"
Dave Morrow a few years after
he left the prairie dog business.
*Courtesy Kansas State Historical
Society*

One day Morrow caught two prairie dogs, the hamster-like, short-tailed ground squirrels that were so named because of their barking calls. The little animals were very numerous on the prairie around Hays City, where their towns were easy to spot.

Wherever the little animals lived the prairie was pockmarked with craters. Each crater had a volcano-like cone, an entrance to the little creature's burrow. The prairie dog would gather soil from the surface, pat it into place forming the cone that served as a lookout post and as protection against floods after heavy rains. Each burrow had many entrances. And each entrance descended steeply for about four yards before meeting radial tunnels. At the end of the tunnels the prairie dogs would build their nests.

Dave Morrow tamed the two prairie dogs he caught. And one afternoon he had them in his pockets when a Kansas Pacific passenger train pulled in from the East. Walking along the station's platform Morrow greeted the newcomers and began to tell tall tales about how lovable his newly found pets were. To his surprise a passenger offered

This turn-of-the-century illustration by Kansas artist Carl P. Bolmar is titled "Playing with a pet prairie-dog." Most plainsmen excepting Morrow thought the prairie dog most worthless. One Kansas newspaper editor wrote: "Procrastinated precipitation and predatory hexapods may destroy the corn and wheat, but the prairie-dog we have always with us. If we can take his hide and sell it to Eastern plutocrats, to be used in the manufacture of beaver muffs and sealskin sacks, we may laugh at hot winds and snap our fingers under the proboscis of the devastating chinch-bug." *Courtesy Kansas State Historical Society*

five dollars for the animals. Morrow gladly parted with them and that day entered the prairie dog business.

To replenish his supply, Morrow hauled barrels of water out from Hays City to one of the nearby prairie dog towns. Selecting a crater, Morrow poured water down the hole. As the little animals floated to the surface, Morrow picked them up. But the method was slow. It took much water and a great deal of time. And it was work.

Morrow decided to invent a better prairie dog trap. It consisted of a barrel full of sand, open at one end. Morrow would place the barrel over a prairie dog's hole, open end down. As the sand flowed into the hole, prairie dogs would surface through the sand into the barrel and find themselves trapped. The sand meantime would fill the hole and cut off their return.

Morrow would set several of these traps over the various entrances.

Then at his convenience he would return to the prairie dog town with a sack and pick up his merchandise. Within a few weeks his prairie dog business was booming. And almost overnight Dave Morrow became known as "Prairie Dog Dave."

But as with any good thing, competition was just around the corner. Morrow had hardly established his monopoly in the field when other men entered the business and soon the prairie dog market at Hays City was glutted. The going price for prairie dogs dropped from five dollars a pair to one dollar, and then to fifty cents and finally a quarter. At that price, trapping prairie dogs was hardly worth the effort. Morrow gave up the prairie dog business and returned to buffalo hunting.

As Morrow began to take up buffalo hunting again, late in 1872, he heard other hunters talking about a white buffalo supposedly seen on the plains southwest of Hays City down toward Dodge City. Most people, including many old buffalo hunters, had some doubts that such an animal really had been seen. But Prairie Dog Dave, always interested in the unusual, decided to hunt the white shaggy. He bought a gallon of formaldehyde, took his gun, some ammunition and supplies, and set out in his wagon to search for the animal.

Just how long he was gone or where he went, no one today is sure. But around January 1, 1873, Dave Morrow drove his wagon into Dodge City, pulled up in front of Robert Wright's general store—the same Bob Wright who years earlier had the adventure with Old Dan the ox—and

Dodge City, Kansas, in 1873, not long after "Prairie Dog Dave" Morrow moved there. It is possible that one of the men in the photo is Morrow. *Courtesy Kansas State Historical Society*

tied his team to the hitching post. Dave Morrow was smiling. In the back of the wagon was the carcass of the white buffalo.

Bob Wright paid Prairie Dog Dave one thousand dollars cash on the spot for the animal's remains, preserved in formaldehyde, and later had the white robe and head mounted and shipped to Kansas City, where it was put on display. Later it was shown in Topeka at the statehouse. It finally ended up in the Hubbell Museum at New York City, where it was destroyed by fire a few years later.

With his money Prairie Dog Dave settled down. A year later, 1874, a reporter for a Topeka newspaper interviewed Morrow where he lived in Hamilton County in far-western Kansas. The reporter later wrote:

> In his personal makeup the "dog" is fashioned very much like a man, walks upright, is solidly and equally constructed, with a pair of black eyes that will go right through a ten foot stone wall, and measuring six feet six inches in his moccasins. In conversation he is fluent, and relates his hair-breadth escapes with that subdued self-gratulation characteristic of old plainsmen. . . . He is an excellent shot, and when he levels his piece on a deer or buffalo it is sure to come down. It is not known that he ever amused himself by shooting the earrings from his sisters' ears. . . . In all his wild and checkered career, where so many have made moral shipwrecks of themselves, Dave has preserved his manhood untarnished, and still carries about him the tokens of a former civilization. He has come to the wise conclusion that a rolling stone will gather no greenbacks, and having taken 160 acres of Uncle Sam's land now whiles away his leisure moments in reading the latest works on agriculture and matrimony.

Prairie Dog Dave—the nickmane was still with him—did settle down for a time and homesteaded, but life was too dull. He became a peace officer at Dodge City. Through the 1870s and '80s, Morrow served as a lawman at Dodge City. Then he retired from law and work and, because of poor health, was admitted to the Kansas State Soldiers Home at Fort Dodge. There he died on October 18, 1893. In reporting his death a Dodge City newspaper observed, "Another old landmark is gone."

Jim Caspion's White Buffalo

Prairie Dog Dave Morrow's white buffalo was one of four known to have been killed on the plains during the 1870s. Another white buff was killed by J. Wright Mooar near where present-day Snyder, Texas, stands, in October of 1876. And James and John Morgan killed a white shaggy about 1870 near the Kansas-Colorado border. The fourth white buffalo was killed by Jim Caspion in 1871, and in that lies a tale.

Caspion and a friend, Sam Tillman, were neighbors in eastern Kansas. When they learned that tanning factories had developed a process to use buffalo hides to make good leather, they became interested. This opened a new market. And when they heard that a buffalo bull's hide had gone up to $3.50 in Leavenworth and Kansas City, they decided to go buffalo hunting.

Teamed up as partners, Caspion and Tillman headed west. In time they found themselves camped east of present-day Wallace, Kansas, about twenty-some miles from the Colorado border. They had been having moderate success killing buffalo for their hides.

On an October morning they rode their horses out of camp. Following them was a hired man with a team and wagon loaded with supplies. The plan was that, if their hunt was successful, they would carry hides back in the wagon.

The morning hours passed without any sign of buffalo. After a midday rest, the men resumed their search, but in order to cover more ground, they decided to split up. They took one precaution. Caspion and Tillman realized they were in Indian country, so they agreed to stay in sight of each other. Also, in that way they could signal each other if buffalo were sighted.

By late afternoon the hunters still had not found any buffalo. Caspion, about to give up, decided to take one last look over a long ridge up ahead. Reaching the ridge and looking over the crest, Caspion saw hundreds, perhaps thousands of buffalo. They were grazing peacefully in a wide valley, perhaps twenty-five miles across. As his eyes scanned the scene, he focused on one spot. On the outside of the herd was a milk-white buffalo. The whiteness of its robe contrasted strangely with the dun tints of the other shaggies around it. The animal was feeding.

Caspion signaled Tillman to join him, and then dismounted. He slowly moved to the crest of the ridge to decide the best way to approach the white buffalo. As he reached the crest he glanced back to see where Tillman was, and at that moment forgot about the white buffalo.

Sam Tillman was riding for his life. About fifty Cheyenne warriors on horseback were after Tillman, riding in the opposite direction.

The chase was a short one.

The Indians shot Tillman's horse, then closed in on him. Moments later, with Tillman's scalp borne aloft on a lance, the Indians turned and started toward Caspion. They were about a mile away.

By then Caspion was atop his horse. He was scanning the countryside. He could not ride to the right or left without giving the Indians the advantage of being able to cut him off. So he headed his horse straight for the buffalo herd.

As Caspion bore down on the buffalo, they stampeded. Within a minute the rider and horse were swallowed up by the mass of beasts, and they were in the rush sweeping across the plains. The last thing Caspion saw over his shoulder, before the dust shut everything from view, was the party of Cheyenne warriors coming over the crest of the hill.

Crowding, jostling, holding on for dear life, Caspion gave his horse his head. The animal held his own among the pushing and shoving buffalo. The dust was so thick Caspion could see nothing. He held his head low. The dust was choking.

After about a mile the buffalo slowed down, but they kept moving at a rapid pace over the plains. The sun soon set, but Caspion could not see the sun. He could only tell by the feel of the ground that the buffalo had moved out of the valley and were now in rough and hilly country, he believed at least twenty-five miles from where the stampede had started.

Then, suddenly, the leaders of the herd divided at a steep bluff. Most turned to the left, but some followed a small valley, which went to the right. Caspion's horse was forced to turn with the buffalo heading into the valley.

After passing through a narrow opening, the valley widened and the buffalo began to thin out. The dust was not so thick. Caspion realized it was dark. A bright moon was coming up. It made the ride seem almost unreal. Then Caspion saw the white buffalo ahead of him, running with other buffalo about one hundred yards away. They came to a place where a deep ravine, worn by water, cut close against the side of the bluff. The animals nearest the bluff kept their footing, but those near the edge were crowded off into space.

As his horse passed the spot safely, Caspion could hear the thuds as the buffalo hit the floor of the ravine twenty feet below, and the painful bellowing of buffalo in the ravine could be heard above the thundering hoofs of the others that passed the spot safely.

Caspion could not see the white buffalo.

When the valley widened, Caspion regained control of his horse. The horse was exhausted, almost ruined, and gave in easily as Caspion slowly reined to a stop outside the dwindling flow of buffalo.

He dismounted, tied his horse and lay down. Exhausted, he fell asleep, paying little attention to the fading roar of buffalo or even thinking about the Indians or the white buffalo.

As faint rays of light crept across the valley floor many hours later, Caspion awakened. Only a handful of buffalo remained in the valley. They were a mile or more away, grazing peacefully.

Caspion untied his horse, mounted and slowly walked the tired animal back over the trail he had been forced to follow the night before. When he came to the ravine, he looked over the edge. Scores of buffalo were lying at the bottom, many of them dead. Others were too badly hurt to move. Among those was the white buffalo.

The animal, a young bull, was leaning against a bank. It had a broken leg. Caspion climbed into the ravine, shot the white buffalo and skinned him. With his prize he decided not to retrace his steps until he could get help.

On reaching civilization, Caspion learned that the Indians had also killed his wagon driver who had been following with provisions. Caspion, with help, returned to the ravine to claim the other buffalo hides. But his real prize was the white robe.

For five years Caspion kept the robe, believing, as the Indians did, that its possession would bring good fortune. For a time it did. But about 1876 Caspion sold the robe for $100 while on a drinking spree one night at Fort Lyon in the eastern part of present-day Colorado. Shortly afterward Caspion was killed by Comanches in New Mexico.

The Saga of Black Kettle

Travel over the Smoky Hill Trail had been hot and tiring for the party of Mormons that June day in 1867. Most were glad when they circled their wagons for the night several miles east of Fort Wallace in northwest Kansas. Soon they relaxed with their evening meal. Grazing just outside the circle of wagons was a group of Kentucky thoroughbred horses. The Mormons were taking them to Salt Lake for breeding purposes. Just how many horses there were is not recorded, but history does mention that one of the animals, a black yearling stud colt, stood out above the rest. He was a magnificent animal. His lines, his conformation—they were those of a champion-to-be.

Under the bright stars the colt and other horses grazed and rested. For everyone the night passed uneventfully, but about dawn a band of Cheyenne Indians under Chief Black Kettle swooped down on the camp. The Cheyennes ran off the stock including the stud colt.

Watching from the protection of their wagons, the Mormons watched as the Indians herded the horses away. At first the Indians had no trouble controlling the animals, but soon the stud colt veered away and hit out cross-country. Three or four Indians gave chase but the colt gave them his tail. After about a mile the Indians gave up. Within a few days the stud colt joined a band of wild horses.

As the weeks and months passed, the colt matured. He fought many battles for leadership with other wild stallions and eventually acquired his own harem. By the early 1870s he ranged over a large portion of Sherman County. The center of his range was near where Goodland, Kansas, stands today. The old government trail—Custer

This photograph of a watercolor painted by the late Byron B. Wolfe in 1972 shows Black Kettle, the wild stallion, racing across the plains of northwest Kansas. The figure on the buckboard to the far right is Frank M. Lockard, the man who eventually captured the wild horse. Artist Wolfe used the author's story as the basis for the watercolor. *Photograph from author's collection; original watercolor owned by Mr. and Mrs. T. N. Luther*

Black Kettle, the Cheyenne chief, after whom the wild mustang was named. *Courtesy Oklahoma State Historical Society*

Road—ran through the center of the horse's range. And by 1873 hardly a week went by that some soldier or buffalo hunter or traveler did not report seeing the noble and beautiful stallion with his harem.

His glossy coat was coal black. It glistened like burnished silver in the sun. He had a long mane that reached nearly to the ground when he stood erect. But when he was in motion with his head, it lay along his back and made him appear about a foot higher than he really was. When he ran across the open plains he was continually tossing his head, throwing his foretop over his ears so he could see.

His tail was also long. When he stood still it would rest on the ground, but when running it stuck straight out behind, which made him appear about twenty feet long from a distance. And his movements, they were described by one man "as graceful like a fawn, while for speed and endurance he excelled any other animal on these plains."

In 1873 the soldiers and traders at Fort Wallace learned the stallion's history from friendly Cheyenne Indians. The Indians related how they had tried unsuccessfully to capture the horse many times. The soldiers at the fort soon began to call the stallion Black Kettle's colt, Black Kettle being the chief of the Indians who ran the horse off from the Mormons. The name spread and soon the horse became known simply as Black Kettle.

Many men tried to capture Black Kettle. One of them was Homer W. Wheeler, post trader and later a cavalry officer at Fort Wallace. With the help of soldiers Wheeler surrounded Black Kettle one night. In a circle around the stallion and his mares, in an area the size of a township, Wheeler posted a soldier every half mile. Wheeler's plan was to chase Black Kettle around the inside of the circle using a fresh horse and rider every hour. Then when Black Kettle became exhausted, Wheeler would send in a cowboy to rope the tired horse.

But Black Kettle was too smart for Wheeler. Before he could begin chasing Black Kettle at dawn, the stallion and his mares broke through the circle. Disgusted, Wheeler returned to Fort Wallace where he offered two hundred dollars to any man who could capture Black Kettle.

Ame Cole, a buffalo hunter, heard Wheeler make the offer.

"By God, Captain, I can walk the tail off the God Dam horse in five days," exclaimed Cole, whose profanity was so natural and unassuming that it soon ceased to be offensive to his listeners.

"I consider the tail the most valuable part of the horse and would not give much for him without it," replied Wheeler with a smile. If Cole gave Wheeler an answer, it is not recorded, but the next morning Ame Cole set out on foot after the horse. His plan was to walk the animal down, crease him and then hobble Black Kettle before he woke up.

Creasing wild horses was a common practice in the 1870s. Mustangers, as the wild horse hunters were called, would fire a rifle ball through the top of a horse's neck just in front of the withers, about a foot from the ears. It would temporarily paralyze but not permanently injure a horse.

A few hours after leaving camp Ame Cole spotted Black Kettle. The stallion and his harem were grazing on a ridge about ten miles southeast of modern-day Goodland, Kansas. But seeing Cole, Black Kettle took his mares and ran northwest. Soon they were out of sight. On foot Cole followed at a brisk walk, sometimes trotting. After nearly two miles Cole had the feeling that Black Kettle had changed course. Walking to a high piece of ground Cole surveyed the countryside.

Far away on the horizon in every direction he saw wild horses. One bunch, larger than the others, was slowly moving west. Cole felt certain it was Black Kettle and his band, but he had no field glass to use to make certain. Taking a chance he began walking west. It wasn't until midafternoon that Cole moved close enough to the horses to see that their leader was not Black Kettle. Tired, hungry and nearly famished for water, Cole headed back to camp near the Smoky Hill River certain that Black Kettle would soon return to the river for water. The horse did not return that night.

What Cole did not know was that Black Kettle was smarter than most wild horses. Instead of running in a wide circle within ten miles of one watering hole, as most wild horses did, Black Kettle had two watering places: one in Wild Horse Draw, near the Smoky Hill River, and the other at the head of Beaver Creek. They were twenty miles apart. And Black Kettle would sometimes run that twenty miles in a straight line when frightened.

The next day Cole again searched for the stallion but without success. That night in camp Cole's partner said it was time the two men returned to buffalo hunting along the Republican River. Cole reluctantly agreed. He said he would return later to capture Black Kettle, but he never did.

Through the 1870s Black Kettle was chased by more men than any other horse on the plains between Kansas City and Denver. He was the subject of countless stories told around campfires on summer nights and in front of warm fireplaces in sod houses on cold winter nights. And one man, William D. Street, wrote a newspaper article about Black Kettle.

Street, an early plainsman and scout for General George Custer and later a pioneer Kansas newspaperman, wrote the article about 1878. Frank M. Lockard, a horse trader, read the article with more than passing interest. At the time Lockard and his partner, Bill Simpson, were selling horses in the Wakeeney, Kansas, area. Lockard clipped the

Frank M. Lockard, who brought Black Kettle's freedom to an end on the western Kansas prairie. *Courtesy Kansas State Historical Society*

article and began to dream of the day when he would capture Black Kettle.

It was a few months before Lockard and Simpson were able to set out to catch Black Kettle from their Norton, Kansas, homes. Lockard was cocksure he would have no difficulty catching the stallion. He had caught hundreds of wild mustangs. The two men pushed west until they reached the Smoky Hill River in present Sherman County, Kansas. South of the river they made camp near a high point on the rolling plains that continue to slope higher and higher until they reach the foothills of the Rockies. Atop the rise on a post, they placed a red undershirt that waved in the almost never-ending breeze. It was a marker that could be seen through a field glass fifteen miles away.

The day after setting up camp Lockard and Simpson rode north to familiarize themselves with the land. They scared up many small bunches of wild horses and watched them through their field glass. It was then, for the first time, that Lockard noticed that nearly all the mares were red roan. "Among the females about one in ten was black while the per cent of roans among the males was a little higher than that. The surplus males were driven out by the leaders and flocked by themselves, usually one, two and sometimes three together," observed Lockard.

It seems entirely possible that many of the black horses were Black Kettle's offspring. "There were hundreds of them on this prairie. . . . These outcasts were called Dog Soldiers by the Indians and the White Men used the same name in describing them. . . . They hunted the herds day and night and the stud who had a family was compelled to keep up a continuous fight or lose them," wrote Lockard.

Late one afternoon, as Lockard and Simpson started for camp, another bunch of wild horses came into view. Although more than a mile away a look through the field glass settled the question as to the leader's identity. It was Black Kettle. There was no mistake about it. His long mane and tail were plainly visible, and Lockard wanted to give chase. But Simpson said, "No, it's late and your horse is jaded now. Wait until morning." Lockard agreed it would be better to wait.

As the first faint light of day was visible in the east, Lockard was in the saddle. He was sure he would take his prize that day. It took him two hours to locate Black Kettle and what happened next is related in Lockard's own words:

"I weighed one hundred and forty pounds at that time and was hardened to the saddle. I could ride a hundred miles without tiring and I had corn fat horses that were as tough as I. . . . I started after him on a stiff lope, going at about ten miles an hour and held that same rate of speed for the next ten hours."

But Lockard did not capture Black Kettle that day. He never got close to the stallion. As darkness closed in the temperature suddenly dropped. A brisk north wind, snow and freezing temperatures swept across northwest Kansas. It was a norther. Lockard lost sight of Black Kettle and wished he had not left his overcoat in camp to lighten his load. Finding a large depression Lockard made camp. He wrapped himself in his saddle blanket, but the sweat-moistened blanket soon froze stiff. Fearing he might freeze to death, Lockard saddled his horse. Alternately riding and walking his horse, Lockard kept moving all night.

It was late the next afternoon before he stumbled upon a ranch on Sappa Creek in southeast Rawlins County. Lockard had traveled more than thirty miles northeast of his camp. He spent the night at the ranch, got food and was given directions. The next day he returned to where Bill Simpson had been anxiously waiting in camp and learned some good news. Simpson had located a deserted corral about three miles away, perfect to hold wild horses. The corral had belonged to the old XY ranch.

Before setting out again after Black Kettle, Lockard said he was going to get a pocket compass. With Christmas only a few days away,

Lockard and Simpson broke camp and headed east to Norton, one hundred and twenty-five miles away. There they spent the holidays and Lockard bought a compass.

Early in January 1880, Lockard and Simpson returned to Black Kettle's range and set up camp near the XY corral. But this time they had six extra corn-fat saddle horses, a wagonload of corn drawn by four horses and driven by Ed Maple. Lockard had hired Maple as cook and driver.

Before preparing to go after Black Kettle again, Lockard went to visit Wild Horse Johnson. While in Norton Lockard had learned of Johnson and his reputation as a successful mustanger. Johnson lived on Goose Creek several miles south of their new camp. Lockard found Johnson, a crusty old plainsman who had caught more wild mustangs than he could count. Wild Horse Johnson was sitting in front of a warm fire in his small ranch house. Nearby in a corral were about fifty horses that he had captured. Johnson invited Lockard to sit a spell in front of the fire. Soon Lockard asked Johnson how he caught wild horses.

"I follow them in a buckboard until they become sore-footed and then corral them. Once in the corral I catch them and tie a clog to the front foot," said Johnson. A clog was made of a forked cottonwood limb about two feet long. It was slipped over the foot just above the hoof and tied with a rawhide thong from the points of the fork. Johnson explained to Lockard that he would then turn his horses out. Once or twice a day he would drive them into the corral to keep them tame. After the horses had worn the clogs for a few days he would take them off. By then the horses would be easy to handle.

When Johnson learned that Lockard was after Black Kettle, he said, "I chased him once for two days and then lost him; he has been run so much that he is very wild and cunning." And then Johnson told Lockard not to bother with Black Kettle. "There are hundreds of horses on the prairie that are worth as much as Black Kettle. There is nothing to him but his mane and tail. He weighs about eight hundred pounds and is getting old. Let him alone," pleaded Johnson.

But Lockard did not heed Wild Horse Johnson's advice. The horse was already an obsession with him. After thanking Johnson for his hospitality, Lockard returned to camp and prepared to resume his plan to capture Black Kettle, then about thirteen years old. With Simpson's help Lockard located Black Kettle and gave chase, but late that January day the weather again turned cold. It was all Lockard and Simpson could do to reach camp before a blizzard struck. For two days Lockard, Simpson and their cook, Ed Maple, struggled to survive on the open plains. All interest in Black Kettle was lost and as soon as the storm passed the three men returned to Norton.

Deep inside Lockard still wanted to capture Black Kettle. By spring Lockard was determined to renew the chase. He had done much thinking about what Wild Horse Johnson had said about capturing wild mustangs and by early June he was back on Black Kettle's range camped with several extra horses and supplies to last him more than a month. Bill Simpson, however, had abandoned Lockard calling his obsession with the stallion foolish. Another young man, Billy Rogers of Norton, had joined Lockard in his quest.

Lockard had decided to follow Wild Horse Johnson's advice. Instead of chasing the stallion on horseback, Lockard would pursue the horse in a light buckboard. It also enabled him to carry food and water for himself and his team.

On the morning of June 2, 1880, Lockard set out in his buggy to find Black Kettle. Within two hours he spotted the stallion and the chase was on. But Lockard didn't try to catch the horse. Instead, he jogged along in his buggy after the stallion and his mares. As Lockard later recalled, "I had learned that speed was not necessary; that if a horse was kept moving constantly his feet soon gave out."

For the first three days Black Kettle and his mares ran away when they saw Lockard, but on the fourth day Lockard could see them limping along and only half a mile away. When the horses went to water in Wild Horse Draw, Lockard returned to camp for a change of horses and a fresh supply of bread. "In my open buggy I carried a five gallon keg of water for the team. A gallon jug of water for myself, a frying pan and coffee pot, for bread I brought a supply from camp but made coffee and fried bacon each time I camped. I carried a Springfield rifle and a field glass, a pair of blankets and a slicker. When night came unless I was near the home camp I made camp on the prairie, put my team on the picket rope and went to sleep," recalled Lockard.

At dawn on the fifth morning Lockard hitched his team to the buckboard and started after Black Kettle. What happened next is told in Lockard's own words:

This was the most beautiful morning I ever experienced. The atmosphere seemed to be impregnated with sweet perfume. I seemed to see hundreds of miles and on the high spots I could see clear across Sherman County. I had driven only a short two miles when I heard something that sounded like distant thunder; the earth seemed to tremble, and as I looked about me, I discovered wild horses coming from all directions. Black Kettle broke into a wild run and other bunches fell in alongside of him. My team wanted to run and I let them out at full speed.

There was a magnificent scene spread out before me and I wanted a close view of it. I was also curious to know the cause, and as I looked out on the panorama, I could see horses coming from everywhere. The herds from each side came in close, then turned west alongside of Black Kettle. We had only run a short time when there were hundreds of them all abreast and running their best. Such a sight I shall never see again. The studs were busy keeping their bunches from mixing, although they were very close together. The almost military discipline of each bunch counted and each herd maintained its own individual number.

After I crossed the Custer Road, I looked to the right and saw a herd of buffalo, about fifty in number, running parallel with the horses and a short time afterwards off to the left there was a small bunch, probably ten or twelve, which soon crossed over behind the horses and joined the other herd. They ran along in this direction for about ten miles and then bore off toward the northwest. These were the last wild buffalo that I ever saw.

Black Kettle was near the center of the long line, which extended half a mile on either side of him. Presently a young colt fell and dropped behind, and when the mother tried to turn back to it Black Kettle put her back in her place and kept her there. As I cast my eyes down the line I could see the little colts dropping behind. The studs paid no attention to them but kept the mares in the bunch by simply shaking their heads at them with their ears back.

We were going very fast. My team soon began to weaken but I applied the whip and kept as near them as I could. About this time I noticed the strangest mirage that I had ever seen. Those horses at times looked to be fifty feet high and then a golden mist would hide them completely. . . . When the mirage dissolved, I found the horses had separated; some went southwest and other bands were moving toward the northwest. Black Kettle had been in a pocket. He could not run fast enough to go around in front and I kept so close that he dared not drop back. Although he was weary and wanted to stop, he had held his place at the front. My team was exhausted and stopped as soon as I laid the whip away. I must have run thirty miles that morning and probably crossed Sherman County quicker than has ever been done since with a team and a buggy. I had killed a team that was worth more than a hundred wild horses. [Lockard's term "killed" means he ruined his team.]

As I turned back for camp I could see many little colts coming. I supposed some of them found their mothers, but the coyotes got a few of them.

Lockard spent most of the afternoon walking his team back to camp. The next morning he left camp at dawn and with a fresh team met Black Kettle and his mares returning to their home range. Lockard again began to follow the stallion and his mares, a daily routine that was to last for twenty-four more days. Each morning Lockard would set out in his buckboard, locate Black Kettle and follow the stallion and his mares. Late in the afternoon, on most days, he would return to camp, spend the night and go out again the next morning with a fresh team.

For Lockard, locating Black Kettle each morning became an easy job. Because Lockard was following and not chasing the stallion, the horse maintained his usual habits ranging in a large circle of perhaps twenty miles. As Lockard later said, "A wild horse never moves very far from his watering place, and when being chased, they would run in a circle and never leave the home range." Black Kettle was no different.

On the morning of the thirtieth day of Lockard's buggy pursuit, he came upon Black Kettle and twenty-nine mares moving along in a slow walk on the south side of the Smoky Hill River. Lockard was able to move close enough to Black Kettle and the mares to touch them with his whip. "Black Kettle had lost interest. His feet were so sore that he would stop for a moment once in a while and hold up one foot while part of the bunch had stopped and was acting as though they did not intend to follow," recalled Lockard, who then slowly moved behind Black Kettle and the mares and drove them along. The horses offered no resistance.

Lockard, although in seeming control of Black Kettle and the others, faced the problem of what to do with the horses. They were moving west. Could he reach Fort Wallace and corral the animals? Lockard made up his mind to stay with the horses and trust to luck. And luck was with him.

Late in the afternoon Lockward came to an abandoned house and corral. He would later learn that it was the Bar Lil Ranch owned by two men named Kibble and Edwards, but when he found it the ranch was deserted. After a few trials Lockard was able to get Black Kettle and sixteen of the twenty-nine mares into the corral. Lockard smiled as Black Kettle calmly moved through the gate. He had finally walked Black Kettle into submission.

The next morning Lockard decided to turn the horses loose and drive them back to his camp, but he didn't want to give Black Kettle any more freedom than necessary. Lockard roped the stallion on the first throw. The horse didn't like the rope and lunged at the fence landing on top with his head and front feet on the outside and the rest of his body inside the corral. Before Lockard could grab the loose rope, Black Kettle slid down on the outside of the fence and started to run north, dragging Lockard's lariat.

Lockard hurriedly hitched his team to the buggy and turned the mares loose. They followed Black Kettle north. What happened next is told in Lockard's own words: "You would have supposed that drag rope would have kept them excited, but except when it touched one of them, they paid no attention to it. . . . Black Kettle brought up the rear; so it was seldom they noticed the rope at all. We reached the Smoky about noon and turned upstream towards the XY corral and camp. I had difficulty at times steering them in the right direction but succeeded late that day in driving them into the big corral at the home camp."

Before nightfall, Lockard succeeded in saddling and riding the weary horse, and within a few days Black Kettle was as tame as Lockard's own horses. Lockard had tasted victory.

Several days later Lockard and his crew headed east to Norton to show off his prize. People came from all over northern Kansas and southern Nebraska; mustangers, settlers and even a few soldiers. They all came to view the legendary Black Kettle, but somehow the romance and adventure that had been associated with the horse was diminished when the people saw the horse under saddle. Black Kettle didn't seem as large in life as he had in legend, especially after Lockard trimmed the horse's mane and tail. Wild Horse Johnson had said there was nothing to Black Kettle but his mane and tail.

Even for Lockard the victory of having the wild stallion in tow was not as sweet as when he captured the horse. In time he sold Black Kettle to Jesse Wright and the once-magnificent horse began the lowly task of pulling a milk wagon. Wright eventually sold the horse to Jim McGinnes, a farmer, who used Black Kettle on a breaking plow. But McGinnes did not keep him long and soon sold Black Kettle to Henry Howard, another Kansas farmer. In the early 1890s Black Kettle passed into the hands of Harlan Day, an old farmer who had the reputation of taking good care of his livestock. It was on Harlan Day's farm, in 1896, that Black Kettle died at the age of thirty years. The end was quiet and peaceful, a far cry from the time two decades earlier when countless men chased the once wild and free stallion across the open Kansas plains.

The German Sisters

The September sun was just peeking over the eastern horizon as John German, his wife Lydia and their seven children broke camp and prepared to continue their journey to Colorado.

The year was 1874.

The German family had spent the night camping along the Smoky Hill River about thirty miles southeast of where Goodland, in northwest Kansas, stands today. But in 1874 that part of Kansas was unsettled.

As German hooked his two oxen to the family wagon, he told his 19-year-old son, Stephen, and 17-year-old daughter, Catherine, to round up the family's six head of cattle. The animals had been left to graze in a nearby hollow during the night.

The two young people set out and were driving the cattle back toward the already moving wagon when a herd of antelope ran across the trail to their front. Stephen was about to shoot an antelope when he heard the unmistakable yells of Indians.

Charging toward the unsuspecting family was a band of seventeen Cheyenne on horseback. The Indians were heading straight for the wagon carrying the mother and five of the six daughters. The father, walking ahead of the wagon, raised his rifle to fire at the Indians. Before he could pull the trigger an arrow struck him. He died instantly and a moment later his wife was dead.

By then Stephen and Catherine had left the cattle and were running away. As Stephen reached a small rise so did an Indian on horseback. The boy never had a chance to use his rifle. Within seconds Stephen was dead.

Another Indian chasing Catherine fired an arrow. It struck the girl in the thigh. The Indian jumped off his pony, pulled out the arrow, put the screaming girl on his bay horse and rode back to the wagon. There he pushed Catherine to the ground in front of her three younger sisters who had not been harmed.

The four girls, scared and crying, huddled together. There was 17-year-old Catherine, 12-year-old Sophia, 7-year-old Julia and 5-year-old Nancy. Nancy cried the loudest. So loud, in fact, that it annoyed one Indian brave. He was about to kill the little girl when one of two squaws with the braves jumped in front and claimed the little girl as her own. The warrior walked away and helped other Indians set fire to the wagon.

Still other braves rounded up the cattle and prepared to leave.

The squaw who saved Nancy's life and her warrior husband placed Nancy and Julia on their Indian ponies. Other braves put Catherine and Sophia on their horses. The Indians and their captives headed south leaving the bodies of John German, his wife, his son and two of his daughters lying on the Kansas prairie. All had been scalped.

That was on Sept. 1, 1874.

John and Lydia German came from Fannin County, Georgia. After serving as a Confederate soldier in the Civil War, John had returned home and found it in shambles. Only his wife, children (he then had only five) and some livestock had escaped a guerrilla raid. It was then that German decided to come west.

The German family spent three months in Tennessee, then crossed Kentucky, arriving in southwest Missouri in August 1870. There German and his growing family took a homestead. But German's health was not good.

In 1873 he traded the homestead for two oxen and a covered wagon and moved to Chautauqua County in southeastern Kansas. There the family was happy, but after ten months they feared their oldest daughter, Catherine, had consumption. So they set out to settle in Colorado. There, they felt, the weather and the climate would be better for Catherine's health.

On August 15, 1874, the Germans left Chautauqua County and headed west in the ox-drawn covered wagon with a few head of cattle, provisions, a feather bed and a coop of chickens.

When asked about Indians, settlers in Ellis, Kansas, assured the German family they would have no trouble. There had been no Indian raids in that part of Kansas for several years. Thus it was that the

Five-year-old Nancy German *(left)* and seven-year-old Julia German about six weeks after they were rescued by the U.S. Army. This photo probably was taken at Fort Leavenworth, Kansas, and is a copy of the one General Miles sent to Catherine German while she was still captive. *Courtesy Kansas State Historical Society*

German family was in northwest Kansas, camped along the Smoky Hill River, only one day from Fort Wallace, Kansas, when the Indian raid came.

The Cheyenne band that swooped down on the family was led by Kicking Horse, one of many warriors under the Cheyenne chief Stone Calf. Not many weeks before, Stone Calf's son had been killed at the battle of Adobe Walls in what today is the Texas panhandle. Losing that battle with buffalo hunters and also losing his son made Stone Calf mad. He declared war on all whites and began raiding over a vast area of the southern plains. The attack on the German family—the worst single Indian attack in Kansas history—was only one of many committed by Stone Calf's warriors.

A few days after the German family attack, a hunter happened upon the bodies. He rushed to Sheridan, Kansas, and reported the massacre. A detachment of soldiers was sent from Fort Wallace to recover the bodies. The soldiers found all five plus the half-burned wagon and the German family Bible. It was unscorched. Inside were the names and birth dates of all nine members of the family. It was then that the soldiers suspected the Indians had taken captives since only five bodies were found.

As news of the attack spread across western Kansas, other soldiers from other posts were sent out to look for the Indians. But the Cheyenne traveled only by night, spoke in whispers at all times and took little time to eat during the daylight hours. The Cheyenne band headed south as fast as they could.

The squaw watching over the two young German girls tried to roast buffalo meat—well done—over a small fire for Julia and little

Seventeen-year-old Catherine German not long after her release from the Indians. *Courtesy Kansas State Historical Society*

Twelve-year-old Sophia German not long after her release from the Indians. *Courtesy Kansas State Historical Society*

Nancy. The squaw also made a mixture of buffalo tallow, salt and some of the flour that the Indians had taken in the raid. But the little girls would not eat.

For the German girls the trip south was rough. The Indians kept running across tracks made by soldiers looking for them. The warrior and the squaw caring for the two younger girls began to grow tired of the children.

Finally, not far from where Pampa, Texas, stands today, the two Indians simply left the two young German sisters on the plains and continued on their way. It was up to 7-year-old Julia and 5-year-old Nancy to fare for themselves miles from civilization.

After the Indians rode off, the little girls wandered until they found a wagon trail. They followed it to a creek and found an old camp used by soldiers, perhaps a week or more earlier. The two girls found some old hardtack, corn and meat scraps that had been left. With these, plus wild grapes, hackberries, wild onions and young blades of grass, Julia and Nancy kept alive.

Meantime the Indians with the two older German sisters had arrived at Stone Calf's main Cheyenne camp of about 300 lodges on the Staked Plains, probably somewhere in northeastern New Mexico. There the two older German girls were separated and forced to do the work of Indian women; they gathered firewood, sewed shirts and dresses with bone needle and thread of buffalo sinew and cooked food.

But not many days after arriving in camp, word reached Stone Calf that the military was demanding the return of the four girls. At once he gave orders to find the two younger girls left on the prairie.

On November 7, 1874, a party of about 200 Cheyenne finally located the little girls in the makeshift camp by the creek. The girls were weak but still alive.

The following day, as the Indians were returning to Stone Calf with the two children, a detachment of nearly 100 soldiers under the command of Lt. Frank D. Baldwin saw the Indians and attacked.

The battle lasted five hours. Some of the Indians escaped, but the two girls were rescued. Their cheeks were hollow and they were almost starved, but they were alive. Nancy showed much anguish and mental suffering. Julia seemed calmer.

The soldiers clothed the little girls and took them to Camp Supply, Indian Territory. There, officers' wives fed and clothed them and began nursing the little girls back to health. Later they were taken north to Fort Dodge, Kansas, and then east to Fort Leavenworth on the Missouri River.

At Stone Calf's camp on the Staked Plains a Mexican trader saw the two older German girls as he passed through the camp one day. When the trader told army scouts, Gen. Nelson Miles lost no time in sending a message to Stone Calf demanding that the Indians surrender and return the two captives—alive.

The winter of 1874 was cold and rough on the southern plains. The Indians had not received their usual supplies from the government. Even their horses were suffering. It did not take Stone Calf long to realize it would be best to surrender. But another lesser chief, Gray Beard, who was holding 12-year-old Sophia, held out for better terms.

General Nelson A. Miles. *Courtesy Kansas State Historical Society*

Thus Stone Calf sent five Indians to Fort Sill, Indian Territory, to see what kind of terms they might get. Stone Calf told 17-year-old Catherine what he was doing.

A few days later a friendly Kiowa Indian visited the Cheyenne camp and gave Catherine a photograph showing Julia and Nancy at Fort Leavenworth. On the back General Miles wrote a message to Catherine telling her "not to be discouraged; efforts are being made for your benefit."

The Kiowa Indian who delivered the message was one of several sent to Stone Calf's camp by General Miles with provisions, blankets and bright cloth in hopes of tempting the Indians to release the girls.

It may have been this tempting or continued bad weather or something else that changed Gray Beard's mind. Within a short time he agreed to surrender.

On February 26, 1875, Stone Calf, the other chiefs and 1,600 Cheyenne surrendered at Cheyenne Agency, Indian Territory. Catherine and Sophia were released.

Catherine German weighed 80 pounds, Sophia, 60 pounds. They were taken to the Mission school where they remained for some time. It was there they were told that their parents, brother and two sisters killed in the Indian raid had since been buried at Monument, Kansas.

When the summer of 1875 arrived, Catherine and Sophia were taken to Fort Leavenworth, Kansas, where they were reunited with their two younger sisters who had since recovered from their ordeal. Congress appropriated $2,500 each for Nancy and Julia, the interest to be used for education and maintenance until they became of age, when the principal reverted to them.

As for the older sisters, Catherine and Sophia, they were given $10,000. The money was taken from government funds appropriated for the Cheyennes.

For a while the German sisters lived with the Patrick Corney family near Wetmore in Seneca County, Kansas. Julia and Nancy later were graduated from the Sabetha, Kansas, high school. Nancy attended the University of Kansas and later married Frank Andrews, a farmer near Bern, Kansas, and became the mother of 11 children.

Catherine married Amos Swerdfeger and lived in California where she died in 1932. Sophia married Albert Feldman and spent most of her remaining life on a farm south of Humboldt, Nebraska, where she died in 1947. Julia married first Howard Reese, and then Albert Brooks, and lived in California where she died in 1959 at the age of 92 years. She was the last of the four German sisters who survived the Indian raid of 1874.

The Ride of Portugee John Phillips

One thing is certain; of all the monuments which the Spaniard has left to glorify his reign in America there will be none more worthy than his horse ... the Spaniard's horse may be found today in countless thousands, from the city of the Montezumas to the regions of perpetual snow; they are grafted into our equine wealth and make an important impression on the horse of the country.

Thus wrote Frederic Remington in 1888 for an article published by *Century Magazine*. Until the arrival of the railroad and later the horseless carriage, mules, oxen and the horse provided man with mobility. Of these the horse was far more than simply a beast of burden. Charles Goodnight, the father of the Texas panhandle, once wrote that "man and horse were one, and the combination accomplished feats that would be utterly impossible under ordinary circumstances."

I have already related the tales of F. X. Aubry's rides and the one by young Bill Cody, but in each case the riders used more than one horse in their rides. There was really more stamina and daring on the part of the man than on most of the horses they used. While certainly impressive they are not as heroic as the tale of Portugee John Phillips and a blooded Kentucky runner. With all due respect to the American Revolution, Phillips's ride even ranks in heroism above the legendary ride of Paul Revere.

The ride of Portugee John Phillips came about because, in 1866, men were traveling to the new gold fields of Idaho and Montana, and

Brevet Brigadier General Henry Beebe Carrington, who gave "Portugee" John Phillips his beautiful white horse with Kentucky blood to ride for help. *Courtesy Wyoming State Museum*

This photograph of "Portugee" John Phillips was taken several years after his heroic ride in the winter of 1866. *Courtesy Wyoming State Museum*

they were traveling over land claimed by Indians. The government in Washington ordered the U.S. Army to build a string of forts along the Bozeman Trail to protect the emigrants from the Sioux and a few Arapahoe and Cheyenne Indians threatening them.

The Bozeman Trail began at Fort Laramie and ran north on the plains along the eastern edge of the Big Horn Mountains in present-day Wyoming. It crossed the Big Horn River in what is today southern Montana and ran west to Virginia City. It was a fast trail. There were few streams to cross, and it was well watered and grassed. But it ran through Sioux country.

Charged with building the forts was Brevet Brigadier General Henry Beebe Carrington. Setting out from Fort Laramie, Carrington established Fort Philip Kearny on the banks of Piney Creek, a branch of the Powder River. The fort was named for General Philip Kearny, a Civil War hero.

Between August and early December of 1866, Indians made fifty-one attacks in the vicinity of Fort Phil Kearny, but the post was not besieged. Each day a wood train managed to go out to find timber to construct the fort and supply trains came and went with little difficulty.

But about 11 o'clock on the morning of December 21, 1866, the post lookout reported that the wood train was being attacked by Indians. Lieutenant Colonel William J. Fetterman led a relief party out of the post to save the wood train. And against orders to do so, Fetterman pursued the Indians over Lodge Trail Ridge along the Bozeman Trail.

It was a trap.

Within a short time every man in the relief party was killed, but the wood train returned to the safety of the fort as did Portugee John Phillips, a civilian, who was engaged in hauling water to fill the post's water barrels at the time the wood train was attacked.

By midafternoon the bodies of forty-nine men had been recovered. Then the weather began to change. The temperature dropped rapidly and soon a blizzard began. Snow started to pile up against the walls of the stockade. Efforts to recover more bodies stopped. By nightfall the snowdrifts were so high along the stockade's walls that details of men were constantly shoveling it away. General Carrington feared the Indians might attack and simply climb the snowdrifts to the top of the stockade walls and jump inside.

At about 9 o'clock that night the temperature stood at near thirty below zero. The cold was so intense that sentries remained on guard duty for only twenty minutes at a time. Even with quick reliefs, however, many a man received frozen fingers, feet, nose and ears.

General Carrigton knew the greatly reduced garrison must get help. And he knew the outside world must be told of the massacre, but there was no telegraph at the fort. The nearest telegraph was at Horseshoe Station more than two hundred miles away near Fort Laramie. Carrington knew he must send a messenger.

The general called for volunteers. At first there were none. A handful of old plainsmen, some scouts and the veteran soldiers shook their heads. They did not want to go. They knew a ride to Fort Laramie through the cold and snow would mean almost certain death. And if the cold did not kill the rider and his horse, certainly the Indians would.

It was then, to the surprise of many, that a swarthy man in his middle thirties, tough and wiry of frame, a native of Portugal, said he would go. It was Phillips—nicknamed "Portugee" because of his native land—who volunteered. Why he did so is unclear. It may have been the challenge and thrill of danger or the desire to help his comrades. Or it may have been the fact that there were a few women and children at the fort, the families of some of the officers.

One of the women was Frances Grummond. She was the widow of Lieutenant Grummond, one of the officers killed in the massacre. She would later write that Phillips was moved by sorrow for her and perhaps a tenderer emotion. Her story is told in the book *My Army Life*. Mrs. Grummond later became General Carrington's second wife and wrote the book in 1910 as Frances C. Carrington.

On volunteering, Phillips asked to have the best horse at the fort for the ride. General Carrington quickly agreed and told Phillips he could have his beautiful white horse with Kentucky blood, the swiftest animal at the post.

Carrington quickly wrote two messages. One was addressed to General Cooke in Omaha asking for reinforcements and supplies and telling of the Fetterman massacre. The other message was addressed to General Grant in Washington, telling of the massacre and asking for new Spencer arms.

Portugee Phillips prepared for the ride. Dressing as warmly as he could, wearing a buffalo coat and several layers of clothing, Phillips slipped a few biscuits—hardtack—into his pockets. He tied a quarter sack of oats for his horse to the saddle. Then, leading the horse, Phillips joined General Carrington and walked to the water gate at the southeast end of the quartermaster yard. A sergeant opened the gate. Carrington and Phillips walked through the gate with Phillips leading the horse.

For about a minute the two men talked quietly. Then Phillips mounted Carrington's horse.

The General was heard to tell Phillips, "May God help you."

A soldier, John C. Brough, standing guard at the gate, later recalled that Phillips "wheeled and started off on a trot. For about thirty seconds we could hear the hoofbeats, and then they ceased. Carrington stood with his head bent on one side, as if listening intently, and then straightening up and speaking to no one in particular, said, 'Good, he has taken softer ground at the side of the trail!' "

The exact route followed by Portugee Phillips has been lost in time, but he did not ride through the timbered valleys nor along the Bozeman Trail where Indians stood watch. Instead, he followed the high shelterless divides where it was colder but where there was less snow and fewer Indians.

A few hours later Phillips reached Fort Reno, a tiny outpost about sixty-seven miles south of Fort Phil Kearny. There Phillips warmed himself, fed his horse and told of the massacre. But he did not stay long.

In the predawn darkness Phillips mounted his horse and left Fort Reno. At dawn he sought shelter in a valley and hid all day among the trees. His horse blended perfectly with the snow. At dusk he again set out for Horseshoe Station.

Riding through what probably seemed like one continuous blizzard, riding only at night, rationing oats carefully to his horse and

This illustration shows John "Portugee" Phillips arriving at Horse Shoe Station, where word of the Fetterman massacre and General Carrington's plea for help were sent over the telegraph. But Phillips didn't trust the telegraph and rode on to Fort Laramie, arriving on Christmas Eve 1866. This illustration, artist unknown, was provided by the Wyoming State Museum.

eating snow for water, Portugee Phillips covered the one hundred and thirty miles from Fort Reno to Horseshoe Station during the next two nights.

At Horseshoe Station, about forty miles north of Fort Laramie, Phillips handed the dispatches to the telegraph operator John Friend. The dispatches were transmitted. But for some reason Phillips did not trust the telegraph. He rebound his legs with sacks, wrapped himself in the buffalo coat, stuffed the dispatches in his pockets and set out at about noon for Fort Laramie.

It was nearly midnight on Christmas Eve when Portugee Phillips reached Fort Laramie. Snow and ice matted his beard and icicles were hanging from his buffalo coat. As Phillips's horse staggered through the gate, music could be heard coming from a large building called "Bedlam"—the post headquarters. A full-dress Christmas Eve garrison ball was being held.

Phillips told the officer of the guard that he had to see the commanding officer at once. The officer of the guard, somewhat shocked by

Portugee Phillips's appearance, sensed something important had happened and told Phillips to follow him. The commanding officer, he said, was at the ball.

As Phillips dismounted, his horse sank to the ground. Before Phillips was to return, the animal would die from exhaustion and the cold. Portugee had not changed mounts during the entire 236-mile ride.

When the snow-covered figure of Phillips entered the ballroom, the music stopped. Everyone stared at Phillips. His eyebrows were twice their normal size crusted with ice and snow. He asked the commanding officer in a trembling voice if he had received the telegraph messages. The officer said he had, but that they were garbled. He had not understood them.

Slowly, his voice weak, Phillips told the story of the massacre and delivered the dispatches.

Aid was sent to Fort Phil Kearny and the post was saved.

As for Portugee Phillips, it took him many weeks to recover from his ordeal. Records show that Phillips was paid three hundred dollars by the government for the ride. The ride, however, supposedly cost him far more than the suffering he had experienced. One tale claims that the Sioux Indians, upon learning of his ride, swore vengeance. Whether this is true is unknown.

Phillips married and settled down on a ranch near present-day Chugwater, Wyoming, north of Cheyenne. There, about six years after his ride, Indians attacked his ranch and killed all his stock. Was it vengeance?

In 1883, Portugee John Phillips died at Cheyenne, Wyoming. He was only in his fifties.

In 1898, thirty-two years after his heroic ride, the government paid his solitary and destitute widow five thousand dollars to settle a claim against the Indian depredation on the ranch of the man who rode one horse 236 miles in four days through driving snow and freezing cold to bring help to Fort Phil Kearny.

Plains Snake Lore

My father told me one evening; when he was a Boy He could
Crack a Harmless Garter Snakes head off; by taking it
    By the Tail, and crack it like a whip.

And so one Day I was crossing the Prairie and came on to
a Harmless Milk Snake about three feet long.
    I had nothing to kill it with; and thought I would
    Try Cracking his head off.

The snake was going into a hole, and I grabed its tail,
Pulled him out of his hole, and swung him around like
    an Ox Whip; and when I reversed and undertook
    to crack his Head off—

I only Succeeded in wrapping it around my neck.
    I was very much Freightened; and so was the Snake.
    I Quickly Jerked it off, and killed it with my feet.

That was the First and Last, time I ever tried to crack
a snakes Head off by the Tail.

These words in this form were written by Harry Jasper Harris
about the turn of the century. Harris, a native of Connecticut, came to
Kansas Territory during the late 1850s when snakes were so plentiful in
some areas that settlers considered them pests much like mice today.
Harris's simple tale is typical of many such snake stories recalled by
early settlers on the plains.

Although Indians had roamed the Great Plains long before the white man arrived, most Indians did not kill snakes. The superstitious Osages and Kaws did not even kill rattlesnakes. They believed it might make the snake tribe of Indians further north mad. Other tribes had similar beliefs. Thus when the white man arrived to settle parts of the plains in the 1850s, snakes were plentiful. They were everywhere.

For the pioneer woman, the sight of a snake in her parlor was usually accepted as another of the inconveniences and drawbacks of frontier life. When she saw a snake she usually killed it. One pioneer mother told how she killed her first rattler:

> Returning from the woods one day with an armful of sticks, I saw a large snake lying across the path in front of my three year old daughter who was with me. I caught and pushed her behind me, then throwing down my sticks, picking out the largest as I did, I went for the snake. The stick was rotten and broke with my first stroke. It enraged the rattler. He coiled himself up on one side of the path, and, rearing his head two or three feet from the ground, ran out a red forked tongue and made such a noise with his rattles that my other daughter in our cabin nearby ran to the door to see what it was.
>
> Without taking my eyes off the snake I called to her to get the hoe. She ran around and came up behind us with it. Then, without moving from my tracks I took the hoe and made short work with his snakeship. We dragged him up to the house and cut off the rattles, sixteen in number, and measured him. He was over five feet in length and as large around as a man's arm.

Another time a settler's wife was cleaning their cabin when she saw a large snake on a log just behind the family clock on a rude shelf. The woman did not dare strike the snake. She would have hit the clock and probably damaged it. "Clocks were too scarce to be broken for a snake," she later recalled. So she grabbed the snake by the tail and with a quick and strong jerk she dashed its head on the carpetless floor. It did not hurt the sod floor but it sure killed the snake.

During the 1850s a settler built a cabin on the edge of a wooded area near Three Mile Creek close to where Junction City, Kansas, stands today. The inside of the cabin was lined with unbleached muslin. Unfortunately, it made a good hiding place for snakes. When the settler would spot a snake moving behind the muslin, he would stab it with his pitchfork, loosen the muslin at the bottom and remove the dead snake. He didn't keep track of how many he killed, but his wife later recalled, "Blacksnakes, rattlers and many other kinds thus met their death."

When it came time for the annual fall housecleaning, many a settler's wife would find snakes in the most unexpected places. Sometimes they might be found in the rafters or behind furniture or under the bed. One woman, during the 1860s, found a large rattlesnake wrapped around the leather straps inside the family's pump organ. "That's why the thing had seemed so hard to pump," she said after killing the four-foot snake.

Homesteaders plowing up the land often found snake eggs in the turned earth. "They were oval in shape," reported one Nebraska homesteader, adding, "and they were about the size of large beans, and I think they were attached together. The little snakes in them were about an inch or so long. The hatched snakes would run into their mother's mouth when discovered."

There's one tale about an old plainsman called Jack Stillwell—his real name was Charles—who one day found himself and a friend hiding in a buffalo wallow from Indians. A large rattlesnake crawled into the wallow and headed straight for the two men. Both men froze. If they tried to kill the snake, the noise might be heard by the Indians nearby. If they did not act, the snake might bite one or both men. An idea suddenly came to Stillwell. He was chewing tobacco. As the snake moved closer, Stillwell expectorated a mouthful of tobacco juice all over the snake's eyes and head. The unwelcome visitor turned and crawled dejectedly out of the wallow. Not long afterwards the Indians left the area and the two men, undetected, went on their way.

Sometimes people were bitten by snakes. If the snake was poisonous, they might die, but then there were the lucky ones. One warm spring day a young girl ran to her mother crying. She said a snake had bitten her on the foot. The mother examined the child's foot. It wasn't injured. But when the mother looked at the little girl's shoe, she found the marks of a snake's fangs on the heel. The stiff leather had been too hard to pierce.

Although many a man was bitten by rattlesnakes, death was not always a certainty. And the cure was often enjoyed. "Red Eye" was recommended for snake bite. Aside from whiskey, some men resorted to a cure of placing gunpowder in the wound and then burning it. This cure is credited to Kit Carson, the early plainsman.

"I cut the bite open and flash powder in it three times and it is all right," Carson is quoted as saying. "One of my men was once bitten on the hand by a big rattler. I cut it open, flashed powder in it three times, and that afternoon he killed and scalped two Injuns."

One of the most unusual snake tales concerns a train that old-timers claimed was stalled by rattlesnakes. It seems that in a cut through much rock a few miles east of Santa Rosa in east-central New Mexico, a train had to stop when it hit a bunch of rattlesnakes on the tracks. In addition to many rattlers killed by the wheels of the engine, the train's crew killed—by actual count—56 of the snakes. The rails, holding the sun's warmth, had attracted the snakes late in the day when the train came through.

But of all the tales about snakes, one of the most fascinating occurred in Cloud County, Kansas, not far south of Concordia. Late one afternoon in September 1876, a young boy was walking over a hill on a neighbor's farm looking for his father's cattle. He stepped into a small hole. When he pulled his leg out several snakes—blue racers—came slithering out of the hole. Scared, the boy ran home and told his father what had happened.

The next morning the boy regained his courage. He persuaded a young friend to go along and returned to the hill. There the two boys saw snakes basking in the sun. Before they left they killed 46. Word soon spread, and the following day several men gathered on the hill to investigate the snake story. Sure enough, they found the hole the boy had stepped into. They discovered it was the entrance to a snake den. With shovels they dug down to a crevice between two upright stones about two feet below the surface. Then for several hours they fought snakes, killing hundreds but seemingly making only a little dent in the snake population.

For nearly three weeks the killing of snakes continued daily. On a Sunday morning men from all over the neighborhood gathered to pick up and count the dead snakes. They piled them near the mouth of the den, all 1,776 dead snakes. Even as they did, still other snakes were killed nearby.

The following day the editor of the *Concordia Empire* rode south of town to see the snake hill. By then at least 2,000 snakes had been piled up. "We killed fifteen in as many minutes and had enough," wrote the editor, adding, "The snakes are of the species called the blue racer, with a sprinkling of adders, and vary in size from the thickness of a man's finger to that of his wrist and in length from a foot to four or five feet. They run with remarkable speed, and at first were cowardly, endeavoring to escape and not much disposed to show fight. They are now, however, becoming vicious, and show fight, and at times get startlingly aggressive. A reasonable theory is that the hole leads to a cavern somewhere in the depths of the hill, where there are many thousands, possibly, of writhing serpents; and that they have gathered here from all directions for a winter residence."

A week later when the count of dead snakes reached nearly 4,000, blasting powder was brought in and the remaining inhabitants of the snake hill were disposed of.

The only other tale that equals the story of the snake hill is one told by Harry Gant. It occurred somewhere in eastern Wyoming or western Nebraska. Gant's story is told in his own words:

> While riding in from the west one evening at a point where I was about to drop off the rimrock to the west, I heard a loud buzzing sound and followed my ears to a pocket under some big rocks. There I saw the rendezvous of what appeared to be at least a thousand rattlesnakes, all twisted and snarled together. They were having an orgy such as cannot be described, not knowing who was whose pardner, nor caring. I was always getting off my horse to kill a rattler, so here was a chance to really kill some snakes. I emptied all my cartridges into the mass and then threw some big rocks into it. That didn't even make one snake leave the party.
>
> When I later told Decker [a friend] about the sight, he said: "Where have you been? Somewhere where they had a lot of whiskey? Those booze hounds are the only ones who see snakes like that!" I insisted that he go with me to the spot next morning. We took a couple of shovels and found a dozen or so dead rattlesnakes, and some cripples. The party had eventually moved to another spot or else they had called it a day. Within a half mile circle, we chopped off the heads of probably a hundred cripples trying to get back to their homes in the rock crannies and prairie dog holes. We couldn't find the main outfit and Decker wouldn't believe me as to the number involved. But if I had had a couple of sticks of dynamite when I first saw them, I could have been St. Patrick II.

The First "Real" Bullfight
in the United States

A. B. Webster was no P. T. Barnum, but during the middle 1880s he gained quite a reputation on the plains as a promoter, and his name even became known on both coasts. He became known as the man who promoted the first real bullfight held in the United States. It was staged at Dodge City, Kansas, the cowboy capital, in July 1884.

The story of Dodge City's bullfight began on a warm spring day in 1884 when Webster, a former mayor, and several prominent Ford County businessmen gathered to plan Dodge City's Fourth of July celebration. Everyone in the group wanted to concoct something new, something unusual, that would attact attention to their fading cattle town. At the meeting it was Webster who suggested they hold a real Mexican bullfight.

Dodge City, at least in the minds of many Easterners in 1884, was still a wild and woolly two-gun frontier town. But it was changing. As one Eastern newspaper reporter who visited Dodge City wrote: "Dodge is a rough frontier town, and it is populated largely by rough people, but they are not at all vicious. They are open-hearted and generous. I would have less fear of molestation in this wild, western town than I would have on the side streets of Kansas City or Chicago late in the evening."

In truth, Dodge City was beginning to grow up. Its lusty youthful days were slipping away. Then too the winter of 1883–84 had been rough. Blizzards and severe cold had taken their toll of cattle. Hoof-and-

A. B. Webster, the man who promoted the Dodge City bullfight. *Courtesy Kansas State Historical Society*

H. B. "Ham" Bell, who owned a Dodge City saloon, was president of the Dodge City Driving Park and Fair Association that staged the bull-fight. This photo of Bell was taken many years later. *Courtesy Kansas State Historical Society*

mouth disease was rampant and quarantines were reducing the num-bers of cattle driven up the trails to Dodge City from Texas. And more and more land around Dodge was being tilled by settlers. Civilization was creeping in on Dodge City and the townsfolk were not sure they wanted it.

The idea of a bullfight triggered the imagination of the town's businessmen. They spread the word and within twenty-four hours ten thousand dollars had been raised in cash and subscriptions. But staging a bullfight in Kansas, where none had ever been held, would be no easy matter. Some residents of southwest Kansas had seen bullfights down in Mexico, but no one knew how to set one up. Thus the businessmen organized the "Dodge City Driving Park and Fair Association" to solve the problems. H. B. "Ham" Bell, who owned a local saloon, was elected president; D. M. Cockey, vice president; J. S. Welch, secretary; and A. J. Anthony, treasurer. A. B. Webster was appointed general manager.

Because everyone wanted "genuine Spanish bullfighters," Webster contacted W. K. Moore, whom he knew in El Paso. Moore, a native of Scotland, was a lawyer who had many contacts in Old Mexico. Moore agreed to locate some bullfighters and to come north as their manager and as the press agent for the fight. But Moore told Webster to find his own fighting bulls in Kansas.

For the bulls Webster did not have to look far. Living in Ford County was D. W. "Doc" Barton, a well-known cattleman, who claimed to be the first man to drive a herd of cattle from Texas to Dodge City

The bullfight was big news in Dodge City as the front page of the June 21, 1884, *Dodge City Democrat* suggests. *Courtesy Kansas State Historical Society*

many years earlier. Webster told Barton to find a dozen "ferocious bulls." Barton began the search. There were many Texas cattle—longhorns—in the grazing grounds around Dodge City. Most were awaiting shipment east. These herds contained many bulls, "about whose fighting abilities and proclivities there was no question." Barton had twelve bulls penned. When Webster, "Ham" Bell and others viewed the bulls, they agreed that Barton had picked some "ugly customers."

One man observed, "By nature, a Texas bull is all the time as mad as he can get." The man added that the mere presence of the townsfolk "was enough to bring them pawing and plunging against the corral fence till the boards bent like paper and the braces creaked with the strain."

Reporting on the selection of the bulls, a Dodge City newspaper noted: "As some of them are liable to be numbered with the dead before our next issue, we deem it proper to give a short sketch of these noted animals, together with their pedigrees. These pedigrees are kindly furnished by the famous bull raiser and breeder, Brother Barton, of the great Arkansas River."

Then the newspaper described each bull. The best of the lot, at least in the newspaper's opinion, was "Ringtailed Snorter." He was the oldest of the dozen bulls. Barton said he had been in twenty-seven different fights. He won each.

Another of the better bulls was "Iron Gall," described as "a famous catch-as-catch-can fighter, and very bad when stirred up." "Klu Klux" was number seven on the list. "He is a four-year-old," reported the newspaper, "and next to Ringtailed Snorter is the oldest noted fighter that will come to the front on next Friday. It is this animal that the bullfighters most fear, having laid out his man in Old Mexico, while playing 'four you see and one you don't.' "

Some of the other "ugly dozen" included "Sheriff," an animal that was never tamed or branded, "Rustler," "Loco Jim," "Long Branch," named after the well-known Dodge City saloon, "Opera," "Cowboy Killer," "Doc," named after "Doc" Barton, and "Eat-Em-Up-Richard." The newspaper tried to give the impression that these bulls had been brought in special for the bullfight from Mexico.

Moore, the El Paso attorney, and his five Mexican bullfighters were present when the bulls were brought into Dodge and placed in stock pens for all to see. They gave their stamp of approval on the selection.

When Moore and the Mexicans arrived in town, Dodge City became more excited than ever. Everyone wanted to meet the "real" bullfighters. "They are a fierce lot, and fear is an unknown sensation to them," reported one Dodge City newspaper. "They have had many narrow escapes from death and have been seriously wounded at times. They understand that the people want an exciting and dangerous fight and they are ready to satisfy them. Some day, they all feel, they will come to their death in the bull pit, but they like the life and would not be satisfied to leave it. Yet they are as intelligent a party of men as any person would wish to meet. Their all-redeeming trait is that they cannot be forced to drink a drop of strong liquor."

The bullfighters' manager, W. K. Moore, may have added the last sentence to give bullfighting and the bullfighters a tone of respectability. From the first day the fights were announced, there had been some talk in Dodge of the "gore in bullfighting." A handful of critics accused the residents of Dodge City of returning to barbarism.

A few days before the fights were to begin, rumors spread through the town that Kansas Governor Glick in Topeka at the other end of the state would stop the fights. Another rumor claimed that the mayor had received a telegram from the U.S. Attorney's office that said bullfighting was against the law in the United States. To this the mayor supposedly said, "Hell! Dodge City ain't in the United States!" Most residents did not take the rumors seriously.

But some residents became more concerned when a handful of reporters from Eastern newspapers arrived in Dodge to cover the bullfights and began sending stories back to their papers. Webster and Moore feared the publicity might cut the number of eastern visitors who were planning the trip, especially after some of the stories repeated the rumors. The two men kept trying to set the out-of-town reporters straight on the facts as Webster and Moore saw them.

The fears of Dodge City's businessmen, especially Webster and

Moore, were forgotten by July Fourth. Dodge City was crammed full of visitors. Cowboys, cattlemen, farmers, gamblers, visitors from the East and women and children filled the town to the brim. It appeared certain that the fight would be a financial success for the promoters.

The festivities began at two o'clock in the afternoon. A. B. Webster, former mayor and manager of the celebration, and W. K. Moore, manager of the bullfighters, led a parade to the fairgrounds. Behind them came the dignitaries of Dodge City followed by the town's cowboy band. Next in line were the bullfighters decked out in "red jackets, blue tunics, white stockings and small dainty slippers."

Just south of town, between Dodge City and the Arkansas River, the Dodge City Driving Park and Fair Association had purchased forty acres. They had built a half-mile track and a four-thousand seat grandstand. In front of the grandstand a bullfight arena had been erected. It was one hundred feet in diameter. Around it stood an eight-foot fence. "At intervals along the fence eight light board screens, or escapes, were provided where the bullfighters could take refuge when too closely pressed. West of the arena was the bull corral, connected with the main enclosure by a chute. Parallel with this chute was a wider passage through which the bodies of the victims would make their exit," was how one Dodge City newspaper described the scene.

The grandstand soon filled with spectators. Of the 4,000 paid customers, nearly 1,500 were women and children. One Ford County deputy sheriff had the job of separating the soiled doves from their "more respectable sisters." He had to draw a line separating the good women from the ladies of the night. Just how successful this frontier Saint Peter was is not recorded.

As the people waited they listened to music provided by the Dodge City Cowboy Band, then well-known on the plains from Texas to Canada. And everyone watched as the "ugly dozen" milled around the arena. Then at half-past two, the bulls were driven back into their pens where "their horns were sawed off and the ends rasped smooth."

The sound of a bugle at 3:30 that afternoon signaled the grand entry. The matadors and picadors, four afoot and one mounted, paraded into the arena. Dressed in their fighting costumes, they circled the arena, bowed to the officials and prepared for the first bull to enter.

Again the bugle echoed across the grandstand and the first bull entered. The animal was hit by two decorated barbs thrown into his neck. This infuriated him, and he charged. Then the matadors began to demonstrate their abilities. For thirty minutes they were in their glory. The crown cheered time after time, but soon the bull tired. The order was given to bring on another.

Four of the Mexican bullfighters who came to Dodge City in June 1884. They are not identified. *Courtesy Kansas State Historical Society*

The second bull came out, but the crowd—anticipating more of the same—was disappointed. The second bull was a coward. He ran from the matadors and was soon taken from the arena. The third, fourth and fifth bulls were also poor imitators of the first.

The crowd began demanding that the first bull be returned. When the announcer said there was time for only one more fight that day, the crowd demanded the first bull. They yelled and screamed and the bull was returned with the announcer saying that the animal—the last bull of the day—would be put to the sword.

The chief matador—Captain Gregorio Gallardo from Chihuahua—was given his sword. The audience became quiet. A tenseness gripped the audience as the advertised "bloodletting" was about to begin. The bull spotted the matador and charged. Gallardo deflected the bull's rush with a graceful sweep of his cape. The crowd cheered. The bull wheeled and headed again for Gallardo. Once more the crowd cheered as the animal found nothing but air. The performance continued. Once Gallardo was almost caught by the bull, but he gracefully escaped the animal's path.

Then it was time for the kill.

Bowing to the crowd, Gallardo slowly began walking toward the bull with his sword in position for the kill. The bull, standing still, watched, his eyes never leaving Gallardo. When the matador was almost upon the animal, the bull shot forward. Gallardo was ready but the angle was wrong. At the last second Gallardo stepped aside. Two more times his position was not right, but the fourth time the sword found its mark.

The bull stopped, staggered a step or two, sank to his knees and moments later rolled to the ground. The first of two days of bullfighting had ended.

That day, Henry Bergh, Jr., president of the American Society for the Prevention of Cruelty to Animals in New York City, had sent Kansas Governor Glick a telegram. It read: "In the name of humanity I appeal to you to prevent the contemplated bullfight at Dodge City this day. Let not American soil be polluted by such atrocities."

Glick ignored the telegram.

And the next day, July 5, the bullfights went on as scheduled at Dodge City. It was the second and last day.

A Dodge City newspaper observed: "The second day's fighting, with the exception of the killing of the last animal in the ring, was more interesting than the first." And after the fights that afternoon the businessmen, celebrating at a local saloon, agreed that the bullfights had been very successful, at least financially, for their town.

A few days later, Governor Glick received a letter in Topeka from Henry Bergh, Jr. Wrote Bergh: "While civilization is striving to extend its peaceful influences over our prosperous and happy country, a spot within the boundaries of your state suddenly invites notice, where humanity and public decency have been trampled under feet and the blood-red flag of barbarism substituted in their stead."

Bergh then went on to condemn the Dodge City fights. He cited a Kansas law passed in 1879 that read: "Every person who shall maliciously or cruelly maim, beat or torture any horse, ox, or other cattle, whether belonging to himself or another, shall on conviction be adjudged guilty of a misdemeanor, and fined not exceeding $50." Governor Glick waited one week before replying to Bergh. When he did, Glick wrote: "The bullfight to which you refer was rather a tame and insignificant affair, and while advertisements gave it some importance it had little or no importance at Dodge City or any place else." With that Glick dropped the subject.

A Dodge City newspaper perhaps reflected the true feelings of most persons who saw the bullfight when it observed: "The matadors showed to the people of America what bullfighting really was. No one could see it and go away saying inhuman punishment was inflicted upon wild animals as the term 'bullfighting' would seem to imply, save and except the single animal that was killed each day. Punishment, torture or cruelty was even less than that inflicted upon animals in the branding pen."

And so the story of the first "real" bullfight in the United States ended. With perhaps only one exception—a bullfight at Cripple Creek, Colorado, in 1895, in which three bulls were brutally killed in a non-bullfight manner—the Dodge City bullfight of 1884 was the only *real* bullfight ever held in the United States.

Comanche

If General George Custer's forces had won at the Battle of the Little Big Horn in June 1876, probably no one would today remember the horse named Comanche. Such was not the case. Comanche is still remembered because he was the lone survivor of the battle from Custer's immediate command.

Just where Comanche was born is unknown, but U.S. Army records suggest the year was 1862. The bay colt was probably foaled by a mustang mare somewhere on the rolling southwestern plains. Like most colts, he kicked and pranced near the side of his dam, gaining strength of wind and limb. By the time he'd been weaned, his future characteristics were becoming apparent—muscular legs, a deep chest, sturdy back, broad forehead with a white star marking and that distinctive coloring of reddish tones, little more bay than sorrel.

As the weeks and months passed, the colt matured. He probably fought other wild stallions for leadership, and eventually acquired his own harem. Comanche may have sired other mustangs. And when mustangers saw Comanche running with his mares, it seems likely that they identified the horse as one of the better specimens.

Comanche was captured about 1868, probably in a wild horse roundup along the present-day border of Texas and western Oklahoma. Comanche and the other stallions were gelded, and the mustangers sought a market for them. When the mustangers heard that the U.S. Army was paying good prices for mounts in St. Louis, Comanche and other horses were sold to the cavalry. It is known that Comanche was purchased by the army for $90 on April 3, 1868.

A week or more later Comanche and an unknown number of other horses were loaded aboard railroad cars and shipped west to Fort Leavenworth, Kansas. At some point, either in St. Louis or at Fort Leavenworth, the horses were branded with a "U S" high on their left shoulders. (The outline of Comanche's brand may still be seen today on his mounted remains in the Museum of Natural History at the University of Kansas in Lawrence.)

The Seventh Cavalry, then stationed in central Kansas, had lost some horses in skirmishes with Indians that spring of 1868. To rebuild the remount herd, First Lieutenant Tom W. Custer, brother of General George Armstrong Custer, went to Fort Leavenworth to obtain replacements. He received forty-one horses including the one that would later become known as Comanche. On May 16, 1868, Tom Custer left Leavenworth by train for the Seventh Cavalry's encampment near Ellis Station, now Ellis, Kansas. He and the horses arrived on May 19. These forty-one horses were the only new mounts received by the Seventh Cavalry that year.

In the spring of 1868, one of the officers of the Seventh Cavalry was Captain Myles Keogh, twenty-eight years old, a native of Ireland and a veteran of the Civil War, where he received the regular army brevet ranks of Major for gallantry at Gettysburg and Lieutenant Colonel for his service at Resaca, Georgia.

It was customary for cavalry officers to purchase their own mounts from private suppliers or from the government. Some writers claim that Keogh purchased the horse that would later be known as Comanche for

Captain Myles W. Keogh, Seventh U.S. Cavalry. This photograph was taken about 1872. *Author's collection*

ninety dollars from the army, but no records of the purchase have been found. It is known that within three months after the arrival of new mounts in 1868, Captain Keogh was riding Comanche in battle. The bay soon became one of Keogh's favorite mounts.

On September 13, 1868, Keogh and some troopers were involved in a skirmish with a small party of Comanches. When it was over, a sergeant supposedly noticed an arrow shaft broken off in the right hind quarter of Keogh's horse. A farrier (blacksmith) was called. While Keogh held his horse's head and talked quietly to the animal, the farrier removed the arrowhead and broken shaft and cleaned the wound. About then a soldier in the troop told Keogh that he had seen the arrow strike. When it did, he said, the horse yelled just like a Comanche.

According to the legend, on that day, Comanche got his name.

By late spring of 1869, the Seventh Cavalry, including Captain Keogh and Comanche, were stationed at Fort Hays, Kansas, but in late summer Keogh took sick leave because of a leg injury and returned to his native Ireland for a visit. He returned to the Seventh Cavalry in Kansas early in March 1870. About three months later, presumably while Keogh was riding Comanche in action against Indians, Comanche received a wound in the right leg. He was lame for several weeks.

In 1871, Comanche, Keogh and the Seventh were ordered to the Southern states to help federal marshals quell civil disturbances between the Ku Klux Klan and Northern carpetbaggers. In Kentucky, on January 28, 1873, while the Seventh Cavalry was chasing moonshiners, Comanche received a flesh wound in his right shoulder, but it healed quickly.

Early in 1873, the Seventh Cavalry was ordered north to guard a Northern Pacific Railroad survey party on what has become known as the Yellowstone Expedition. But two troops, including Keogh and Comanche, were assigned to escort the International Boundary Survey Commission working along the Canadian border.

By the summer of 1875, Keogh and Comanche were back with the regiment trying to eject miners from the gold fields of the Black Hills. Miners, prospectors and settlers were ignoring the Laramie Treaty of 1868 that had created the Great Sioux Reservation covering that portion of present-day South Dakota lying west of the Missouri River. The Sioux, who considered the Black Hills sacred, killed many intruders.

The Seventh Cavalry joined a large campaign against the Sioux in May 1876. Three large columns of troopers converged on Indian country. One group marched east from Fort Ellis, in western Montana. Another column moved north toward the head of Rosebud Creek in southeastern Montana. The third and strongest column under Brigadier

General Alfred H. Terry, marched west from Fort Lincoln. The back-bone of Terry's forces was Custer's Seventh Cavalry, including Co-manche and Major Keogh. They pushed through the Badlands region of Dakota and Montana and emerged in the Powder River Valley not too far above its confluence with the Yellowstone.

After fresh Indian signs were found, Terry, Custer and other officers met aboard the supply steamer *Far West* lying along the bank of the Yellowstone at the entrance to the Rosebud. It was decided that the Seventh would push up the Rosebud, cross the Wolf Mountains and move on the Little Bighorn from the south, while Terry's forces would ascend the Bighorn and enter the Little Bighorn Valley from the north, thereby crushing the Sioux from two sides.

But, as nearly everyone knows, that did not happen. One of the greatest concentrations of Indians ever gathered on the North American continent was in the Little Bighorn Valley. Some authorities believe there were as many as twelve thousand Indians, including more than two thousand warriors, in the area.

On Sunday, June 25, 1876, General George Custer, Captain Myles Keogh and every officer and enlisted man in five companies of the Seventh Cavalry were killed. Two other columns from the Seventh—one under the command of Captain Frederick W. Benteen, the other under Major Marcus A. Reno—also fought the Indians. They were some distance south of Custer's column and did not see the Custer fight.

What actually happened to Custer and his men during the battle is a matter of speculation. But from stories told later by Indians who were there, Myles Keogh's troop, among others, fought a brave fight. One historian, D. H. Miller, who gathered much Indian evidence, said Indians recalled seeing a black-mustached officer, probably Keogh, riding his horse back and forth between two separated platoons of troopers trying to bring them together. Miller has suggested that Custer was killed at an early stage of the battle and that Keogh atop Comanche took command.

On June 28, 1876, two days after the battle, a burial party moved into the area. Who first spotted Comanche is unknown, but the horse was severely wounded. The late Theodore Goldin of Kansas City, Missouri, was a member of the burial party. In 1921, Goldin wrote:

"Many of us went over and recognized Comanche, the favorite mount of Major Keogh. . . . The poor fellow was too weak to stand, and many of the men mounted, galloped to the river and returned with water carried in their hats which was given the poor famished horse. Later, he was able to get to his feet and in time was brought into camp where his wounds were washed and the soreness relieved as much as possible. The story is that Dr. Pauling of Terry's medical staff sacrificed the larger part of a bottle of Hennesy brandy in concocting a mash for the wounded horse."

It is believed that Comanche suffered seven wounds in the battle. Three were severe: one in the neck just behind the left shoulder (a bullet passed clear through the neck), another in the front part of the neck and one in the flank. The four others were flesh wounds.

Captain Henry J. Nowlan, a close friend of Keogh's who had been acting as quartermaster on the staff of General Terry away from the field of battle, soon took charge of Comanche. He had Gustave Korn, a farrier, walk the horse about fifteen miles to where the steamer *Far West* lay moored. There the horse was bedded down along with 52 wounded soldiers from Major Marcus A. Reno's engagement with the Indians. The steamer then carried the wounded to Fort Lincoln. The 950-mile trip was made in 54 hours, a record.

At Fort Lincoln, Comanche was too weak to walk. Soldiers placed the horse in a wagon and took him to the stables at the fort where he was placed in a sling. Under the careful attention of Gustave Korn and Captain Nowlan, Comanche was nursed back to health. By the spring of 1877, nearly a year after the battle, Comanche had recovered.

Early the following year, on April 10, 1878, Colonel Samuel D. Sturgis, who had assumed command of the Seventh Cavalry, issued General Orders Number Seven at Fort Abraham Lincoln. They read:

1. The horse known as Comanche being the only living representative of the bloody tragedy of the Little Big Horn, Montana, June 25, 1876, his kind treatment and comfort should be a special pride and solicitude on the part of the Seventh Cavalry, to the end that his life may be prolonged to the utmost limit. Wounded and scarred as he is, his very silence speaks more eloquently than words of the desperate struggle against overwhelming numbers, of the hopeless conflict and of the heroic manner in which all went down on that fatal day.

2. The commanding officer of Troop I will see that a special and comfortable stall is fitted up for him, and he will not be ridden by any person whatsoever under any circumstances, nor will he be put to any kind of work.

3. Hereafter upon all occasions of ceremony (of mounted regimental formation), Comanche, saddled, bridled, draped in mourning, and led by a mounted trooper of Troop I, will be paraded with the regiment.

Farrier Samuel J. Winchester poses with Comanche at Fort Riley, Kansas, in 1890 or 1891, not long before Comanche's death. *Courtesy Kansas State Historical Society*

Pride in the history of the Seventh Cavalry may have played a role in the issuance of the orders. Personal sentiment also may have been involved since Colonel Sturgis lost a son in the Custer battle, but there appears to have been another reason.

Henry Inman, a retired army officer turned writer in Kansas, wrote in 1891 in a little-known account, that "the daughter of the colonel of the regiment was in the habit, every pleasant afternoon, of sending her compliments to Captain Nowlan, requesting the use of 'Comanche' to take a lope on the beautiful prairies surrounding the fort." Inman wrote that one day the daughter of another officer, a major, asked to ride Comanche and was given permission to do so. The colonel's daughter, said Inman, became extremely bitter when she saw the other lady riding Comanche.

"That was the last time," according to Inman, that Comanche was ridden. The next day the colonel of the regiment issued the general orders. Inman was a close friend of Captain Nowlan. It seems likely that Nowlan, who at the time was stationed nearby at Fort Riley, Kansas, was Inman's source.

If correct, Inman's account destroys the myth that Comanche was never ridden after the Custer battle.

Regardless, Comanche led a free and peaceful life after the orders were issued. Theodore W. Goldin remembered that the horse "was allowed the freedom of the Post, the only living thing that wandered at will over the parade grounds at Lincoln without a reprimand from a commanding officer, and the old fellow was a great pet of the soldiers."

Goldin recalled, "Several times when the band would be out, or the bugles sounded for squadron formation, I have seen the old fellow trot to his old place in front of the line of his master's troop."

And others remembered stories about how Comanche would beg sugar lumps at the doors of the officers' quarters and wait at the enlisted men's canteen for buckets of beer.

Comanche adopted Gustave Korn as his new master and would sometimes follow Korn around like a pet dog. When the Seventh Cavalry went into the field, Comanche went along, traveling with the lead horses. But he was never ridden. When the regiment was ordered to the newly established Fort Meade in the Black Hills in 1879, Comanche marched overland with the regiment under the watchful eyes of farrier Korn. The horse was then about seventeen years old.

In 1888 the Seventh Cavalry regiment was ordered back to Fort Riley, Kansas. There Comanche continued to receive full honors. Each June 25 was an official regimental day of mourning. All duties were suspended and a ceremonial parade was held. Comanche participated and led Keogh's old troop. The horse was draped in a black mourning net with saddle reversed and a pair of riding boots in the stirrups.

Comanche remained in good health at Fort Riley until late in 1890 when the Seventh Cavalry was ordered from Fort Riley to the Pine Ridge Agency in South Dakota. Although some accounts suggest that Comanche went along with the regiment, it is doubtful. He was getting old.

On December 29, 1890, Gustave Korn, Comanche's adopted master, was killed along with thirty other whites and about two hundred Sioux men, women and children in what became known as the Battle of Wounded Knee.

When Gustave Korn did not return to Fort Riley with the Seventh Cavalry, Comanche, some said, lost interest in life. Whether or not the horse really missed Korn is unknown, but by the summer of 1891 the horse was failing rapidly.

#7 of series—how the mounted remains of Comanche appeared soon after the work was completed by Professor Dyche and his staff at the Museum of Natural History, University of Kansas, Lawrence, in 1892. *Courtesy Museum of Natural History, University of Kansas*

In a letter to Henry Inman at Topeka, Kansas, dated June 5, 1891, Captain Nowlan wrote: "I fear that the famous horse will not last much longer."

At 1:30 in the morning on November 7, 1891, Comanche died.

Farrier Samuel J. Winchester was with Comanche. Later that morning Winchester wrote the following note to himself:

"Fort Riley, Kansas, Nov. 7, 1891—in memory of the old veteran horse who died at 1:30 o'clock with the colic in his stall while I had my hand on his pulse and looking him in the eye—this night long to be remembered."

The official cause of death was listed as colic. Comanche was about twenty-nine years old.

The officers of the Seventh Cavalry wanted to preserve Comanche. They sent a telegram to L. L. Dyche at the University of Kansas in Lawrence to come to Fort Riley at once. Dyche took an early train to Fort Riley where he agreed to mount the remains into a lifelike figure for four hundred dollars. He returned to Lawrence with Comanche's skin and major bones and completed the task.

Exactly what happened next is unclear. If Dyche kept records of the transaction, their whereabouts are unknown. But General W. H. Sears, writing in 1931, observed that Dyche told him he "sent a bill to the officers of the 7th Cavalry for $400 for his services; but told them if they would leave Comanche at the Dyche Museum at the University, there would be no charge for the mounting. The officers held a meeting at which it was decided to give Comanche to the Dyche Museum, and property rights are now vested in the University through the generosity of Lewis Lindsay Dyche."

General Sears confirmed an earlier statement by General Edward S. Godfrey that "Captain Nowlan called the officers together and they decided to let the University have him, principally because they had no way of transporting him when changing stations."

Comanche became the property of L. L. Dyche and the University of Kansas. Dyche displayed the horse with a university exhibit at the Chicago Exposition in 1893. The horse was the center of much attention. Comanche was then returned to the university where, early in this century, he was placed in the newly constructed Museum of Natural History.

For many years Comanche stood silently just inside the main entrance to the museum, but he suffered. Nothing kept visitors from touching him. Souvenir hunters plucked hairs from his mane and tail, and the changing humidity caused his hide to deteriorate.

Early in 1939 residents of Hardin, Montana, requested that Comanche be placed in a new museum to be constructed at the nearby Custer battlefield. Congress had just authorized funds to build the museum. But members of the Kansas legislature, visiting the university campus several days later, viewed Comanche and, according to one account, "agreed the famous horse was in no condition to be moved to Hardin, Montana."

All remained quiet until late 1946 when General Jonathan M. Wainwright, hero of Bataan and an old cavalryman, led a movement to persuade the University of Kansas Chancellor, Deane W. Malott, to return Comanche to the U.S. Army at Fort Riley, Kansas. The story made national headlines. For a time it appeared the Seventh Cavalry might storm Mount Oread, the site of the University at Lawrence, to obtain Comanche.

But Chancellor Malott said no and held his ground.

"Even assuming a vested interest by the Army in Comanche, which the University does not assume," wrote Malott to then Kansas Governor Frank Carlson, "it would be a dangerous precedent to return a 'bona fide' gift at the behest of the donor; such a policy would mean that all gifts are merely loans returnable at the instigation of the donor, and thus complicate our relations with hundreds of donors who occasionally might change their minds."

Malott wrote one well-wisher, "I should almost as soon think of giving away part of the library as to part with Comanche. He's almost an alumnus of the institution!"

Malott wrote another person supporting the university's position of ownership: "I dropped by Dyche Museum the other day and Comanche seemed to be quite unconcerned and calm about the hullabaloo which has been blowing about his ears. He seemed to want to stay right where he is . . . and I am confident that he will remain there."

The university kept Comanche.

In 1951, South Dakota Senator Francis Case asked for the loan of Comanche to use the mounted animal in the South Dakota 75th-anniversary celebration. Chancellor Malott declined, saying Comanche could not possibly survive the trip. And that same year a well-known publishing company in New York City asked to borrow Comanche for a display in a large Chicago department store in conjunction with an autograph party for a new book.

Chancellor Malott said no.

Two years later, in 1953, the Lewiston, Montana, Kiwanis Club led an effort to move Comanche to the then recently completed museum at the Custer Battlefield National Monument. And they charged that most people in Kansas had never heard of Comanche and that the university

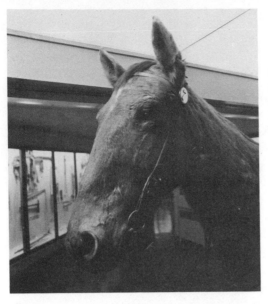

Comanche as he appears today on exhibit in the Museum of Natural History at the University of Kansas in Lawrence. *Photo by author*

had allowed the horse to get dusty and moth-eaten in the museum.

Dr. E. Raymond Hall, then museum director, denied the charges and pointed out that Comanche was being preserved with much care. (A few years earlier Comanche had been placed in a humidity-controlled glass case.) Hall added that thousands of persons visited the museum annually to view the old horse.

Franklin Murphy, then chancellor of the University, followed the example set by Chancellor Malott and refused to give up the horse. Kansas Governor Edward Arn got involved and supported the university's claim to perpetual possession of Comanche.

The controversy soon cooled and all remained quiet until the early 1970s when a group of young Indians objected to the wording of a placard that had long been beside the mounted horse. The wording read, in part: "Comanche was the sole survivor of the Custer Massacre at the Battle of the Little Big Horn on June 25, 1876." The Indians pointed out that quite a few of their ancestors had survived the battle.

The Indians were obviously correct and the wording of the placard was changed. Comanche was the only living thing from Custer's immediate command found on the battlefield two days later. Certainly thousands of Indians survived the battle.

There is evidence today that other cavalry horses survived the battle but were led away by the Indians. Many years after the battle Indians told how the battlefield was picked clean of the soldier belongings, including a few horses that survived. One Indian said that Comanche was not taken from the battlefield because he was too badly wounded, but his saddle and bridle supposedly were taken by Indians.

Museum officials at the University of Kansas discovered that the wording on the old placard had been taken, in part, from the wording of the orders issued in 1878 by Colonel Sturgis and from old newspaper accounts. The wording of the new placard placed inside the glass case on the fifth floor of the Dyche Museum began thus:

"Comanche stands here as a symbol of the conflict between the United States Army and the Indian tribes of the Great Plains that resulted from the government's policy of confinement of Indians on reservations and extermination of those Indians who refused to be confined."

Whether the Army or the Indians or both were at fault is for historians to decide. As for Comanche, he became famous because of a military conflict.

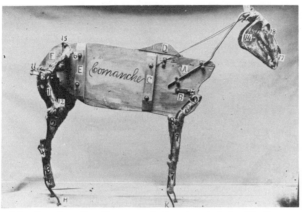

#1 of series—the framework constructed by Professor Lewis Lindsay Dyche for the mounting of the horse Comanche. *Courtesy Museum of Natural History, University of Kansas*

#2 of series—the completed second step of the framework constructed by Professor Dyche for the mounting of the horse Comanche. *Courtesy Museum of Natural History, University of Kansas*

#3 of series—the third step of preparation for the mounting of the horse Comanche. Here the body is being built by winding twine around the framework. *Courtesy Museum of Natural History, University of Kansas*

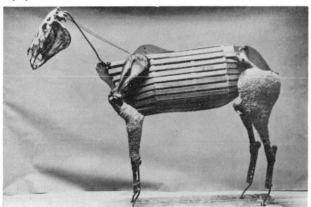

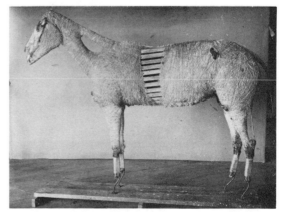

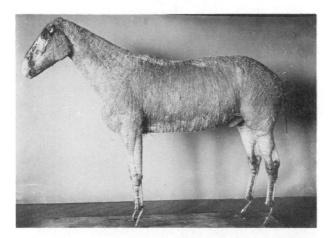

#4 of series—the nearly completed body frame for the horse Comanche. *Courtesy Museum of Natural History, University of Kansas*

#5 of series—the completed body—clay molded over the framework—for the horse Comanche. *Courtesy Museum of Natural History, University of Kansas*

#6 of series—museum workers (Professor Dyche is on the left) pulling the skin of Comanche over the completed framework. *Courtesy Museum of Natural History, University of Kansas*

Lilly's Escape and Unbelievable Ride

It was a bright June morning in 1867 when a settler named Babb said goodbye to his wife and three children and a family friend. He was taking a small herd of cattle, perhaps a dozen, to market in central Texas.

The family friend was a pretty young widow of twenty-five years. Her husband had died a few months earlier, and she was spending the summer with the Babbs on their ranch near the headwaters of the Colorado River south of where Lubbock, Texas, stands today.

In 1867 the Babb Ranch consisted of nothing more than a snug little frame cabin in the sparsely populated region of West Texas. The nearest neighbor was 15 miles east, and for more than 100 miles to the south, west and north, there were no white settlements. It was unsettled land frequented by Indians, mostly Comanches.

Indians had not bothered the Babb family during the many months they had lived on the frontier. Whether Babb gave any thought to hostile Indians before he left is unknown. There is no indication that Babb feared leaving the women and children alone.

For a few days everything was fine. But then one morning after breakfast the two older children went outside the cabin to play in a nearby dry creek bed. Mrs. Babb and her friend—I will call her Lilly in this story—began the household chores.

About midmorning the children called to their mother and pointed toward the west. The mother, stepping outside the cabin, looked in that direction. In a flash a feeling of fear filled her body. A group of mounted horsemen were rapidly approaching the cabin. They were Comanches.

Mrs. Babb yelled for her two children to run to the cabin as fast as they could. Inside, hearing the alarm, Lilly had hurriedly climbed the ladder into the loft to hide. She reached the loft as Mrs. Babb entered the cabin and shut the door, but she didn't bar it. She was waiting for her two children to come dashing in before doing so.

What she didn't know was that the two children had hid in some brush near the dry creek bed. Before she realized they were not coming, it was too late. The Indians reined up outside the cabin. Some of them had seen the two children trying to hide and went after them, while others stormed into the cabin.

Mrs. Babb's third child, a baby of perhaps twelve months, was torn from its mother's arms and thrown to the cabin floor. The Indians, apparently resenting the mother's resistance, seized her by the hair, pulled back her head and slit her throat.

Above in the loft, Lilly, who was watching the scene below through cracks in the loft's floor, screamed as the Indians killed Mrs. Babb. Instantly two Indians vaulted up the ladder and overpowered Lilly.

Fearing for her own life, Lilly gave no resistance as she was dragged from the cabin. Outside were the two older Babb children guarded by other Indians. Lilly and the children were placed on horses and soon the Indians headed north leaving Mrs. Babb dead and the Babb baby, still alive, on the cabin floor.

Whether the baby lived is unknown.

For several days and nights the Indians and their captives rode rapidly northward stopping only long enough to graze and rest their ponies and to get a little food and sleep for themselves.

The captives were given little else but water. The children suffered from harsh treatment, fatigue and want of food, but Lilly was strong. She had been raised on the frontier and had a robust constitution. She fared much better than the children.

As the days passed the party continued north crossing the Brazos, Wichita, Red and the Canadian rivers. They covered many miles. The Indians guarded Lilly and the children carefully until they passed the Canadian River. Their guard then slackened and Lilly and the children were permitted to roam short distances from their nightly camps.

Realizing the Indians might slacken their guard even more, Lilly began to look for the opportunity to escape. She spent time studying the speed and endurance of the different Indian ponies. She knew good horseflesh and, having ridden from an early age, was an accomplished rider.

A few nights later the opportunity came after all the Indians were asleep. Lilly crawled out of camp and made her way to where the ponies were grazing. Quietly she tossed a lariat around the neck of the best pony, leaped upon its back and without saddle or bridle started off at a slow walk in the direction of the North Star.

As soon as she was some distance from camp, she jabbed the pony with her feet and took off at a gallop. All night she rode stopping only when necessary to let her animal rest.

At dawn she rode to the crest of a rise where she could see for miles around. There was not a human being in sight, only the broad open plains. Lilly felt free at last. The sensation of loneliness that one finds on the plains was a good feeling, in spite of the fact that Lilly did not know where she was.

She continued north using the sun as a guide during the day and the North Star at night. By the second day she would have given anything for sleep. She feared losing her horse and by then had tied the end of the lariat around her arm. Should she fall asleep and fall off the pony, she wouldn't lose the animal.

By the middle of the second day wolves had picked up the scent of her pony. Trailing Lilly, perhaps half a mile away, the pack of wolves grew in number. They kept their distance, perhaps hopeful that something would happen to Lilly or the pony.

As the third night began, Lilly realized her horse needed rest. He was barely able to continue at a slow walk. Toward morning she could go no farther. With the lariat tied to her arm, she slid off the pony's back and fell to the ground. The pony stopped. As Lilly fell into a deep sleep, the pony slowly grazed on the short grass around where Lilly slept.

How long she slept is unknown, but as the sun climbed high in the sky, her pony commenced dancing around. The lariat pulled on her arm. She sat up quickly only to find herself surrounded by a group of Indians.

Lilly fainted.

When she came to a few minutes later, the Indians placed her on her pony and rode to their camp a few miles away. There Indian women gave Lilly food and put her to bed in a tepee. It was several days before she had sufficiently recovered and was able to walk about the camp. And it was then that she learned the Indians were Kiowas, part of Lone Wolf's band.

Although these Indians treated her with more kindness than had the Comanches, she was their captive. It was clear they intended to keep her. Again she began to think of escaping.

She became more optimistic about her chances of finding help when a small party of Indians left camp and traveled to the north. They returned six days later with ears of green corn. She knew the Kiowas did not grow corn and that chances were good the Indians had visited a white settlement only three days away.

A few nights later after the Indians were asleep, Lilly crawled out of camp toward where the Indian ponies were grazing. But the Kiowas had dogs. They began barking before she could reach the ponies and she slipped back into camp without being seen.

Two nights later she tried again and this time reached the ponies. She roped one of the better ponies, jumped on its back and slowly moved the animal away from the Kiowa camp. Soon she was galloping north, the direction the Indians had taken to obtain the corn.

Through the next day she stopped only to rest the pony. She kept riding as the last rays of sun disappeared in the western sky and the stars began to twinkle in the night sky above. There was something about riding at night that Lilly enjoyed. Perhaps it was the sensation of moving through the darkness. As she gave her pony his head, she kept her eye on the North Star.

About dawn she came upon a buffalo wallow. Here buffalo had rolled on the ground to remove their winter robe. The depression in the ground was perhaps two or three feet deep. In the center of the wallow rainwater had accumulated, but now only a couple of inches deep.

Lilly let her horse get a drink after she drank some from her cupped hands. The taste was awful but it was water.

Through that day and one more night she continued to ride north. About midmorning of the third day she reached a large river flowing across her line of travel. The river was bank full. The water was cold. Pausing a few moments, fearful of trying to cross the rapidly flowing stream, Lilly quickly realized she had little choice. She had to cross.

She directed her pony into the cold water. The animal hesitated but Lilly gave encouragement and forced the pony through the water to the other side. The stream wasn't as deep as she first thought. But the water nearly touched the pony's back.

Once on the river's northern bank, she paused to let the horse rest. She felt cold as the southerly breeze blowing up from the Staked Plains of Texas brushed past her wet body. But she had met the challenge and won.

A few minutes later she began riding north again. A short distance from the river she struck a broad and well-beaten wagon road. It was the first evidence of the white man's civilization that she had seen since leaving Babb's ranch in Texas.

Moments later, as her eyes followed the wagon road toward the horizon, first to the west and then the east, she could hardly believe her eyes. To the east in the distance was a long train of wagons. They were coming toward her.

Half smiling, half crying, she galloped toward the wagons. The man in charge, Robert Bent, rode ahead to meet her. He was surprised to find a woman in the middle of nowhere. He stopped the train and immediately ordered that Lilly be given food and water. Robert Bent was the son of George Bent, a pioneer trader on the southern plains.

Bent asked Lilly where she lived. When she replied, "In Texas," Bent could hardly believe his ears. Texas was several hundred miles to the south. But it was easy to see that Lilly had been through some kind of ordeal.

It was then that Lilly told her story.

When she finished Bent shook his head almost in disbelief. He then told her she was in Kansas. And the stream she had just crossed was the Arkansas River. Bent said that about fifteen miles east on the trail was a settlement on Big Turkey Creek. He told her she could find help there and even offered to send someone with her. Lilly declined and cast a graceful kiss with her hand toward Bent as she got on her pony and slowly headed toward Big Turkey Creek.

The spot where Lilly met Bent appears to have been on the line between present Rice and McPherson counties in central Kansas. The location is not far from where the city of Hutchinson now stands.

Bent, meantime, continued west with his wagon train to Fort Zarah near where Great Bend, Kansas, is today located. There Bent told the Indian agent about Lilly and her story. Ironically, the Indian agent was then holding council with the band of Kiowa Indians from whom Lilly had last escaped.

The Indian agent immediately dispatched an employee to find Lilly at Big Turkey Creek and to escort her to Council Grove, Kansas, farther east. This was accomplished.

During the months that followed, Indian agents located the two captive Babb children still being held by Comanches. The children were ransomed and sent home to Texas and their father. As for Lilly, she supposedly stayed in Council Grove.

Although her real name is unknown, Lilly, it is said, met a young man at Council Grove and soon remarried. The couple was still living there late in the nineteenth century.

Randolph Marcy, the well-known plains soldier, trailblazer and mapmaker, who first related the story of Lilly's incredible adventure in 1872, said she traversed at least five hundred miles of the plains on horseback. "If any other woman, either in ancient or modern times, has performed as signal an equestrian achievement as this, I have yet to learn it."

Lilly's identity remains a mystery today. If it is ever learned, perhaps someone will build a statue to this noble plainswoman whose courage and perseverance deserve a lasting place in the history of the American West.

Part V

THE FAMOUS AND OBSCURE

To many fame comes too late.

—Camoëns

The Hermit Priest of Belfry Hill

A Santa Fe-bound wagon train came creaking into Council Grove, Kansas, one early spring day in 1863. Walking alongside one of the wagons was a rather handsome looking man about fifty-five years old. But he was shabbily dressed and he had the appearance of one who spent much time in the out-of-doors. The man was Matteo Boccalini, an Italian by birth.

Boccalini had joined the wagon train a couple of days before, but he refused all offers to ride in the wagons. He insisted on walking. And Boccalini kept to himself.

When he arrived in Council Grove the town's few hundred residents paid him little attention at first. He probably looked like many of the other travelers who passed through their community each week. Council Grove was then an important stop on the Santa Fe Trail, about one hundred and ten miles southwest of Westport, Missouri, the eastern terminus of the trail.

But soon it was obvious to the townspeople that Boccalini was different. For one thing, they learned that he had been a Catholic priest—and they understood he might be out of favor with the Church. When the wagon train resumed its journey toward Santa Fe, Boccalini remained behind. He climbed the eastern face of Belfry Hill on the western edge of Council Grove and there, near the summit, he constructed a shelter. He laid up a rude wall of loose rocks until it met the brow of an overhanging ledge. He made the cavelike structure his home.

On the walls inside he carved his name, a cross, and the words *Gesu*

A view of Council Grove, Kansas, early in this century. This photo was taken from near the top of Belfry Hill close to where Matteo Boccalini made his home under an overhang. *Courtesy Kansas State Historical Society*

Maria and *Capri*. His new home was not far from the spot where towns-people had placed a large alarm bell to be rung in the event of Indian raids, fires or other trouble. Belfry Hill was named for the bell.

Boccalini had few possessions. Aside from the clothing on his back and a few religious articles, his only earthly belongings were a half-dozen well-thumbed books and an old mandolin. One evening soon after he set up housekeeping on the hill the sound of mandolin music floated down over Council Grove. The songs—they were Neapolitan in origin—were unfamiliar to most of the townsfolk, who began to talk about the strange man living on the hill.

As the sun came up each morning Boccalini would usually seat himself at the entrance of his cavelike home and read from his books. From time to time he would pause to survey the town and the valley below, especially the trail winding into Council Grove from the east. Almost every night at dusk he would put his books away, eat some supper and then play his mandolin.

A Council Grove newspaper story dated April 27, 1863, notes, "He refuses to eat bread or meat; his food consists of corn meal mixed with water or milk without cooking."

One early-day resident of Council Grove later recalled that "Boc-calini was always restless and alert, as though awaiting some dreaded, yet expected event. He avoided everyone and went down into town only when it was necessary to buy a little food. He either could not, or would not, speak English. But he spoke both Spanish and Italian." His sense of impending danger was regarded by some as hallucinatory.

Many townspeople began to call him a hermit, but a few of the residents who spoke Spanish felt differently about the newcomer. They had gained his confidence and talked with him. Two or three men in Council Grove chose to call him "El Solitario," meaning "The Solitary Man," instead of hermit. They said that Boccalini argued that solitude was the nurse of enthusiasm and that enthusiasm was the parent of genius. He told them that it was the inspiration of the dominant religion of every nation. Those who had solitude, said Boccalini, had visions of the beyond.

Once or twice a week Boccalini would invite one of the trusted few to his cavelike home, where they would talk in Spanish and enjoy mandolin music. In time Boccalini's friends pieced together the story of "El Solitario." Boccalini was born about 1808 on the island of Capri. There he spent his youth. At the age of eighteen he was sent to Rome where he studied and took his holy vows at the age of twenty-one. Soon he was ordained.

Young Boccalini became Father Francesco. And for one so young he was an eloquent speaker who boldly spoke his mind. He soon came to the attention of the Pope, who named him one of his secretaries. But the Congregation of the Propagation of the Faith refused to confirm him. They believed Boccalini was too outspoken, and he was placed on trial. Boccalini defended himself and was so eloquent that the charges were dropped. He then assumed his Vatican duties.

But according to Boccalini's story, jealous priests plotted his downfall. During the early 1830s they supposedly saw to it that a dark-haired young lady befriended Boccalini. He fell in love with the young girl "in a most earthly and fleshly way," according to one account. Boccalini was immediately charged, prosecuted and denounced, but before he could be sentenced he fled Rome and soon became a wanderer upon the face of the earth.

More important, he feared for his life. The priests had accused him of disgracing the Church. He believed or perhaps imagined that they wanted to take his life in revenge. We have only the hand-me-down tale from Boccalini as evidence. Whether it was fact or fantasy is unknown.

For a time he campaigned with Garibaldi, the Italian general and nationalist leader. But Boccalini's enemies discovered him—or he imagined they did—and he made his way to Mexico. There, according to the tale, he lived a life of solitude in the mountains for many years. He made his way to the United States in the early 1850s and traveled as far east as Indiana. There he spent nearly five years living in further solitude.

After the Civil War began, he headed west. For a time he supposedly lived in a large hollow tree near Westport, Missouri. Then, moving west again, he tried to help the Kaw or Kansas Indians on their reservation in the Neosho Valley southeast of Council Grove. But the Kaws were superstitious. They did not trust the strange man who acted unlike other whites. His asceticism and self control made them suspicious. The Indians did not understand. It was then, early in the spring of 1863, that Boccalini headed north, met the wagon train on the Santa Fe Trail and followed it into Council Grove, where he made his home on Belfry Hill.

Although Boccalini told his few close friends about his difficulties with the Church, he still practiced his religion and on occasion served as a priest. One day a Mexican was stabbed in a gambling quarrel among some drivers of a train of freight wagons stopped at Council Grove. The Mexican was dying. He wanted a priest. Boccalini hurried to the man's side and administered the last sacraments in Spanish much to the satisfaction of the dying Mexican.

But late in August 1863, about five months after Boccalini arrived in Council Grove, he saw a man dressed in clerical garb. Boccalini believed that the man was looking for him and hurriedly returned to his hilltop perch. His old fears, based on his fugitive status, were with him again. His apprehensions moved him to quick action.

Early the next morning before the sun came up Boccalini gathered together his meager personal belongings and joined a caravan starting for New Mexico. The Mexican don who owned the wagon train—one account says he was a brother-in-law of Kit Carson—recalled many years later that Boccalini refused to ride "either on horseback or in one of the wagons, despite the earnest invitation extended to him each recurring morning by the master of the wagon train."

Boccalini also refused to sleep in a tent or in a wagon when the train stopped for the night. He preferred to roll himself up in a single blanket under the stars some distance from the wagons. Then he would pray or play his mandolin long after the camp had gone to sleep. Sometimes Boccalini caught and cooked prairie dogs or he would eat his cornmeal mixture. Only when he was hard pressed for food would he accept a meal from the Mexican teamsters.

When the wagon train neared Santa Fe he thanked the Mexican don and disappeared. For nearly a year Boccalini reportedly wandered through New Mexico and parts of Arizona. Early in 1865, while wandering along the eastern edge of the Sangre de Cristo mountains northwest of present-day Las Vegas, New Mexico, he came upon a cave near the summit of Rincon de Tecolote—"The Owl's Corner"—a mountain peak more than nine thousand feet high, not far south of the headwaters of the Mora River. There Boccalini made his new home.

As before, he carved his name, a cross and the words *Gesu Maria* and

Capri on the cave's walls. He divided his time between solitude in the cave or among nearby piñon trees and religious work among the poor Mexicans who lived in the valley below. For nearly four years he lived a peaceful life helping the depressed and ill in the Sangre de Cristo area. One day in 1869 he failed to make an appearance among the natives. After more than a week's absence, a search party was sent from the valley into the mountains. They found his body near the entrance to his cave home. A knife was stuck in his heart. No one knows if Boccalini's death was suicide or murder. It is one mystery that probably will never be solved.

Today in New Mexico, near Las Vegas, people still refer to a nearby mountain as Hermit's Peak. And in Council Grove, Kansas, Belfry Hill still stands, but there is no trace of Boccalini's rock wall shelter under the overhang near the summit. All that is left are the bits and pieces of a man's life found on the dusty pages of a few old newspapers and old books, and the philosophy that he who has solitude has visions of the beyond.

The Day Chief Old Wolf
Nearly Lost His Scalp

John L. Hatcher was a wiry little man, full of muscle and as fearless as any plainsman or mountain man of the Old West. He had red hair and blue eyes that were piercing. He was a good shot. He also was a good poker and euchre player.

John Hatcher was born in Virginia, and went west as a young man. At St. Louis he joined up with the Bent Brothers and St. Vrain. That was in 1835. He worked for them at Bent's Old Fort on the Arkansas River in what is today eastern Colorado and then lived for a time among the Indians before becoming a scout for the army.

By the summer of 1857, John Hatcher had become a trader. He made his headquarters at Taos. Hatcher, then about forty-five years old, set out early that summer with a caravan of fifteen wagons and about as many men. His destination was Westport.

A few days after leaving Taos, Hatcher's caravan reached Wagon Mound, a rocky mesa that resembles something like an old covered army wagon. Wagon Mound may still be seen today near Interstate 25 about sixty miles south of Raton in northeastern New Mexico. A small town nearby is named for the mesa.

Hatcher's men had been driving their wagons two abreast for protection. They were in Indian country, but as they approached Wagon Mound, Hatcher gave the order and the wagons began to move in single file. On the open rolling plains ahead, Hatcher knew that Indians, if there were any, could be seen at a far distance.

The wagons had hardly had time to move into single file when suddenly a large band of Indians rode over a small rise in the ground and headed straight for the caravan. They were Comanches, but they were not attacking. The Indian chiefs—there were six or seven leading the Indians—were giving the peace sign.

Hatcher knew the ways of the Comanches, and he suspected they were coming to murder and rob. Hatcher, however, returned the sign of peace. He had little choice. Then he quickly gave the order to his men to corral their wagons in a circle and to stand by for trouble.

As the Indian chiefs came ahead of their braves, Hatcher saw that the leader was Old Wolf. The old Indian had been responsible for many raids on the southern plains. They had made Old Wolf's name a terror, especially among Mexicans traveling the Santa Fe Trail.

Hatcher cautiously welcomed Old Wolf and the other chiefs and invited them to have some refreshments. A blanket was thrown to the ground and Hatcher seated himself beside Old Wolf. Sugar was served.

As Old Wolf and his chiefs finished eating, Hatcher asked Old Wolf to send his young braves away, over the hill. The braves were standing beside their horses not far from the wagons. At this Old Wolf and his chiefs stood up. So did Hatcher who already sensed the old Indian's answer.

Not waiting for a reply, Hatcher grabbed Old Wolf's hair with his left hand. With his right hand Hatcher took his knife from its scabbard and thrust it to the chief's throat.

"Send your braves over the hill now, or I'll kill you right where you are," demanded Hatcher.

Old Wolf shook his head back and forth.

"Send them on or I'll scalp you alive as you are!" said Hatcher in a firm voice.

Again Old Wolf shook his head.

A second later Hatcher began to carry out his threat, but he started slowly. Blood trickled from a tiny incision on Old Wolf's hairline down the Indian's forehead. Moments later Old Wolf weakened. He ordered his next in command to send the young braves over the hill. The order was given and the astonished braves quickly mounted their horses and rode away.

Still holding Old Wolf's hair, Hatcher ordered his men to unload their wagons. They did, piling bundles of pelts and furs inside the circle of wagons as a barricade. Then Hatcher's men climbed behind their barricade, passed out ammunition and prepared for the battle they all knew was coming.

When Hatcher saw that his men were ready, he let go of Old Wolf's hair, gave the Indian a swift kick in the seat of his pants and told the chiefs to leave. They did and with haste. Hatcher quickly joined his men and prepared for the attack.

Thirty minutes passed. Then an hour. The expected Indian attack still had not come as the sun began to set. Hatcher and his men remained on watch until darkness, but there was no sign of Old Wolf and his band.

The night passed uneventfully. By dawn there still were no signs of the Indians. It was then that Hatcher made the decision to move on. He gave the order and the men reloaded their wagons and the caravan continued slowly toward Westport. The remainder of the journey was peaceful. Not an Indian was seen.

Why Old Wolf and his band did not attack the wagon train is unknown. They outnumbered Hatcher and his men. It may have been that Old Wolf had lost face among his chiefs and braves or that he had lost the element of surprise against Hatcher and his men.

Colonel Richard I. Dodge, plainsman and soldier, wrote in 1877, "As a rule, the Indian relies upon surprise, upon the effect of a sudden and furious dash ... to demoralize his enemy and render him sure prey."

If surprise had been Old Wolf's aim, he had not succeeded.

But a more likely reason appears to have been Hatcher's bravery. His actions undoubtedly gained him sudden respect from Old Wolf. Comanches placed great importance on acts of bravery, and it probably was this sudden respect for Hatcher on the part of Old Wolf and the other Indians that saved Hatcher and his men.

Hatcher returned to Santa Fe later that summer and made another trip over the trail the following year in 1858. Never once was he troubled by Indians.

What became of Old Wolf I am unable to learn, but Hatcher later moved to California where he bought a large ranch and settled down. Still later he moved to Linn County, Oregon, where he died at the age of eighty-five in about 1898.

Frederic Remington: Sheep Rancher and Saloon Owner

It was late March 1883. The calendar said it was nearly spring, and the rolling Kansas Flint Hills were showing their first green tint. But winter's chill was still in the air as the Santa Fe passenger train pulled into Peabody, Kansas.

For the youth of twenty-two years who stepped off the train, the long journey from northern New York State was over. Fred Remington had come to Kansas to "get rich" raising sheep. Rich he would become on the plains, but not in dollars.

That cold March day when Remington got off the train at Peabody, in Marion County northeast of Newton, Kansas, he had a sheep ranch on his mind. He was a stocky young man with a spirit for adventure. He had gone to the Yale art school for a year and a half, but had to quit when his father died. From his father's estate he had inherited $10,584. He spent some of this money looking into the cattle business in Montana, but he found cattle too costly.

Bob Camp, a school friend from Yale, had then sold Remington on the idea of raising sheep in Kansas. Sheep cost less than cattle, said Camp, but they were just as much fun to raise. Camp had come to Kansas for his health a few months before. He had bought a sheep ranch in northwest Butler County, south of Peabody, and was on hand to welcome his friend Remington to Kansas as he stepped off the train.

Camp had found a ranch for Remington next to his own. It was

Fred Remington, Kansas sheep rancher, poses proudly for this photograph taken in Peabody, Kansas, in 1883. *Courtesy Kansas State Historical Society*

160 acres, had a three-room frame house, two barns, a corral and water well. Remington apparently was satisfied with Camp's choice because within a few days he bought the ranch and within several weeks purchased an adjoining quarter section to give him 320 acres, a half section.

The young New Yorker then set about the task of becoming a sheep rancher. He purchased several horses including "a nervous little half-breed Texas and thorough bred," as he later described her. The mare was "a beautiful light gold-dust color, with a Naples yellow mane and tail." Remington named her "Terra-Cotta."

The closest settlement to Remington's ranch, the tiny community of Plum Grove, had only a school, a couple of houses and a general store with a limited stock. Remington had his major supplies freighted in from Peabody.

Young Remington hired a ranch hand named Bill Kehr. He was about the same age as Remington, and one of Kehr's first chores was to remodel the barns to handle several hundred sheep that Remington purchased. In short order, Kansas sheep rancher Fred Remington was in business.

Remington soon became moody, however. He was almost melancholy. The young New Yorker may have had second thoughts about his Kansas venture. The girl he loved, Eva Adele Caten, was more than one thousand miles to the east. She said in letters she would wait, but would she? Then too he had used up most of his inheritance plus two thousand dollars he borrowed from his mother. And there was the land which may have had an effect on Remington. Certainly the plains were different from the rolling woodlands of northern New York State where he had been reared. The vast expanse of almost treeless open plains perhaps made Remington feel uncomfortable and a little humble.

But the fresh air and the wide-open spaces were undoubtedly good for Remington. As the newness of Kansas and sheep ranching began to wear off, Remington fell into a routine. He let Bill Kehr do most of the hard and dirty work. Remington assumed the job of watching his sheep. It was a lonely job, but sitting atop his horse, hour after hour, or squatting on a grass-covered knoll catching the breeze on a hot summer day gave him time to think and to sketch. For young Remington, however, art was not easy. It never had been and it offered little satisfaction. As Remington would write many years later, "Art is a she-devil of a mistress, and, if at times in earlier days she would not even stoop to my way of thinking, I have persevered and will continue."

As the days passed he frequently hired a neighbor boy and his dog to look after the sheep so that he could go riding off across the plains on a horse. Of one such ride to Bob Camp's adjoining ranch one morning, Remington would later write: "The gallop across the prairie was glorious. The light haze hung over the plains, not yet dissipated by the rising sun. Terra-Cotta's stride was steel springs under me as she swept along, brushing the dew from the grass of the range."

While Remington found satisfaction in riding his horses—at one point he owned fifty—he did not shun all work. He pitched in to help when it was time to dip the sheep and he liked to do the cooking. Remington usually got the meals for himself and Bill Kehr and whoever else might drop by. But there are some doubts about his cuisine.

Remington's watercolor of his Butler County, Kansas, sheep ranch in 1883.
Courtesy Frederic Remington Museum, Ogdensburg, N.Y. ➝

Left: These sketches by Remington depicted work on his Kansas sheep ranch in 1883. The drawing in the lower right-hand corner is a self-portrait of Remington and his horse with a feedbag. *Courtesy Kansas State Historical Society*

Below: This panel of Remington's Kansas sketches, drawn in 1883, is owned by Harold McCracken, the well-known writer and authority on Remington and other Western artists. *Courtesy Harold McCracken*

A quiet evening on the Ranch.

Below: "Any thing for a quiet life" is Remington's caption on a sketch he drew of a neighbor boy and his dog watching over the artist's sheep herd in 1883. *Courtesy Frederic Remington Museum, Ogdensburg, N.Y.*

Any thing for a quiet life.

my Ranch

One day a neighbor lady sent her daughter to Remington's ranch with a couple of loaves of freshly baked bread. As the girl arrived, Remington was dumping a large basket of dirty potatoes into a huge pot on the stove.

"Mr. Remington," exclaimed the young girl, "don't you wash your potatoes before cooking them?"

"Wash them? Heavens no. I've tried them both washed and unwashed and they taste better unwashed. Have *you* ever tasted boiled unwashed potatoes?"

The young girl shook her head.

"Well, tell your mother to try them this way, and you'll see they're good. Anyway," added Remington, "it takes time to wash them."

As ranch life became routine, Remington spent more time sketching. Everything was his subject. He entertained Bob Camp and Bill Kehr and anyone else who happened to be around with his drawings. And before many weeks passed, nearly everyone in the neighborhood knew Remington could draw.

Frequently someone would ask him to make a sketch. One day a neighbor brought over a new trotting horse he had just purchased and asked Remington to make a sketch of the animal. Another time, at Bob Camp's ranch, Remington made a drawing on brown wrapping paper of a cow defending her calf from a wolf. He gave the sketch to Camp's cook. And one day at Camp's ranch, Remington supposedly took his knife and sketched on a barn door the picture of a cowboy roping a steer.

Remington's Kansas sketches are crude, however, when compared to his work of a decade later. As they show, he was still learning.

As the spring of 1883 eased into summer, Remington became more restless. In July, he left the ranch in the hands of Bill Kehr and with George Shepherd, a newfound friend from Peabody, set out on horseback to see the Southwest. Just how far they went is unknown. They may have gone as far as New Mexico. A few weeks later, Remington returned to his Kansas ranch, hardened even more by the outdoor life.

When fall arrived, the first of a series of events occurred that would eventually cause Remington to quit sheep ranching. About the middle of October 1883, he, Bob Camp, Jim Chapin and three other young friends from the neighborhood, decided to run jackrabbits. Each armed himself with a lance. Then, mounted on their best horses and using dogs, the riders spent several hours chasing rabbits across the plains. The object was to touch the rabbit with the lance but few came that close.

About midday they lost a rabbit near the house of a newcomer in

These four sketches by Frederic Remington, titled "Agriculture in Kansas," were drawn in 1883 when he was owner of a Kansas sheep ranch. *Courtesy Kansas State Historical Society*

"Boss of the 'Badger State' in Spring Lambing" is the caption Remington gave this sketch of Bob Camp, his Yale school friend and Butler County, Kansas, neighbor. It was drawn in 1883. *Courtesy Frederic Remington Museum, Ogdensburg, N.Y.*

the community, John Mitchner. Old John, as the young men had come to call him, saw the horsemen approaching and invited them to stay for dinner. The tired riders accepted, tied up their horses and went inside Old John's house. Everyone sat down in front of the warm stove and smoked and talked and waited for the bacon and eggs to cook. Soon the conversation turned to horses.

Old John gazed at the stove and listened for a few moments, then said—as Remington quoted him later—"Wall, my horse stock ain't nothin' to brag on now, because I hain't got the money that you fellers down the creek has got fer to buy 'em with, but I've got a little mare down thar in the corral as I've got a notion ken run some shakes."

It was an open invitation for a race. Before very many minutes passed, Remington's friend, Jim Chapin, had bet that his horse Push-Bob could beat Old John's mare. Bill Kehr said his horse Prince, a beautiful gray, could beat both Push-Bob and the mare.

Everyone left the bacon and eggs to burn on the cook stove and headed for the corral. By the time they got to Old John's horses, Remington and the others had made wagers on the race. Remington put up Terra-Cotta, his favorite mare, against another mare and a colt in Old John's corral. And Remington's other friends put up their horses against some of Old John's other stock. Then a course was laid out and the horsemen prepared to race.

What happened next is told in Remington's own words:

> The three racers came up to the scratch, Bill and Jim sitting on their sleek steeds like centaurs. Old Prince had bristled up and moved with great vim and power. Push-Bob swerved about and stretched his neck on the bit. The boys were bare-footed, with their sleeves rolled up and a handkerchief tied around their heads. Old John came prancing out, stripped to the waist, on his mare, which indeed looked more game when mounted than running loose in the corral. The old man's gray thin locks were blowing loose in the wind, and he worked his horse up to the scratch in a very knowing way. We all regarded the race as a foregone conclusion and had really begun to pity old John's impoverishment, but still there was the interest in the bout between Prince and Push-Bob. This was the first time the victors of the Whitewater bottoms had met, and was altogether the greatest race which that country had seen in years. How the boys from the surrounding ranches would have gathered could they have known it, but it is just as well that they did not; for as I fired the gun and the horses scratched away from the mark, Old John went to the front and stayed there to the end, winning by several lengths, while Prince and Push-Bob ran what was called a dead heat, altogether there was considerable discussion over it for a long time afterwards. There was my dear little Terra gone to the hand of the spoilsman, and the very thought almost broke my heart, as I loved that mare as I shall never love another animal. I went back to the corral, sat down and began to whittle a stick.

When Old John pulled up at the corral he jumped to the ground and drawled out "Thar now; I've been a-layin' for you fellers ever since I came inter these yar parts and I recon as how I've sort of got ye. If ye'd had more horses with ye, I'd a hade a right smart horse herd after this race."

Remington and his friends said nothing. They piled their saddles on the mule Bob Camp's cook had been riding, the only animal not lost in the wagering. Then Remington and his friends walked ten miles home.

This drawing by Frederic Remington shows the artist, Bill Kehr, Jim Chapin, and Robert Camp racing across the Kansas prairie. The drawing appeared in *Outing Magazine,* May 1887. *Courtesy Kansas State Historical Society*

That night Remington and Bill Kehr saddled two fresh horses to go into Plum Grove to get some groceries. It was dark when they arrived at Hoyt's old stone store. As they looked in they saw a crowd of men gathered around one lone kerosene lamp listening to none other than Old John. Remington and Kehr stopped to listen. When Old John finished, the men inside broke into laughter. Remington and Kehr looked at each other. Without a word, they turned, got on their horses and rode home without the groceries.

Remington brooded over the loss of Terra-Cotta and having "been taken" by Old John. When Halloween came not too many days later, it gave him the chance to let off some steam. The morning after, the local preacher at Plum Grove found his buggy on top of the church and his cow inside the front door.

"No one knew who did it, but Fred Remington paid for getting that buggy down, cleaning up the church, giving it a fresh coat of paint and made the pastor a present of $10 or $15," recalled Jacob DeCon, a Plum Grove resident, many years later.

But that was not the end of young Remington's exuberance.

On Christmas Eve, 1883, Remington and four of his young friends rode into Plum Grove to attend the Christmas party at the schoolhouse. The white frame building, with double doors at one end and windows along two sides, was jammed with people. First, there were a few songs, then some readings. Everything went smoothly until a little girl in a flutter and white dress stood up and began reciting "Hang Up the Baby's Stocking."

At that point Remington and his friends became noisy. From their seats in the back of the room, they started throwing paper wads. The program came to a stop. Remington and his friends were told to leave. They did, and the program resumed.

In a few minutes the lamps inside the schoolhouse were turned out and the candles on a large Christmas tree were lit for the arrival of Santa Claus. Squire Duncan, a large bald man, was Santa. He made his appearance wearing a buffalo robe, which covered his usually shiny head, and from his chin hung homemade cotton whiskers.

Just as he was about to speak, the double doors behind the audience swung open. Someone outside yelled "Fire," and as everyone turned to look flames filled the doorway.

In seconds the audience was in panic. Everyone scrambled for the only exit not blocked, the windows. In less than a minute the building was emptied, save one old maid whose long dress got caught on a window sash. But by then everyone outside realized the schoolhouse was not on fire. It had been a prank. Hay from wagons nearby had been piled on a dry goods box in front of the schoolhouse door, then set afire. The flames had shot harmlessly toward the sky. But from inside the school, there had been the illusion that the schoolhouse was afire.

Blame was immediately laid on "that Fred Remington and his gang." Before the night was over charges were filed and the five young men arrested. By the time their case came to trial in El Dorado, the county seat, it was early in January 1884. Just about everyone in Butler County had heard what happened Christmas over in Plum Grove. The courtroom was packed. Justice of the Peace Charles E. Lobdell presided. Remington must have felt like a dangerous criminal, especially when he was referred to as "Billy the Kid" by the prosecuting attorney. There is little doubt that he was shaken by the experience.

After two days the jury failed to reach a verdict. The vote was six to six. Lobdell dismissed the case on the condition that the young men pay the court costs, attorney's fees and all expenses. Remington paid everything.

Even before the trial and perhaps before the incident on Christmas Eve, Remington apparently had made up his mind to call it quits in Butler County. Only a few days before the trial, young Remington had written Arthur Markley, a friend from the East then living in Colorado, that "I am going farther West—I do not like Kansas—and then tackle

Frederic Remington as he appeared in 1884, not long after he sold his Kansas sheep ranch. This photograph was taken in Kansas City. *Courtesy Amon Carter Museum, Fort Worth, Texas*

some business. I don't care whether it is stock, mercantile—either hardware or whisky—or anything else."

At the same time wool prices were dropping just as Remington was about ready to sell his first wool. Things looked bleak.

The disillusioned youth put his sheep ranch up for sale. For a time no one expressed an interest, but then in April 1884, D. M. Greene expressed an interest in buying the spread. When the bargaining ended and the sale was completed, Greene had the ranch and Remington had made a slight profit.

Remington said goodbye and headed west, but in not too many weeks he turned up in Kansas City with a portfolio of sketches. In 1884 Kansas City was a town of about 75,000 and a large cattle-trading center. Remington, then twenty-three years old, located a place to live on Southwest Boulevard and began to sketch and to soak up the color of Kansas City.

With money from his ranch sale probably in the bank of Franklin B. Hough in the New Journal Building and only himself to support, Remington began to look around the town for ways to invest his money. His first investment may have been a small house in Pendleton Heights, then almost in the country off Southwest Boulevard. It is known that Remington invested several thousand dollars in Bishop & Christie's saloon, 116 West Sixth Street. Remington became a silent one-third partner with no active role in management.

Apparently confident that his saloon investment would be profitable, Remington began to sketch. And he frequented the haunts of the cowpunchers including Gillis's, Gaston's, the palatial Pacific and Bishop & Christie's, where he silently watched his investment.

A man who had worked in Bishop & Christie's at the time, the late S. E. Ellis, remembered in 1909 that Remington "used to spend a good deal of time in the saloon and poolroom. . . . but it was a long time before I learned he was one of the proprietors."

Ellis remembered that Remington was always "drawing sketches of men in the place and always talking of the rides he took." Remington kept a big horse on his property off Southwest Boulevard and regularly used the animal under saddle.

Another of Remington's Kansas City acquaintances, Al Hatch, who in 1884 ran a clubhouse near the state line, recalled that Remington "sketched a whole lot." Hatch said, "He used to ride out in the hills mornings and evenings, and draw pretty near everything he saw. He was great on drawing things around the place, too. He'd be standing quiet over in the corner, kind of watching the crowd out of the corner of his eye. Then, all of a sudden he'd take a piece of paper out of his pocket and begin sketching. When he got through it'd always be a picture of one of the bunch. He gave me a whole lot of 'em," said Hatch in 1910, "but they've kicked around and got lost some way. I wish I'd taken more care of 'em. Some were real good."

Hatch observed that Remington "knew a lot about horses. He could draw a picture of a bucking pony that was livelier than the original, and that's saying something," said Hatch, who added, "They all looked like horses, too, not like stock advertisements. . . . Fred's horses are the real thing."

Young Remington didn't limit his acquaintance to saloonkeepers. Inside of six months he was acquainted with most of the persons worth knowing in Kansas City including George Gaston, an ex-Bavarian colonel who was a connoisseur of music, art and roast beef, and a man who spoke five languages.

It is believed that Gaston, after viewing some of Remington's sketches, encouraged the young man to become a professional artist, certainly something that Remington had undoubtedly thought of before. And similar encouragement apparently came from artist John Mulvaney, then well known for his painting *Custer's Last Rally*. The painting was completed by Mulvaney in Kansas City after a trip to the Custer battlefield in 1879. The full extent of Mulvaney's influence on Remington, however, is unknown, but it is likely that the young New Yorker was attracted to the forty-year-old native of Ireland in part because of his Custer painting.

A photograph of Frederic Remington working in his New Rochelle, N.Y., studio taken a few years after he gave up sheep ranching in Kansas. Remington is shown working on a painting he called "An Indian Trapper." The original is now in the Amon Carter Museum, Fort Worth, Texas. *Courtesy Kansas State Historical Society*

Mulvaney may also have introduced Remington to a Kansas City art dealer, W. W. Findley. In 1911, Findley's son, W. C. Findley, recalled that Remington gave W. W. Findley "three pictures" to sell. Young Findley remembered that "Father sold the three for $150. Later a man came in and offered $100 to Remington for a duplicate of one of the three," said young Findley, who recalled that his father then told Remington, "You've got a start now. Don't duplicate anything. Keep conceiving new pictures." Remington did and so far as is known he never duplicated any of his sketches or paintings after that.

His success in selling art in Kansas City appears to have prompted Remington to spend more time as an artist. He rented a small room in the Sheidley building and began to spend a great deal of time sketching and doing some painting. But he still enjoyed visiting the bars where he sometimes put on the boxing gloves with anybody willing to do so.

Saloonkeeper Al Hatch recalled that the artist-to-be was built "just like Jim Corbett, only broader. He was a boxer, too," said Hatch, adding, "I've got a notion that if he hadn't a taste for art, he could have made a good living as a fighter, for it's my opinion he never saw the man he was afraid of." Hatch remembered the time when he put the gloves on with Remington and, as Hatch said, "stayed sorry for two weeks."

Remington's growing equity in the small house he was buying, the sales of his drawings plus what he undoubtedly believed was a wise saloon investment probably gave him a false sense of security. About mid-September, 1884, less than a year after he arrived in Kansas City, Remington headed east. On the first of October, he and Eva Adele Caten were married at Gloversville, New York, and the next day they took a train west to Kansas City to make their home.

For a time all went well for the Remingtons, but his new wife—he called her "Missie"—was anything but happy in Kansas City and the West. And when Remington went to collect his dividends on his saloon investment, there was nothing. Exactly what happened is unknown, but it appears that the owners of Bishop & Christie's had moved the saloon to 511 Delaware Street, probably upstairs above J. T. Tarney's basement billiard hall. Somehow in the shuffle Remington lost his share of the saloon. According to one account, it amounted to seven thousand dollars.

W. C. Findley, the Kansas City art dealer, remembered in 1911 that "that made a great change" in Remington. The young artist suddenly realized he was dependent on himself and income from selling art was simply not sufficient to support two persons. He and "Missie" talked about the situation and soon agreed that she would return to the East until he could get back on his feet again.

As for Remington, he moved in with friends, settled his Kansas City business and headed west to draw. During the months that followed he frequently returned to Kansas City, where he had left his belongings with friends. And he probably continued to sell art through W. W. Findley. And in the fall of 1885 Remington collected his possessions and, with a little money in his pocket, headed east. He would never take up residence in the West again although there would be more trips.

The Remingtons settled in New York City close to where he could sell his art. And within four months one of his western sketches made the cover of *Harper's Weekly*. Frederic Remington, the artist, was on his way.

During his remaining years Remington produced nearly three thousand sketches, paintings and drawings. At least two of his major works are believed to have had their beginnings in rough sketches drawn in Kansas. His oil *The Cowboy* now in the Amon Carter Museum in Fort Worth, Texas, appears to have started as a sketch drawn on his sheep ranch. Later it became the model for his first bronze sculpture called *The Bronco Buster*. Remington drew an early sketch of *The Last Stand* on his Kansas sheep ranch as well, although it was not his first such sketch. He had produced one as a teenager in the East. *The L t Stand* later

"Texas Cattle in a Kansas Corn Corral" is the title of this sketch by Frederic Remington that appeared in *Harper's Weekly,* April 28, 1888. Such scenes were familiar to Remington when he lived in Kansas. *Courtesy Kansas State Historical Society*

became the frontispiece of *Pony Tracks,* the first of six books written and illustrated by him.

At the age of forty-eight, the day after Christmas, 1909, Remington had an attack of appendicitis and died after surgery. But his legacy to America and her people was great. He had documented the Old West through art, which today is more popular than ever. Like that of the late Montana artist Charlie Russell, Frederic Remington's work is considered by many to be "the best there is."

When Abe Lincoln Came West to the Plains

The last day of November 1859 was unusually warm. The afternoon sun was still high in the sky as the train from the East pulled into the railroad station at St. Joseph, Missouri. The tall and lanky man in the stovepipe hat appeared tired as he stepped down from the coach. The man was Abe Lincoln, and he was going to Kansas Territory where he would make several public appearances.

As Lincoln's feet touched the ground, he looked around. His eyes met those of two men rapidly approaching the train to meet him. There was a smile of recognition on Lincoln's face as they neared. They were from Kansas Territory, just across the Missouri River to the west. One of the men was Daniel W. "Web" Wilder, a leader of the new Republican party in the territory, who ran a free-state newspaper in Elwood, Kansas Territory. The other man was Mark W. Delahay.

Delahay, a former Illinois newspaperman and later a lawyer at Springfield, had often ridden the circuit with Lincoln. Delahay had helped to raise the regiment of volunteers that drove the Mormons out of Nauvoo and started them, with Brigham Young as leader, on the long journey to Salt Lake. When Delahay came to Kansas to support the free-state movement, he started a newspaper at Leavenworth, but a proslavery mob sacked his office and threw his printing press into the Missouri River.

Perhaps of more importance, Delahay's wife was Lincoln's cousin. Mrs. Delahay's grandfather, Joshua Hanks, was a near relative of Nancy Hanks, the mother of Lincoln. As a young man Delahay had lived for a time with Joshua Hanks, in Scott County, Illinois. Lincoln

Daniel W. Wilder, a leader of the Republican party in Kansas Territory in 1859. He settled in Kansas in 1858 in Elwood, Donipan County, and became the editor of the *Elwood Free Press*. He was one of the men who invited Lincoln to Kansas. *Courtesy Kansas State Historical Society*

Mark W. Delahay of Leavenworth and Wyandotte City (now Kansas City, Kansas) was an early Kansas City newspaperman. He was one of the men who invited Lincoln to Kansas. His wife was Lincoln's cousin. *Courtesy Kansas State Historical Society*

frequently went there to go fishing with Hanks, other relatives and Delahay.

The three men shook hands and exchanged pleasantries. Then Lincoln, who had ridden all day in the coach over the recently completed Hannibal and St. Joseph line, told his hosts he was tired and would like a shave. The trio took an omnibus to a barbershop in the business district where Lincoln got his shave. Then the Kansans bought him a Chicago and New York newspaper on their way to the bank of the Missouri River to wait for the ferry to take them across to Kansas Territory.

As they waited, the three men sat on a log in the afternoon sun, dangled their feet in the mud and talked. Wilder studied Lincoln's features, especially his legs, and later he wrote:

"They were legs you could fold up. The knees stood up like the hind joints of a Kansas grasshopper's legs. He wore a hat of stovepipe shape, but made of felt, unglazed, not shining, and needing no brush. The buttons were off his shirt. . . ."

To the unknowing who saw the ungainly figure with weathered and wrinkled face in St. Joseph that day, Lincoln might well have been taken for a farmer who dressed up for a spree in town. But on that November day in 1859, Lincoln was the new political leader of the nation's antislavery forces and an important figure in the newly formed Republican party.

This photograph of Abe Lincoln was taken soon after his visit to Kansas Territory in 1859. *Courtesy Kansas State Historical Society*

He began to gain national attention when Illinois Republicans nominated him as their candidate for the United States Senate in June of 1858. Lincoln sounded phrases at the convention in Springfield that thundered across the land. The phrases—"A house divided against itself cannot stand"—"Kansas must be free"—"This country cannot exist half slave and half free"—stuck in the minds of men and became the slogans of the new Republican party.

The now-famous debates with Senator Stephen A. Douglas of Illinois, his opponent, began in August of 1858. The nation followed them with much interest as Lincoln put into plain language the things people had been thinking but could not express in words. It was Lincoln who said: "Although volume upon volume has been written to prove slavery a good thing, we never hear of the man who wishes to take the good of it by being a slave himself."

Thus, by late October of 1859, Lincoln was a national figure. Persons talked of his humble background and of the possibility that he might be the next president. Invitations to speak poured into his Illinois home, and at least one of them came from Kansas Territory where the new Republican party was beginning to take shape.

By then the fight to make Kansas a free state was about over. The free-staters had won and Kansas Territory was knocking for admission to the Union as a free state. The struggle in Kansas had, in part, been responsible for lifting Lincoln into the national spotlight.

It was late afternoon on November 30, 1859, when Lincoln, Delahay and Wilder crossed the Missouri River on the ferry to Elwood, Kansas Territory. They went immediately to the Great Western Hotel. Lincoln had not planned to speak at Elwood, but when residents heard he was in town, they asked him to speak. He agreed to speak that evening.

The time and place were set. Then a man walked the streets of Elwood ringing the hotel's dinner bell and crying, "Abe Lincoln of Illinois will speak at eight o'clock in the dining room of the Great Western Hotel. Everybody invited."

The small dining room was crowded that night. Lincoln, feeling a little under the weather, made a short speech, had dinner and then went to bed. During the night the weather changed. The next morning, December 1, 1859, it was bitterly cold. Because there were no railroads in Kansas Territory yet, Lincoln was driven in a one-horse open buggy across the rolling plains to Troy, some twelve miles to the west.

Old newspaper accounts report that Judge J. B. Maynard, Carter H. Wilder, Daniel W. Wilder, Henry Boder, Joseph Hayton, Frank Kotsch and Albert D. Richardson, an Eastern newspaper correspondent, went along, most of them in other buggies. Delahay apparently returned to Leavenworth to prepare for Lincoln's arrival there.

About midway between Elwood and Troy, Lincoln's party met a two-horse wagon going east. The wagon was driven by a man in heavy corduroy clothes and wrapped in several buffalo robes. And there were icicles hanging from the man's heavy beard.

As they met, the man in the wagon called out, "Hello, Mr. Lincoln." At that the wagon and buggies stopped.

Lincoln didn't appear to recognize the man.

"Don't you know me, Mr. Lincoln? I'm Henry Villard."

"Good gracious," replied Lincoln, adding, "Villard, you look like a real Pike's Peaker."

"That's where I've been," replied Villard, then a well-known correspondent for an Eastern newspaper.

"Why, Mr. Lincoln, you're blue with cold, and shivering," exclaimed Villard, seeing that Lincoln was wearing only a short overcoat and no other wraps. Villard loaned Lincoln two buffalo robes which were later returned, and both parties went their separate ways.

Lincoln spoke that afternoon at Troy. About forty persons gathered in the little, bare-walled courthouse to hear him talk. The following day John Brown was to be hanged in the East, and Lincoln said Brown's attack on Harpers Ferry had been wrong for two reasons: the act was a violation of the law, and it was futile.

"We have a means provided for the expression of our belief in regard to slavery. It is through the ballot box, the peaceful method provided by the Constitution," said Lincoln.

Lincoln noted that Kansans had recently adopted a state constitution. "Kansas will be free," he said, adding, "but the same questions aroused here in regard to freedom or slavery will arise with regard to other territories—and Kansas will have to take a stand in deciding them."

Lincoln *talked* to his audience and said the general feeling in regard to slavery had changed entirely since the early days of the Republic. He told his audience to examine the debates under the Confederation, in the convention that framed the Constitution, and in the first session of Congress—and "you will not find a single man saying Slavery is a good thing. They all believed it was an evil."

Newspaperman Albert D. Richardson, who was in the audience, later wrote:

"In the imaginative language of the frontier, Troy was a town—possibly a city—but, save a shabby frame courthouse, a tavern and a few shanties, its urban glories were visible only to the eye of faith. It was intensely cold. The sweeping prairie wind rocked the crazy buildings, and cut the faces of the travelers like a knife. . . ."

Of Lincoln's speech at Troy, Richardson observed: "There was none of the magnetism of a multitude to inspire the long, angular, ungainly orator, who rose up behind a rough table. With little gesticulation—and that little ungraceful—he began, not to declaim, but to talk. In a conversational tone he began to argue the question of slavery in the territories in the language of an average Ohio or New York farmer. I thought, 'If the Illinoisans consider this a great man their ideas must be very peculiar.' But in ten or fifteen minutes I was unconsciously and irresistibly drawn by the clearness and closeness of his argument. Link after link it was forged and welded, like a blacksmith's chain.

"The address lasted an hour and three-quarters. Neither rhetorical, graceful nor eloquent, it was still very fascinating. The people of the frontier believed profoundly in fair play, and in hearing both sides, so they now called for an aged ex-Kentuckian, who was the heaviest slave holder in the territory; responding, he thus prefaced his remarks: 'I have heard, during my life, all the ablest public speakers, all the eminent statesmen of the past and the present generation, and while I dissent utterly from the doctrines of this address, and shall endeavor to refute some of them, candor compels me to say that it is the most able—the most logical—speech I ever listened to.' "

After his speech at Troy, Lincoln traveled to Doniphan to speak. And the next day he was driven to Atchison where he was slated to make an address at the Methodist Church at the corner of Fifth and Parallel streets. A brass band paraded through the streets drumming up a large crowd. Then, when things were about ready, the band—playing loudly—escorted Lincoln to the church.

The late Franklin G. Adams, an Atchison pioneer, was there. He later wrote:

"I still remember the appearance of Mr. Lincoln as he walked up the aisle on entering the church and took his place on the pulpit stand. He was awkward and forbidding, but it required but a few words for him to dispel the unfavorable impression, and he was listened to with the deepest of interest by every member of the audience."

The next morning, Saturday, Lincoln was taken to Leavenworth where he took a room at the Planter's Hotel and then went to visit his cousin, Mrs. Mark W. Delahay. That night he spoke at Stockton's Hall. Afterward, he joined a few men in an upstairs room across the street from his hotel. Years later Daniel R. Anthony, one of the men present, recalled:

"The room contained two beds, a cot, some plain chairs, and an old box stove. That stove could eat wood enough to keep one man busy carrying fuel up the stairs and two or three men poor paying for it. Lincoln and Marcus J. Parrott, the Kansas delegate in Congress, were our guests, and they stayed until all the wood in the room had been devoured by the glutton stove.

"It was a cold night, as I remember it, and nobody was willing to leave the room long enough to go for wood. Mark Parrott had sent us great sacks full of patent-office reports from Washington to distribute among the boys. Times were not dull enough in the town, however, to make government reports popular reading matter, and many sacks full of bound papers were unopened in the room. Some had already served for fuel, and when the fire died down two or three bulky books went into the stove. . . ."

"As the books were heaved into the stove one of the men asked, 'Mr. Lincoln, when you become president will you sanction the burning of government reports by cold men in Kansas Territory?'

" 'Not only will I not sanction it,' said Lincoln, 'but I will cause legal action to be brought against the offenders.' He smiled good naturedly as he said it. That was the only reference to the presidency made that night although every man in the room was a politician."

Lincoln sat and talked with the men for several hours. There was nothing to drink but some of the men smoked. Lincoln's great feet were against the stove, his long, lean, ungainly form hunkered down in his tilted chair. "He was made up of head, hands, feet and length. The lines that gave his face and figure a majesty of sadness were yet to come," recalled Anthony.

The next day was Sunday. Lincoln went to the home of his cousin to stay a few days. His talk at Stockton Hall, however, had given him such a reputation in Leavenworth that many who had not heard him asked to hear him speak. He agreed to do so Monday night, December 5, 1859, following a public reception for him at Planters House.

An engraving of the Planters Hotel in Leavenworth made ten years after Lincoln stayed there. Lincoln delivered his address from the hotel steps to people standing in the street. *Courtesy Kansas State Historical Society*

A few hours before the reception, Lincoln sent out for a pitcher of lager beer brewed in Leavenworth. He had heard about the locally famous beer and wanted to taste it. Mark Delahay's young daughter, Mary, poured the beer for Lincoln and saw him drink it. The pitcher was carefully preserved by the Delahay family until the 1920s when it was given to the Leavenworth Chapter of the Daughters of the American Revolution. Today it is in the Fort Leavenworth Museum.

That night the assembled crowd was so large that no room or hall in Leavenworth could hold everyone, so Lincoln stood on the steps in front of the Planters Hotel while the people of the town massed in the street. August Uebline, the Leavenworth brewer, was in the crowd and listened to Lincoln. Years later he was quoted as saying, "It was my good beer that inspired Lincoln and helped him withstand the cold."

Whether the beer had an effect on Lincoln is unknown, but his speech was impressive. Henry Villard, the Eastern newspaperman, wired his paper, "It was the largest mass meeting that ever assembled on Kansas soil, and the greatest address ever heard here."

On Wednesday, December 7, 1859, Lincoln, after spending nearly seven full days in Kansas Territory, took a steamboat from Leavenworth to St. Joseph and then traveled by train to his home in Illinois. Two months later, on the evening of February 27, 1860, Lincoln made his famous speech at Cooper Union in New York City. The theme of that speech was a formulation of the principles on which the Republican party should face the voters in 1860. But instead of attempting to cover all issues, Lincoln spoke only of the slavery question. He inquired into what the fathers who framed the government thought of and did about slavery. And Lincoln showed, by conclusive and irrefutable argument and citations from history, that the fathers acted as though they believed that the Federal Government had no power to put slavery into the territories.

Lincoln then directed a portion of his remarks to the people of the South and advised fellow Republicans to yield to Southerners wherever possible. "Wrong as we think slavery is," he urged, "we can yet afford to let it alone where it is . . ." Then Lincoln concluded his speech with the following: "Neither let us be slandered from our duty by false accusations against us, nor frightened from it by menaces of destruction to the government, nor of dungeons to ourselves. Let us have faith that right makes might, and in that faith let us to the end dare to do our duty as we understand it."

Many persons, back in Kansas Territory, subscribed to the *New York Tribune,* Horace Greeley's paper. When it printed Lincoln's Cooper Union address, those who had heard Lincoln speak were surprised to see that it was essentially the same speech he had given in his various appearances in Kansas. He had changed it only slightly. They realized that they had first heard the speech that would lead Lincoln to the presidency.

Three months after making the Cooper Union speech, Lincoln was nominated for the presidency in Chicago, and on November 6, 1860, Abraham Lincoln was elected the sixteenth president of the United States.

Jim Lane and His Frontier Guard

On April 17, 1861, Virginia seceded from the Union, and when the news from Richmond reached Washington, tension mounted. Fears grew that Confederate soldiers might attack the capital at any time.

Only a few days before, James H. Lane of Lawrence, Kansas, had arrived in Washington. Lane and S. C. Pomeroy had been chosen by the legislature in Topeka as Kansas's first United States senators. As a state, Kansas was only a few months old.

When Lane heard the rumors that the capital might be attacked, he hurriedly contacted those Kansans he knew in the city and a few other trusted acquaintances. Within twenty-four hours he had organized a force of more than fifty men. Then, on April 17, he advised the War Department of their availability.

Two days later saw the first bloodshed of the Civil War. A mob of Southern sympathizers attacked the Sixth Massachusetts Infantry as it passed through Baltimore, about thirty miles northeast of Washington. On the day before, the War Department had received secret information that an attempt would be made to seize President Lincoln and overturn the government.

It was then that Lane was ordered to muster his men. Their mission, said the War Department, was to protect the President of the United States.

Shortly before 9 p.m., April 18, Lane and his men arrived at the White House where they were given arms and ammunition, and Lane received a gleaming saber. Then, until nearly midnight, Lane put his

James "Jim" Lane, one of the first two senators from Kansas, and the energetic organizer of the "Frontier Guard." *Courtesy Kansas State Historical Society*

men—he called them the Frontier Guard—through "rudimentary squad drill under the light of the gorgeous gas chandeliers" in the East Room of the White House.

"Late in the evening," as the *Washington Evening Star* reported the next afternoon, "the President attempted to enter the East Room, but as the sentinel at the door had received orders to admit no one without the countersign, Mr. Lincoln was forced to beat a retreat, to the no small amusement of the company."

Sometime after midnight, Lane and his Frontier Guard "disposed themselves in picturesque bivouac on the brilliant-patterned velvet carpet—perhaps the most luxurious cantonment which American soldiers have ever enjoyed."

President Lincoln may not have liked the idea of soldiers bivouacking in the East Room of the White House, or it may have been that additional Union soldiers from the North were arriving in the capital. In any event, the next night, April 19, Lane and his men were "excused from serving on guard," and dismissed with orders to rally with their guns in the White House at the first alarm.

For the next eight days the Frontier Guard remained on duty during the daylight hours in the area around the Executive Mansion. During that time the group grew in size from about fifty to one hundred men, most of them from Kansas.

On Tuesday night, April 22, Lane and about half the Frontier Guard paraded down Pennsylvania Avenue. It must have been quite a show. The *Washington Evening Star* reported on April 24: "This company is armed with Minie rifles, several bayonets, and navy-sized revolvers,

United States of America

Headquarters Frontier Guard,
Washington City, April 27, 1861.

To Hon. S. Cameron, Secretary of War:

Sir: In consequence of the arrival of large numbers of troops in this city, I am satisfied the emergency has ceased that called our company into service.

If you concur in this opinion, I should be pleased to receive authority from you to disband said company, and to honorably discharge the members thereof from the service.

Very truly,

J. H. Lane
Capt. Comdg.

War Department, April 27, 1861.

Gen. James H. Lane:

Sir: In reply to your letter of this day's date, stating that, in consequence of the arrival of large numbers of troops in this city, the emergency has ceased which called the company commanded by you into service, and that you would be pleased, therefore, to have authority to disband your company, and have an honorable discharge from service for it.

Concurring fully with you, I readily grant you the authority asked for, and, in doing so, I beg to extend to you, and through you to the men under your command, the assurance of my high appreciation of the very prompt and patriotic manner in which your company was organized for the defence of the Capital, and the very efficient services rendered by it during the time of its existence.

Very respectfully,

Simon Cameron

Cheerfully approved.

A. Lincoln

By authority vested in me as Captain of the Frontier Guard, I, JAMES H. LANE, do hereby certify that Sidney Clarke a Member of said Company, served his Country in defence of the National Capital, at a time of great peril, when threatened by hordes of traitors; said service commencing on the eighteenth day of April, 1861, and ending on the date hereof.

I also, by virtue of said authority, do hereby HONORABLY DISCHARGE the said Sidney Clarke from the service of the United States.

Given under my hand at the East Room of the Executive Mansion, at Washington City, this third day of May, 1861.

Attest

M. W. Delahay Lieut.

J. H. Lane
Capt.

One of the two original discharge papers now in the files of the Kansas State Historical Society. This was the discharge of Sidney Clarke of Lawrence, Kansas, and is signed by Jim Lane and "cheerfully approved" by Abraham Lincoln. *Courtesy Kansas State Historical Society*

and are among the most skilful marksmen connected with the present service." Back home in Kansas, newspapers were reporting the events in Washington. A Leavenworth newspaper claimed that Lane had been "called upon by the War Department to take charge of one thousand Union Guards." The newspaper added: "It does not surprise us that the Defender of Freedom in Kansas is honored with a high position the moment he arrives at the seat of Government."

Washington was not attacked, and Lane's Frontier Guard proved to be short-lived. By Thursday, April 25, more Union troops had

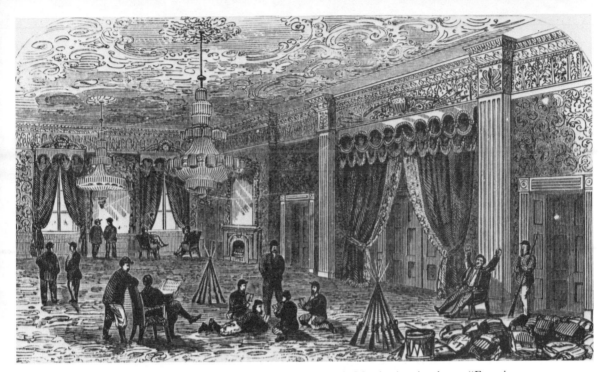

This illustration from Benson J. Lossing's book *Civil War in America* shows "Frontier Guards" luxuriously bivouacked in the East Room of the White House in 1861. *Courtesy Kansas State Historical Society*

reached Washington from the North and reinforced the capital's defenses. That afternoon, the emergency over, Lane formed his Frontier Guard—now about 120 in number—at Willard's Hotel on Pennsylvania Avenue. They marched the few blocks to the White House and into the East Room, where they stood in formation. When President Lincoln entered the room, the Frontier Guard snapped to attention. Then, walking down the rows of men, Lane introduced each man to the President. Lincoln thanked them for their services and officially disbanded the unofficial group. Each member received an elaborately printed "honorable discharge" certificate signed by Lane, President Lincoln and Secretary of War Simon Cameron; and the Frontier Guard, which had existed for little over a week, was no more.

Officially, the guard never existed. It was a voluntary organization serving without pay. Neither the adjutant general's office in Washington nor the state adjutant general's office in Kansas have records showing that the Frontier Guard ever existed.

But it did. Tucked away in the files of the Kansas State Historical Society at Topeka are two original discharge papers of former Frontier Guardsmen. And the whereabouts of two other such papers and the names of at least fifty other members are known: members of what must have been one of the most unusual military units to have ever existed in the United States.

What Happened to Boston Corbett?

About seven miles south of Concordia, Kansas, is a stone marker. It stands between two small cedar trees in a pasture a few yards off a county road. A plaque on the marker reads:

1878
BOSTON CORBETT'S DUGOUT
SIXTY YARDS SOUTH IS THE SITE OF THE
DUGOUT HOME OF BOSTON CORBETT, WHO AS
A SOLDIER SHOT JOHN WILKES BOOTH,
THE ASSASSIN OF PRESIDENT LINCOLN

From the dirt road there is no sign of Corbett's dugout. Only a small mound of rocks can be seen from the road on what was once Corbett's eighty-acre Cloud County, Kansas, homestead. But south beyond a barbed-wire fence and the stone marker, I found a depression in the ground when I visited the site several years ago. There Corbett's dugout once stood, where the quiet but nervous little man, with graying chin whiskers and mustache, lived for several years.

Boston Corbett—his real name was Thomas H. Corbett—came to Kansas in about 1878. Ten years later, after a series of strange events, Corbett vanished, his disappearance still a mystery. The story of Boston Corbett's place in history began on the fateful evening of April 14, 1865, when President Lincoln went to Ford's Theater in Washington to see a performance of the play *Our American Cousin*. That night one shot was fired. Lincoln was struck in the head. His assassin, an actor named John Wilkes Booth, escaped across the stage. Outside the theatre, Booth jumped onto a waiting horse and fled. Meantime President Lincoln was taken to a house across the street where he died at seven o'clock on the cold and rainy morning that followed.

By then orders had reached a detachment of the Sixteenth New York Cavalry, stationed near Washington, to assist Colonel E. J. Conger and three other detectives in tracking down and capturing Booth. Lieutenant Edward P. Doherty asked for twenty-five volunteers. Corbett, a sergeant, who had been released from Andersonville prison only five months earlier on an exchange of prisoners, was the first man to volunteer.

Through the woodlands, swamps and fields the detectives and the soldiers trailed Booth. Twelve days later, early on the morning of April 26, 1865, Booth, with an accomplice named David Herold, was found hiding in a tobacco barn near Bowling Green, Virginia, about sixty miles south of Washington. The soldiers surrounded the barn. Booth and Herold were ordered to come outside. Herold came out, hands stretched high above his head, but Booth refused.

What happened next is told in Corbett's words. "When Lieutenant Doherty demanded Booth's surrender, he shouted, 'No!' Three times the lieutenant gave the order, three times he refused. The lieutenant then gave the command to fire the barn. A torch was lighted and touched to it. In the flickering light, I could see Booth through cracks between boards, standing on a pile of hay. He was leaning on a crutch with his carbine in hand. As fire mounted up, he suddenly raised his carbine. I saw the move, took aim, and fired. In an instant, he crumpled on the hay. He was dragged outside and carried to the back porch of the nearby house. He died there, some time later," said Corbett.

"I was straightaway placed under arrest for daring to disobey orders. They disarmed me and took me to Washington. There the officers treated me with scorn . . . because I shot Booth! General Howard asked me, 'How in the world did you happen to send the bullet to the same spot, exactly to the tilting of a hair, where Lincoln was shot?'

" 'The Lord directed it,' I told him," said Corbett.

Boston Corbett was brought before Edwin M. Stanton, secretary of war, on the charge of having disobeyed orders. But Stanton freed Corbett saying, "The rebel is dead—the patriot lives—he has saved us continued excitement, delay and expense—the patriot is released," related Corbett.

Corbett was then discharged from the army.

Because he fired the shot that killed Booth, Corbett felt the $75,000

Photograph of Boston Corbett. Date unknown. In the files of the Kansas State Historical Society, Topeka. This photo was probably taken in the East, before Corbett came to Kansas.

reward posted by the government for Booth's capture should be his. The decision was placed before a committee on claims of the House of Representatives. When it became evident their deliberations would be lengthy, Corbett went to Camden, New Jersey, and returned to his prewar occupation, that of a hatter. He waited.

Corbett—who later would be called the "Mad Hatter"—waited more than a year. On July 26, 1866, the committee announced that the reward money would be distributed among all members of the search party. The largest amount went to Colonel Conger, the detective, who received $15,000. Corbett was given only $1,653.95.

Returning to Camden, Corbett continued to make hats and to preach the gospel. In 1869 he became a full-time minister of the Siloam Methodist Episcopal Mission at Camden. A correspondent for the Philadelphia *Sunday World* visited Corbett a few months later and reported, "He lives alone in his little house, doing his own cooking and housekeeping, and seeing nobody but members of the little flock of Methodists, which meet nightly at his house. . . . He preaches and exhorts himself and uses a Windsor chair for a pulpit."

Corbett was then thirty-eight years old.

He had not always been a religious man. He was born in England in 1832, and emigrated to America with his parents, settling in Troy, New York. After his schooling he served as an apprentice to a hatter in Danbury, Connecticut. After working in Albany, Boston, Richmond and New York City, Corbett married. His wife, however, died about 1855 and Corbett went to Boston. There he attended a revival and soon became so imbued with fanatical zeal that he changed his name from

Thomas to Boston when he was baptized in honor of the city where he was converted.

Then stranger things began to happen. On July 16, 1856, after reading chapters eighteen and nineteen of the book of Matthew in the Bible, Corbett took a scissors and emasculated himself. It took him nearly a month to recover in Boston's Massachusetts General Hospital, according to the records.

Why Boston Corbett then chose to settle in Kansas in 1878 is still unknown. Some historians believe he may have come west to escape the publicity of being John Wilkes Booth's killer. In the East he was visited frequently and received countless letters from persons praising him for killing Booth. Writers asked him to send them his autograph or to write a description of how he killed Booth. Another reason may be the fact that he knew one or two persons in Kansas who urged him to settle in the West.

And there is still a third possibility. There are reports that Corbett received threatening letters signed "Booth's Avenger." Someone told Corbett that Booth had belonged to a secret order whose members had taken a vow to avenge Booth's death. Perhaps fearing for his life and to escape further publicity, Corbett headed west in the spring of 1878. One morning, many days later, he drove swiftly into Concordia, the county seat of Cloud County, Kansas, in a buckboard pulled by a black pony named Billy.

The late Albert T. Reid, newspaperman and artist, then a young boy growing up in Concordia, saw Corbett arrive. Reid later remembered that Corbett swung down from the buckboard, fed Billy some lumps of sugar and quickly strode away. "Corbett was a small, insignificant-looking little man, with a thin, scraggly beard, and he wore an old army cap such as the ex-soldiers of those days often wore as souvenirs of their part in the war," recalled Reid.

"One thing which attracted my attention was his long hair. It strayed from under his cap and hung down to his shoulders. Around his waist was an old army belt, and from the belt dangled two pistols," wrote Reid.

Corbett filed a soldier's claim to an eighty-acre homestead about seven miles south of Concordia. There was a good spring on the hillside land, one reason, according to old-timers, why Corbett chose the spot. Soon he hired four men including a stonemason named Grigsby to build a one-room cabin, nine by ten feet, over the spring in the side of the hill. Inside the dugout the stonemason built what looked like a fireplace over the spring to catch the fresh spring water. The overflow ran under a wood plank floor.

Corbett furnished the cabin with an old cot, stove and several old chairs. He cut small holes in the walls of the cabin through which he could observe the surrounding countryside and perhaps fire a gun. As the days passed neighbors noticed that the stranger who kept to himself trenched his cabin as though it were a fort.

In filing his claim Corbett gave his real name. Soon someone realized who he was and people began to call on their famous neighbor. But Corbett never invited them inside his dugout, though a few persons later claimed they had been inside while he was away. Corbett rejected friendship.

In an effort to make his land pay Corbett hired four men to break the ground and plant corn. The men brought their own food and Corbett never went out where they were working until the job was finished. He paid them in cash.

From the beginning Corbett apparently had no money worries. He paid for everything in cash including milk and butter purchased from a Mrs. Randall who lived nearby. It was Mrs. Randall and another woman to whom Corbett showed a blanket that he said he wanted to be wrapped in when he died. He also showed them a grave on top of the hill behind his dugout where he wanted to be buried. Corbett had already dug his own grave. Nearby he planted a cottonwood tree. Today there is no sign of the grave nor the tree.

A drawing of Boston Corbett's dugout in Cloud County, Kansas, made early in this century. Artist is unknown. *In the files of the Kansas State Historical Society*

Whether Corbett expected to be killed by one of "Booth's Avengers" or felt he would soon die of natural causes, no one knows. He did little work, spent much of his time wandering about aimlessly on his pony. He did not work his land and soon limited his agricultural interests to raising chickens and a few head of livestock.

Corbett apparently spent much time answering letters after the news spread that he had moved to Kansas. Many of the letters Corbett received are today preserved by the Kansas State Historical Society at Topeka. Nearly all were from persons requesting his autograph or a description in his own words of Booth's killing. One writer from Indiana wrote, "Please send your picture as a momento [sic] of your bravery." Another writer from Michigan: "I truly hope you will not treat this with the contempt you may think it merits, I have but a simple request to offer. Can I be honored with your autograph."

The Bible was Corbett's constant companion. One Sunday he was driving slowly along behind his pony, his guns strapped about his waist, reading the Bible. Up ahead he saw a group of farm boys playing baseball in a pasture. The local boys had organized a team and were playing another team from across the county.

"It's wicked to play baseball on the Lord's day," yelled Corbett as he reined his horse and buckboard to a stop. "Don't play it anymore. Get out," he yelled then, waving his gun in the air.

The farm boys left, but the next day a warrant was sworn out against Corbett. He was told to come to town on a certain day and stand trial. When the day arrived Corbett went quietly to the office of the justice of the peace at Concordia. He sat moodily listening as witnesses told what had happened. The expression on Corbett's face grew more and more serious. The late Fred W. Sturges, a former district court judge at Concordia, was in the room and recalled the scene:

"There was Boston Corbett, a little slender, wary-eyed chap, his hair hanging down long behind, sitting there quietly, while these fellows told how he had threatened to shoot them. Suddenly he jumped up, whipped out his army revolver and began pointing it at one man after another.

" 'That's a lie, a lie, a lie,' he shrilled. 'I'll shoot any man who says such things about me,' exclaimed Corbett.

"I can tell you there was scattering," remembered Judge Sturges in 1913. "Most of the townspeople had come to the trial and they trampled each other getting to the doors and windows. One old attorney, who was crippled up with rheumatism and knew he could not make much showing in a run, crawled under a small table. But Boston didn't shoot, and nothing was done to him, either. They quieted him down and talked to him, and he went back to his hillside eighty, the cabin and the pony," remembered Sturges, who had other memories of Corbett.

"Often enough, as I was driving along I have seen this Boston Corbett slip quickly off his horse as he caught sight of me and lie motionless in the grass, his long revolver in one hand, waiting to see what was coming. He never made any attempt to hurt me, or indeed to hurt anyone, but he was always wary," added Sturges.

Soon after moving to Kansas Corbett attempted to get a pension for his military service. It was not until 1882 that it came through in the amount of $7.50 a month.

Although many persons in Cloud County felt something was wrong with Corbett, most were sympathetic toward him. They felt he had been neglected by the government. Trying to do him a favor and perhaps to help bring him out of seclusion, a local politician got Corbett a job as an assistant doorkeeper in the House of Representatives at Topeka. A collection was taken to give him clothes and money, and early in January of 1886, Corbett left his hillside eighty and traveled to Topeka.

For a time everything went well, but Corbett was the object of great curiosity. Many times visitors paid more attention to Corbett than the lawmakers and the business at hand. Then one day two employees did something to make Corbett mad. He pulled his gun and threatened them. Police were called and Corbett was led away to jail. The next day he was brought before the probate judge and pronounced insane. He was sent to the state insane asylum in Topeka.

Corbett remained in the asylum for more than a year. In the official hospital records Corbett is described as "a very civil and comfortable patient . . . but full of cranky notions; and makes frequent demands for liberty . . ." At one point in March of 1887, he assaulted an attendant with a knife in an apparent attempt to escape. Corbett was disarmed without causing any injury.

But one spring day in 1888, while guards were taking Corbett and other inmates for a walk, the son of the hospital's superintendent rode up to his father's office on his pony. The boy tied the animal to a hitching rail and went inside the building. Corbett, who was at the head of the procession, gradually began to fall back. He paused to pick flowers, then to examine plants, until he was almost the rear man. When the procession neared the pony, Corbett bolted from the ranks and ran to the animal. Jumping on the pony he rode away.

News spread quickly that Boston Corbett had escaped. Flyers were sent across Kansas and elsewhere warning that Corbett was dangerous, but there was no word of his whereabouts until a letter came from a livery-stable operator at Neodesha, in southeast Kansas. The operator

The site of Boston Corbett's dugout about seven miles south of Concordia, Kansas. All that remains today is the depression in the ground where the dugout once stood. It is partly visible to the right of the stone marker, left of center. The cottonwood tree planted by Corbett on the hill behind his dugout is no longer there, and the trees that once stood around the dugout have since been cut down. When this photo was taken, the tree limbs, branches and trunks were still on the ground where they fell. *Photo by author*

said that a man had left an Indian pony with him, requesting that the asylum be notified of its whereabouts.

Later authorities learned that Corbett had stopped in Neodesha to visit Richard Thatcher, superintendent of schools, and Irvin DeFord, son of Captain Harvey DeFord with whom Corbett had spent time in prison during the Civil War. Corbett was hid in DeFord's barn at Neodesha. Irvin DeFord's daughter, Helen DeFord Bush, told me in 1972:

"My mother said for several days she kept missing food and leftovers from meals. After questioning my father for several days, he admitted they were hiding Boston Corbett in the barn. He said to her, 'Don't worry, tonight we are starting him west.' She then asked him to have Corbett autograph her memory book (which all women had in those days). He did, and I now have it. It is dated June 1, 1888.

"Boston Corbett . . . left on a horse or pony procured by Uncle Dick Thatcher and my father. Probably, Capt. Harvey DeFord was also there. They gave him food, a blanket and some money, with the promise he would keep going and not come back. He told them, 'I won't. I'm going to Mexico,' They never heard from him after that," wrote Mrs. Bush.

What became of Boston Corbett remains a mystery to this day. Over the years a few men claimed to be Corbett, but their claims were proved false. Some people believe Corbett died in Mexico. Others believe he lies in an unmarked grave near the site of the long vanished town of Seapo in Republic County, Kansas. A few others claimed he drowned in the Kansas River near Topeka, but no one knows for sure.

The Song "Home on the Range"

Lugging a heavy Edison recording machine, John Lomax, a rather large man, walked into the Buckhorn Saloon in San Antonio, Texas. It was a hot summer day in 1908. The Buckhorn's proprietor, Albert Friedrich, a German, frowned as he looked at the strange object Lomax was carrying. Walking to the bar, Lomax introduced himself and said he was searching for cowboy songs. Friedrich smiled.

Sipping a glass of beer, Lomax explained that he was a professor at the University of Texas in Austin, and how, as a Sheldon Fellow for the Investigation of American Ballads at Harvard University, he was crisscrossing the Southwest in search of cowboy songs and frontier ballads. Lomax said he wanted to record them for posterity. He added that he knew the Buckhorn Saloon was a meeting place for the old Texas trail drivers, and he asked Friedrich for his help.

"Well, if you want cowboy songs," said Friedrich, "you go see the Negro singer who runs the beer saloon in a scrubby mesquite grove out beyond the Southern Pacific depot. He was a camp cook for years. He made the trip up the Chisholm Trail to Kansas half a dozen times. He can give you a lot of cowboy songs if you can get him to sing."

Lomax thanked Friedrich and left. A little while later he found the Negro out behind his saloon in the mesquite grove. He was sitting on the ground, his hat pulled down over his eyes, his head tilted back against a mesquite tree. As Lomax later recalled, "When I shook him awake and told him what I wanted he muttered as he looked at me with bleary eyes, 'I'se drunk. Come back tomorrow and I'll sing for you.'"

Lomax returned the next morning and spent all day with the man.

Recalling that day, Lomax said, "Among the songs he sang for me was 'Home on the Range.' It was the first time I had heard the melody." He recorded the song with his equipment and a few weeks later asked Henry Leberman, a blind teacher of music at the state school for the blind in Austin, to set the musical notes on paper. Leberman used earphones and played the record over and over until he felt sure that he had captured the music as the Negro saloonkeeper had sung it.

About two years later, in late 1910, Lomax wrote a book that was published under the title *Cowboy Songs and Other Frontier Ballads*. It was a 326-page collection of 112 songs that he had gathered on his travels. Included in the book—the first edition of which is a collector's item— were the words and music to "Home on the Range." Looking back in time the publication of the song in Lomax's book may have saved it from oblivion.

When Lomax's book was published, the singing of cowboy songs was becoming popular, even in the East. But it was not until 1933 that "Home on the Range" became the vogue. President Franklin Roosevelt is credited with making the song popular. According to one version of the story, a group of newspaper reporters sang "Home on the Range" on Roosevelt's doorstep in New York City the night he was first elected president. When Roosevelt heard them he asked to hear the melody again. Then he supposedly said, "That's my favorite song."

When the news spread that the President liked the song, every singer began including "Home on the Range" in his or her program. By early 1934 nearly every radio station in the country was playing the song on the air. Record companies, music publishers—everyone connected with the music business—were taking advantage of "Home on the Range" since there were no royalties to pay. The song was not copyrighted. The author was unknown.

It was then that an Arizona couple—William and Mary Goodwin of Tempe—dropped a bombshell. In June, 1934, they brought suit in the United States District Court in New York City against several music publishers, the radio networks, motion picture producers and many singers who had sung the song in public.

The Goodwins asked for a half million dollars in damages alleging that they had written the words and music to the song under the title "An Arizona Home." The copyright, they said, had been registered on February 27, 1905. The records showed it was registered.

Quickly music publishers pulled "Home on the Range" sheet music off music store shelves. Recording companies stopped selling records of the song and radio stations were warned not to play the tune on the air. Most stopped doing so.

As these things were happening, the Music Publishers Protective

Association, then headed by John G. Payne, took over the defense of the suit. Samuel Moanfeldt, the association's attorney, was called in and told to find out if the Goodwins had, in fact, written the song, or had someone else.

Moanfeldt's investigation was to last three months.

Attorney Moanfeldt soon discovered that all popular versions of the song could be traced to John Lomax and his 1910 book. Moanfeldt contacted Lomax, who told how he found "Home on the Range" in Texas. From this Moanfeldt was certain the song was known long before the Goodwins claimed they wrote it, but he needed evidence—proof—to back this up.

News of the lawsuit brought a letter from a Chicago woman who told how she remembered singing the song in Missouri in 1880. Moanfeldt went to Missouri and found other people who had sung the song. They confirmed that they knew the melody before 1890.

It was then that Moanfeldt began to suspect that the song had been written in the West, perhaps in cowboy country. He headed west to Dodge City, Kansas. Even in the 1930s the town was still considered a cowboy capital. Between 1875 and the early 1890s, Dodge City was the rendezvous for cowboys from Texas who brought cattle up the trail, and those men who came south from Wyoming and Montana to buy animals and sometimes sell. It was in Dodge City that Moanfeldt hoped to find some old-timers who remembered the cowboy songs of the late nineteenth century.

He found them.

Many persons at Dodge City remembered "Home on the Range." Some signed statements that the song was well known to them before 1890. Still others remembered hearing it before 1880.

With the statements in hand Moanfeldt was certain he had enough evidence to successfully defend the case in court. But he wanted to establish the author or authors of "Home on the Range." It was then that Moanfeldt asked for the help of a newspaper in Dodge City. The newspaper not only printed a local story on page one, but the story was picked up by the Associated Press news service. Within days it appeared in newspapers from California to Maine.

"A great deal of information started to come to me about this song," wrote Moanfeldt. One letter, from Miss Florence Pulver of Osborne, Kansas, said the song had been written by a Dr. Higley. Moanfeldt went to Osborne and talked with Florence Pulver. She was an invalid and liked to listen to the radio. She enjoyed hearing old songs but told Moanfeldt she missed hearing "Home on the Range."

Miss Pulver told Moanfeldt her mother had sung the song to her as a child; that her mother had lived in Gaylord, Kansas, at the same time as Dr. Higley.

Moanfeldt lost no time in going to Gaylord, not far north of Osborne in Smith County. There Moanfeldt found other persons who confirmed Miss Pulver's story. Moanfeldt knew he was getting warm.

At Smith Center, the county seat, Moanfeldt learned more, including the fact that the original words to "Home on the Range" were first published in December of 1873 in the *Smith County Pioneer,* a newspaper, under the title "My Western Home." The words, as printed in 1873, were:

> Oh, give me a home where the buffalo roam,
>   Where the deer and the antelope play,
> Where never is heard a discouraging word
>   And the sky is not clouded all day.
>
> CHORUS
> A home, a home, where the deer and the antelope play,
>   Where never is heard a discouraging word
> And the sky is not clouded all day.
>
> Oh, give me the gale of the Solomon vale
>   Where life streams with buoyancy flow,
> On the banks of the Beaver, where seldom if ever
>   Any poisonous herbage doth grow.
>
> Oh, give me the land where the bright diamond sand
>   Throws light from the glittering stream,
> Where glideth along the graceful white swan,
>   Like a maid in her heavenly dream.
>
> I love the wild flowers in this bright land of ours,
>   I love, too, the curlew's wild scream,
> The bluffs of white rocks and the antelope flocks
>   That graze on our hillsides so green.
>
> How often at night, when the heavens are bright
>   By the light of the glittering stars,
> Have I stood there amazed and asked as I gazed,
>   If their beauty exceeds this of ours.
>
> The air is so pure, the breezes so light,
>   The zephyrs so balmy at night,
> I would not exchange my home here to range
>   Forever in azure so bright.

Moanfeldt learned that Dr. Brewster Higley had probably written

Dr. Brewster Higley, who wrote the words to "Home on the Range." *Courtesy Kansas State Historical Society*

Dan Kelley, the man who wrote the music to "Home on the Range." *Courtesy Kansas State Historical Society*

the words in his one-room dugout home along Beaver Creek about fourteen miles northwest of Smith Center. Higley who was born in Ohio, had moved to Smith County in 1871. But in 1886, after finding the winter weather in Kansas too severe for his failing health, Higley had moved to Arkansas and later to Shawnee, Oklahoma, where he died at the age of eighty-six in 1909. He is buried there.

Moanfeldt soon learned that the music to "Home on the Range" had been written by Daniel E. Kelley, a native of Rhode Island, who came to Kansas in 1872 at the age of twenty-nine years. Kelley was a carpenter by trade. In his spare time he liked to hunt wild game and play in a dance orchestra. And like Dr. Higley, Kelley had left Kansas. In 1889 he moved to Waterloo, Iowa, and it was there he died at the age of sixty-two in 1905. Kelley was thirty years old and Dr. Higley about sixty when "Home on the Range" was written.

At Smith Center Moanfeldt talked with A. L. Headley, editor of the *Smith County Pioneer*. Headley showed Moanfeldt the old issues of the newspaper including an article by W. H. Nelson, an earlier editor of the newspaper. The article, written in 1914, reads:

"I remember well when this song, 'Oh, give me a home where the buffalo roam,' first came out, and I was well and intimately acquainted with the author of it. It was written by Dr. Brewster Higley, who was an early settler in Smith County, having homesteaded in section No. 17, in Pleasant Township, about fourteen miles northwest of Smith Center, on the land now owned by Mrs. L. C. Ahlhorn.

"The poem was published in the *Smith County Pioneer* in the fall of 1873, and soon attained popularity among the young people of that time. A tune was arranged for it and it was sung at every gathering in those early days. Its cheering words helped to dispel the gloom of the grasshopper days. I well remember hearing it many times," wrote Nelson.

The article added that Dr. Higley had been "an eccentric character, rough in appearance, but with a heart that was filled with poetry and compassion for suffering humanity."

Putting down the old newspaper, Headley told Moanfeldt, "Now I'm going to take you to the man who was the first to sing 'Home on the Range' in public." Headley did. He took Moanfeldt to the home of Clarence "Cal" Harlan, then eighty-six years old and almost blind. Harlan told the New York lawyer how he once sang with the Harlan Bros. Orchestra, the same group Dan Kelley played with. Harlan told how he sang "Home on the Range" the first time it was performed in public. Moanfeldt learned that Kelley was Harlan's brother-in-law.

As Moanfeldt later wrote, " 'Cal' Harlan brought out his guitar and played and sang this song from memory, using the tune as he knew it in 1874. . . . I procured a recording machine and made phonograph records of this rendition of the song."

Moanfeldt found other old-timers around Smith Center who remembered the song and he had them sign statements about the song's author. Most were indignant over the Arizona couple's claim to authorship.

As he was preparing to return to New York City, Moanfeldt was asked if he had enough evidence to win the case.

"Enough," he asserted jokingly, "why I have everything but the quill the song was written with."

Moanfeldt and the Music Publishers Protective Association did win the case, but it was twelve years before Kansans—using the evidence uncovered by Moanfeldt—decided it would be a good thing to adopt "Home on the Range" as their official state song. The Kansas legislature made it official in 1947. Not all Kansans approved, however. The more commercially minded contended that the song "failed to sell the state and its products." And two years later, in 1949, attempts were made to jazz up "Home on the Range" and to give it snappier words. A token effort was made to remove it as the official state song, but Kansans—those who liked the original version—besieged state lawmakers, newspapers and radio stations with letters and calls of protest demanding that the ballad be left alone. It was and has not been changed.

But if it had not been for John Lomax, the Texas college professor, and Samuel Moanfeldt, the New York City attorney, the official state song of Kansas might not be "Home on the Range" today.

The First White Woman
to Climb Pike's Peak

Julia Archibald Holmes was the young and, some said, pretty wife of James Henry Holmes of Lawrence, Kansas. He was a free-stater who in October of 1856 narrowly escaped with his life when two hundred and fifty Missourians swooped down on the free-state stronghold of Os-awatomie, Kansas, where Holmes happened to be. In retaliation, James Holmes joined several free-state raids into Missouri and in the process "borrowed" a few horses belonging to those "Southern Gentlemen" in the neighboring state.

In November, 1856, on order from Kansas Territorial Governor John Geary, Holmes was arrested by a U.S. marshal. U.S. Army soldiers were given the task of escorting Holmes to Missouri to stand trial for horse stealing, but Holmes escaped and fled to Emporia, then only a tiny village on the edge of the frontier in Kansas Territory.

Early in 1857 the free-state legislature met in Lawrence. Most minds, however, were not on the business at hand. Rumors were whispered that a Delaware Indian named Fall Leaf, a burly fellow who lived on the reservation north of Lawrence, had brought some fine specimens of gold from the Rocky Mountains. Almost overnight the gold fever replaced politics.

One Lawrence man, John Easter, a butcher by trade, organized a party to go west to the Rockies, then part of Kansas Territory, to strike it rich. When the party left Lawrence on May 23, 1857, young Julia Holmes hurried to Emporia to meet her husband. Telling him about the gold party, he decided that they should join in. A few days later Julia

A photograph of Julia Holmes. Where and when it was taken is unknown. The author believes Julia Holmes wrapped herself in a sheet for this photograph to symbolize the feelings of many American women during the last half of the nineteenth century. The sheet is a far cry from the tight pants Julia Holmes wore when she became the first woman to climb Pike's Peak in 1858. *Courtesy Kansas State Historical Society*

and James met the Lawrence party at a point not too far west of where Burlingame, Kansas, stands today.

The forty-seven persons in the party knew nothing of the land to the west nor what route they should follow once they left Council Grove. They pushed ahead, however, and by early July sighted Pike's Peak and the towering Rockies. On July 6, 1857, they camped near what is today Colorado Springs at the entrance to the Garden of the Gods. Almost immediately a few men set out in search of gold, but three others, fascinated by the mountains, decided to climb Pike's Peak. When they returned to camp a few days later their stories stirred Julia Holmes so much that she coaxed her husband into trying the climb.

On August 1, Julia and James set out to duplicate the feat. They planned to be gone one week. Julia carried a seventeen-pound pack. James's pack weighed thirty-five pounds. Between them they carried six quilts, a tinplate, a pail, a change of clothing, nineteen pounds of hardtack, one pound of sugar, one pound of hog meat, three-fourths pound of coffee and a book. The book contained essays by Emerson.

For three days Julia and James slowly pushed up the steep and sometimes gravelly slopes. They pushed on through canyons and among the trees until they reached the timberline. Just above it they found a cave and made camp. They called their camp "Sun Dale," and there they rested. Julia wrote a few letters while James read Emerson. Then, after a light supper, they went to sleep.

At the first light of dawn they broke camp and moved toward the summit. As Julia later wrote, she and James were fascinated by the "tiny blue flowers most bewitchingly beautiful." She called them "children of the sky and snow." Shortly after noon they reached the summit, and Julia, dressed in black tight pants, a hickory shirt and a pair of moccasins, became the first white woman to climb Pike's Peak.

From the summit James and Julia saw the breathtaking panorama before them. To the east lay the flat plains. Perhaps one hundred or more miles away they melted into the blue horizon, and to the west she saw South Park. Farther on was the Continental Divide where peaks seemed to touch the round white puffs of clouds on a field of blue. The view was magnificent.

Sitting on the summit, forgetting the cold, Julia read Emerson aloud to James. One poem was titled "Friendship." When she finished, she wrote a letter to a friend observing, "Just being up here, fills the mind with infinitude, and sends the soul to God." After a little while snow flurries began falling. Hurriedly, not wishing to get caught in a snowstorm, they began the long climb down, back to their camp near the Garden of the Gods, far below.

A few days later, after no one found gold, the Lawrence party broke camp. A few members decided to go north to Cherry Creek—the present site of Denver—to spend the winter and to continue their search for gold. Some of them would later be successful. But Julia and James Holmes and a few others headed south to winter at Taos in what today is New Mexico.

When spring came the Holmes did not return north to search for gold. Instead, they remained in New Mexico where James became territorial secretary and Julia became the New Mexico correspondent for Horace Greeley's *New York Tribune*. The bonds that had held the young couple together as they had climbed Pike's Peak did not last. They soon separated. James remained in New Mexico for many years, but Julia traveled east where she plunged into the suffrage movement and soon became secretary of the National American Woman Suffrage Association in Washington, D.C. Later, still climbing to new heights, Julia Archibald Holmes, the first white woman to climb Pike's Peak, became the first woman member of the U.S. Bureau of Education.

The Legend of Smoky Hill Thompson

They called him "Smoky Hill" Thompson. And those who knew him said he could shoot straighter, hunt more game and ride a horse faster and longer than any other man on the Great Plains. But then he was made of the same stuff that legends are made of.

His real name was P. M. Thompson. What his initials stood for is not known. The P may have been for Phillip. And where he came from, when he was born and what he looked like have been lost in time. Thompson did not care for publicity. He did not like to talk about himself, even to his friends. His background seems to have been a closed book. Whether he was a fugitive from the law or trying to forget a broken marriage is a matter of conjecture. It appears he did not think of himself as being any different from other men on the plains during the nineteenth century. If he had, perhaps today the name "Smoky Hill" Thompson would rank with those of "Buffalo Bill" Cody or Kit Carson or even "Wild Bill" Hickok.

If if had not been for Bill Ziegler, a onetime partner of Thompson's, the name "Smoky Hill" Thompson might not be known today. Ziegler, however, left some meager reminiscences and in them the legend of "Smoky Hill" Thompson takes shape.

Thompson first arrived in Kansas Territory about 1856, two years after the territory was created. He came from somewhere back East. Instead of settling in the thinly populated areas of eastern Kansas Territory along the Missouri border, Thompson continued west past the last outposts of civilization to the unsettled country of the Smoky Hill

River—where he picked up his nickname—and the Arkansas River. It was near the Great Bend of the Arkansas River that Thompson met Bill Ziegler.

Both men had come west to escape civilization and to start life anew. The two men, having similar tastes, hit it off from the start and soon became hunting partners. During the years that followed Thompson and Ziegler made the area that is today western Kansas and eastern Colorado their home. They slept under the stars and hunted and trapped along the Arkansas and Smoky Hill rivers. Only during the cold winter months did they seek shelter in a dugout or lean-to which they would build near water and wood.

For the most part the two men lived off the land. They earned money for the few supplies needed by selling wolf pelts. In those days wolves were plentiful in Kansas where the critters followed the buffalo herds killing the weak and ailing shaggies, thereby keeping the buffalo a vigorous species.

Thompson and Ziegler sold the pelts to a hide man at Leavenworth. But they did not have to deliver the pelts in person. When they had enough pelts for a shipment, they would take them to any one of several points along the Santa Fe Trail. There they would make camp and wait until a freighter's wagon train bound for Leavenworth would come along. If there was enough room on the wagons, the freighter would give them a receipt for their pelts and take them to Leavenworth, then the nearest market. There the hide man paid the freighter for his trouble and credited the rest of the money to the trapper's account.

About once a year Thompson and Ziegler would go east to Leavenworth to collect their money and buy supplies. It was then they would pick up a large batch of poison—strychnine—which they had ordered from a Philadelphia manufacturer the year before. They used the strychnine to kill wolves.

The two plainsmen would stay in Leavenworth only long enough to collect their money, pick up supplies and spend a night or two in Leavenworth's numerous saloons. They then would head west again, back to the open plains.

For nearly four years "Smoky Hill" Thompson and Bill Ziegler trapped along the Smoky Hill and the Arkansas. Of those years, Ziegler recalled the time when Thompson, trapping alone, was surrounded by an Indian scouting party. Ziegler said Thompson killed six Indians before escaping unharmed.

Another time Thompson and Ziegler were trapping along a small stream when suddenly Thompson, who was leading on the trail, came face to face with a huge grizzly bear. The bear was as surprised as the plainsmen. Ziegler said the old grizzly charged Thompson who fired his rifle at point-blank range. The bear fell to the ground.

Thinking the grizzly was done for, Thompson walked up to inspect his kill. But the bear, although dying, was not dead. The animal got to its feet and lunged forward toward Thompson. "Smoky Hill" side-stepped the beast and jumped on the bear's back. Thompson began hitting the grizzly over the head with his rifle until the bullet inside the bear finished its job. That night, in camp beside the stream, Thompson and Ziegler feasted on bear steak until they could eat no more.

The sight of grizzlies on the plains was not uncommon during the 1850s. Like wolves, grizzlies often came down from the mountains to follow the buffalo herds. But as the buffalo began to vanish, the grizzlies returned to the rugged Rocky Mountains.

About 1860 Thompson and Ziegler began to tire of trapping. Anyway, more and more people were crossing the territory en route to the gold fields along the western edge of Kansas Territory—now Colorado. Hunting and trapping was not the best.

One day Thompson told Ziegler that he was going to become a buffalo farmer.

"Ziegler, why don't you join me," said Thompson.

Ziegler said he told Thompson he would.

In what is today southern Ellsworth County, Kansas, not many miles south of present Ellsworth, Kansas, Thompson and Ziegler built a dugout. There they commenced to "buffalo farm."

First they constructed a large corral out of lumber cut from trees found nearby. Then Thompson went out and caught a number of buffalo calves.

Finding buffalo calves in 1860 was not difficult on the central plains. Vast herds of buffalo still roamed the plains. Tanners had not yet discovered that buffalo hides could be a source of fairly good leather.

Catching buffalo calves was rather easy. First Thompson located a herd. He would give chase on horseback. Soon the calves would drop behind their mothers. Thompson would rope a calf and lead it back to the corral where they let the animal suck a milk cow. Catching calves took time but it was easy.

Within a matter of weeks the two men had a quite respectable looking herd of buffalo calves. There were more than a dozen of the little shaggies in their corral. It was a good start toward a buffalo herd.

As Thompson told Ziegler, "We can sell buffalo meat to all them wagon trains headin' west, and them soldiers at the forts along the Santa Fe Trail, they'll buy the meat too."

But their dreams of buffalo farming were shattered a few months later. One morning a large herd of wild buffalo stampeded across their "buffalo farm" smashing through the corral and scattering the herd of buffalo calves in all directions. That day Thompson and Ziegler gave up trying to raise buffalo and decided to try their hand at "ranching."

Now in 1860 the word "ranch" did not have the same meaning as today. The word "ranch" then meant a combination general store, bar, watering hole, camp ground and sometimes hotel. And sometimes it meant even more including ladies of the night who would entertain soldiers, hunters and others passing through the country. But Thompson and Ziegler had no plans to include painted ladies in their ranch business.

Perhaps two or three miles from their buffalo farm dugout, closer to the Santa Fe Trail, Thompson and Ziegler cleared a site for their "ranch" beside a creek. The stream is still known today as Thompson Creek. They hauled cottonwood logs from the Smoky Hill River some distance away and set about the task of building a respectable "ranch."

One morning, as their "ranch" was nearly finished, a wagon train from the east came along. One of the drivers or bullwhackers, suffering from an injured hand, talked Bill Ziegler into taking his place with the train. The bullwhacker promised to wait at the "ranch" until Ziegler returned with the wagon train several weeks later. Meantime, he said, he would help Thompson, as best he could, to finish the "ranch."

The wagon train had been gone from the ranch only a few hours when it was attacked by Indians, but not before the wagons could be pulled into a circle for defense. One man was sent for help. He rode a fast horse through a hail of arrows and headed as fast as his horse would carry him back to the ranch.

As he pulled his horse up at the nearly completed ranch building, he fell to the ground. The rider had not escaped all the arrows. One was sticking in his back. He died a short time later in "Smoky Hill" Thompson's arms, but not before telling about the Indian raid.

Thompson wasted no time in saddling his horse. Leaving the bullwhacker to bury the dead man, Thompson raced to Fort Larned for help. Soon soldiers rescued the wagon train. But in the meantime a small party of Indians had followed the wounded man's trail to the Thompson-Ziegler ranch.

Fortunately, the bullwhacker with the injured hand was away from the ranch burying the dead man when the Indians arrived. He took cover and from some distance watched as the Indians first looted the ranch building taking everything they could carry. The Indians then put the torch to the nearly completed ranch building. The bullwhacker was helpless. He could only watch the flames engulf the building.

When Thompson and Ziegler returned to their ranch a day or two later—Ziegler having quit the wagon train—there was nothing left but ashes. The wagon train driver, who had set up camp nearby, told them of the Indian raid.

Thompson and Ziegler looked at their ranch and shook their heads. And before the sun went down on the western horizon, both men agreed to give up the idea of running a "ranch." A few days later they shook hands and went their separate ways: Thompson back to hunting and Ziegler to nearby Rice County.

Just where Thompson went is unknown, but Ziegler spent a few years in Rice County. About 1870 he became a buffalo hunter after hides became valuable as a source of leather. Three years later, while visiting Dodge City for supplies, Ziegler saw "Smoky Hill" Thompson. He too was buying supplies, and like Ziegler, Thompson was hunting buffalo for a living. They had a good visit that day in 1873. But it was the last time Ziegler saw "Smoky Hill" Thompson.

The story of "Smoky Hill" Thompson, however, does not end here. An extensive search for information uncovered the fact that Thompson was chosen by W. D. Lee, Charles Rath and a man named Reynolds to lay out a trail from Dodge City south to the area of the Double Mountains in northwest Texas.

Lee, Rath and Reynolds—partners in business—wanted Thompson to pick a place where there was plenty of buffalo for the end of the trail. This was important because their company sold supplies, guns and ammunition to buffalo hunters. It seems likely that Thompson was chosen because he knew the area. If so, "Smoky Hill" probably spent much time in the region after leaving Ziegler and their burned-out ranch.

Thompson picked a site late in 1876. It covered two to three hundred acres. The site was located in what is today Stonewall County, Texas, one mile north of the Fisher County line and about ten miles northwest of modern Hamlin, Texas, about one hundred and fifty miles west of present Fort Worth, Texas.

Rock from a nearby outcropping was hauled to the spot and used as a foundation for the company's store. Adobe blocks were then placed on the rock foundation. The sides were constructed and the roof was stayed with cedar poles and covered with lumber, then sod. Across from the entrance to the store George Aiken built a combination saloon and restaurant. Nearby Thompson and others constructed temporary shelters of buffalo hides stretched around cedar poles. The new community became known by at least three names—Reynolds, Camp Reynolds and Rath City.

It was there another incident in Thompson's life is reported. A little distance from the new settlement was a creek that provided water for men and stock. "Smoky Hill" Thompson, realizing the value of water, dug a cistern in front of Aiken's saloon and filled it with water hauled from the creek in barrels. Thompson reportedly made a good profit selling buckets of water from his cistern.

By the spring of 1880 most of the buffalo on the southern plains were gone. So was the need for the trading outpost to serve the hunters. W. S. Glenn, a Texas buffalo hunter who knew Thompson, recalled that "Smoky Hill" stayed around Camp Reynolds until the buffalo were gone. Glenn's recollections then contain the last reference to Thompson this writer has found.

Glenn wrote that he had heard that Thompson had "gone to Dallas and was running a restaurant" early in the 1880s. Whether "Smoky Hill" Thompson actually did is unknown. But many men who came west to the Great Plains to, as some said, "escape civilization" eventually returned to the civilized life because they could not escape it. "Smoky Hill" Thompson may not have been an exception.

Battle at Pawnee Rock

History books, old records and narratives of pioneers are filled with numerous stories of adventure connected with Pawnee Rock, a massive rock formation covering about four acres, located southwest of Great Bend, Kansas, on the old Santa Fe Trail. About a mile south of the formation is the modern town of Pawnee Rock. None of these tales, however, hold a candle to one related by Kit Carson not many years before his death in 1869. It's a story, according to Carson, that he heard from an old trapper named Gibson.

The year was 1836. Kansas was not yet a territory. It was simply part of what some persons then called the "Great American Desert." Jim Gibson and his partner—a young man known only as Bill—had had a successful season trapping in the Powder River country up north in what today is Wyoming. They had packed their pelts and supplies on three mules weeks before, followed the eastern slopes of the Rocky Mountains south and then headed east, walking all the way behind their mules.

Gibson and his partner reached Pawnee Rock and were picketing their mules on the west side when a band of about sixty Kiowa Indians attacked them. The two trappers had plenty of powder, a pouchful of bullets each and a couple of jackrabbits for food.

The Kiowas, atop their ponies, circled Pawnee Rock and gradually tightened their circle. Their arrows fell like a hailstorm around the trappers but missed their mark. And each time the Indians closed their circle, the trappers made each of their bullets count. When dead or

• 251

Kit Carson about 1865, the year he
told the story of the Battle of Pawnee
Rock to Henry Inman while they
camped in the Raton Range. Carson
died about two years later. *Courtesy
Kansas State Historical Society*

wounded Indians fell from their ponies, the rest of the Indians would
pull back.

By late afternoon a few Indians on foot tried to move close to
Pawnee Rock to remove the bodies of their dead brothers. The trappers
unleashed volley after volley forcing the Indians to retreat.

At dusk most of the Indians withdrew to a makeshift camp on a
nearby creek. Only a few mounted patrols circled Pawnee Rock to make
certain the two trappers would not escape.

When darkness came, Jim Gibson slipped down through the rocks
to the prairie below where the tall grass hid his movements from the
Indian patrols. He located some dried buffalo chips to use as fuel for a
fire. Returning to the protection of the rocks that then covered the top
of Pawnee Rock, the two men built a small fire and cooked a jackrabbit.

After the meal the two trappers quietly made their way to where
they had picketed their mules and moved the animals to another spot
closer to the top where grass was more plentiful. The mules, like the
trappers, had had no water for several hours. The nearest water was in
the creek where the Indians made camp. Both men knew it would mean
certain death if they tried to reach the creek. They could only hope their
mules would survive.

There was plenty of grass for the animals, but it was very dry. This
fact concerned Gibson who knew well that under such conditions the
Indians might try to fire the prairie to smoke or burn them out. The
night, however, passed uneventfully as the two trappers took turns
standing watch.

At dawn, as the first rays of light appeared in the eastern horizon,
Jim and Bill saw the Indians leave their camp and come charging
toward Pawnee Rock, yelling loudly. The Indians began circling the

rock, but they kept their distance just outside the range of the trappers' rifles.

A light breeze out of the northwest soon gave way to strong winds. It was as though nature was conspiring with the Indians against the trappers. Gibson and his partner watched as a group of Indians rode off to the northwest of Pawnee Rock. There was no question in the trappers' minds—the Indians were preparing to fire the prairie.

Gibson crawled to the spot where their mules were picketed. He quickly led the animals around the north side of Pawnee Rock to the area on the east side where the rock wall was the highest. There he tied the mules securely. He hoped the flames and smoke would pass over the mules once the wind fanned the fire toward the southeast and Pawnee Rock.

Just as Gibson tore away the nearby grass and undergrowth near the animals, Bill yelled that the Indians had fired the prairie. Gibson crawled back to the top of Pawnee Rock and with his partner watched what was for a moment a scene that was indescribably grand.

To the northwest huge clouds of smoke climbed into the crystal blue sunlit sky. As the wind pushed the fire along in the tall grass toward the Rock, the sun tinted the rolling clouds of smoke a bright crimson color.

But the trappers didn't have time to watch the spectacular scene. The fire was picking up speed. Within seconds the two men ran for shelter under a large overhanging rock on the east side. They crouched against the rock wall under the overhang and within a minute were enveloped in darkness as smoke covered the area. And a moment later a sheet of flame passed within a few yards of where the two men huddled.

Then, as if by magic, clear blue sky suddenly appeared above them. With their watery and smoke-filled eyes, the two trappers watched as the prairie fire pushed southeast at what seemed like an ever-increasing speed. And suddenly they saw two Indians on horseback engulfed by the flames. The Indians, while attempting to reach the trappers' mules, had apparently misjudged the swiftness of the fire.

It was a horrible sight.

As Gibson would later recall, the path of the fire was marked with the crisped and blackened carcasses of coyotes, turkeys, grouse, wolves and many small birds.

The trappers watched as the widening line of fire reached the Arkansas River, about two miles to the southeast. Even the river did not stop its forward advance. The flames jumped the stream. Gibson figured that the fire traveled about eight miles in fifteen minutes.

But the two men did not stop to talk about the fire. While Bill watched for Indians, Jim crawled to where the mules had been picketed. They had been singed but not seriously hurt. Jim quickly returned to Bill in time to see the Indians approaching the Rock, apparently intending to make certain the trappers were dead. The two men, to the surprise of the Indians, fired a volley of shots and the Indians retreated.

For two or three hours the two trappers could see the Indians gathered on the prairie talking. It was late morning when they began to move. The Indians tied their horses together, covered the animals with branches of trees cut from the nearby creek, packed their lodgeskins atop the branches and began driving the makeshift fortification toward Pawnee Rock. The Indians, walking behind their ponies, had good protection.

Quickly the two trappers decided there was only one course of action: to kill the Indians' ponies if they were to stop the moving wall. Moments later, as the row of Indian ponies came within rifle range, the two trappers opened fire. A few ponies dropped and the Indians were thrown into confusion.

Some of the Indians kept moving toward Pawnee Rock without the protection of their ponies, Jim and Bill made every shot count. They succeeded in forcing the Indians to retreat, but when the two men stopped firing, they realized their ammunition was almost gone.

As the trappers discussed their next move, they saw a lone Indian carrying a piece of white blanket walking boldly toward Pawnee Rock. He was giving the sign of peace as he came within the range of the trappers' rifles. He wanted to talk.

From their high perch the trappers motioned for him to come ahead. He did. As he stood below the trappers, he explained that the Indians were part of White Buffalo's band of Kiowas, that their war chief was O-ton-son-e-var—meaning "herd of buffalo"—and that the war chief had praised the two trappers as being very brave. The Indian said the chief wanted the trappers to come to their camp where they would be treated kindly and adopted as members of the tribe. He added that the band of Indians were on their way to Sioux country in the north to steal Sioux ponies.

The two trappers looked at each other. They knew their answer without talking. Gibson yelled to the Indian below that they would not accept the invitation, that they were on their way to Missouri and would get there or die trying. Gibson told the Indian that the white man's God looked with favor on the trappers. If the Indians wanted to continue to fight, so be it.

The Indian turned and headed back toward his camp. Before he reached it other Indians came out to meet him. They talked for a few

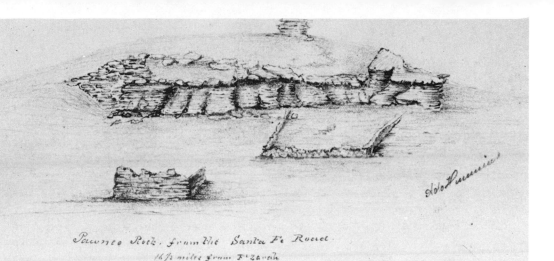

Pawnee Rock in Barton, Kansas, a century ago was a massive rock formation covering about four acres located on the Santa Fe Trail. Man and nature have since torn away at the formation until it is no longer as high or massive as it once was. This drawing by Ado Hunius was made in April 1867. It is perhaps the earliest known illustration of Pawnee Rock. *Courtesy Kansas State Historical Society*

moments and then hurried into camp. Soon the Indians, atop their ponies, were again charging toward Pawnee Rock.

Each trapper had three or four loads for their rifles. They made each shot count. Then their ammunition was gone. The trappers, anticipating that moment, had stacked loose stones in piles nearby. They were about to pick up some of the stones to throw them at the Indians when the brave with the piece of white blanket appeared again and asked to talk.

Again the trappers motioned for him to approach. They had no choice but to listen. They were well aware that they had to come to terms with the Indians if they wanted to survive.

The Indian said the trappers were indeed brave men and that the Indian warriors would not kill them even though the prairie grass was red with the blood of other Indians. He then offered to give the trappers a chance for their lives and an opportunity to prove that the Great Spirit of the white man is powerful and could save them.

There, said the Indian, pointing toward a cottonwood tree perhaps two miles away on the bank of the Arkansas River, you must run the knife gauntlet from that large tree two hundred steps of the chief out toward the open prairie. If the one who runs escapes, both are free. O-ton-son-e-var has said it, and the words of the Kiowa are true.

Gibson asked the Indian when the race must take place. The Indian replied that it would begin when the sun begins to shine on the western side of Pawnee Rock.

The trappers told the Indian to tell O-ton-son-e-var that they accepted the challenge and would be ready. The Indian nodded, turned and headed back to the Kiowa camp.

Gibson told his partner that he would run the race, but Bill said he would. He told Gibson how he had traveled the same race once after being captured by the Apaches. He said their knives never struck him and he could do it again.

Almost before the two men realized it, the sun had moved across the cloudless sky and was shining down on the western edge of Pawnee Rock. The trappers realized it was time to go. They left the protection of the rocks and made their way to the prairie below and headed toward the cottonwood tree some distance away.

There, ahead of them, they could make out the Indians, perhaps thirty of the band that had numbered sixty the day before when the battle began.

Not a word was said as the two trappers bravely walked past O-ton-son-e-var and the other Indians. The trappers stopped at the cotton-wood tree. As they watched, O-ton-son-e-var paced off the two hundred steps, arranged his warriors on either side and then ordered the warriors to strip to the waist. They did, with each man seizing his long scalping knife.

Each Indian braced himself and then raised his knife high over his head, so as to strike a blow as the runner tried to move the length of the line.

When all was in readiness, Gibson stepped forward to run the race. But O-ton-son-e-var pointed to Bill. The younger of the two trappers was to run the race. Bill was to get his wish.

Bill stripped to his drawers and nodded when he was ready. Then, when the chief gave the signal, Bill sprang forward like an antelope. The Indians yelled and crowded one another and brought their knives down with tremendous force, but Bill's speed helped him. Although he had to strike some of the warriors, pushing them out of his way, he managed to evade their cold steel knives. And Bill passed almost twenty feet beyond the mark where the Chief stood. Bill was unhurt.

As he caught his breath, some of the warriors started toward Bill, but O-ton-son-e-var motioned for them to stay away. He kept his word and told the two happy trappers they were free to leave. Slowly the two men walked back to Pawnee Rock where they loaded their mules and in the heat of the midafternoon sun headed east.

Gibson and his partner camped that night on the north bank of the Arkansas River, a few miles east of Pawnee Rock. As they sat in front of a small fire of buffalo chips cooking a jackrabbit, they could hear the faint sound of the Kiowas chanting their death song for the warriors who had died in the battle at Pawnee Rock.

How Kansans Came to Be Called Jayhawkers

The small group of men moved cautiously as they got off their horses and mules some distance from the small cabin. They fanned out in a line. On a signal from one of the men, they moved toward the cabin that was situated close to the banks of the Osage River. It was midday. The smoke curling from the stone chimney was a sure sign that someone was home.

The men, perhaps a dozen or more, were free-staters under the command of Dr. Charles Ransford Jennison, a surgeon, and Rev. John E. "Plum" Stewart. Inside the cabin was a man named Van Zumwalt, a proslavery settler.

Suddenly, as the men neared the cabin, the door opened slightly and the muzzle of a long rifle appeared. Then a shot rang out. One of the free-staters fired at the door. As the ball tore into the cabin, there was a yell. Moments later a man emerged from the cabin holding one of his arms. It was bloody.

The wounded man was Zumwalt. Some of the free-staters hurried to his side while others rushed to check the inside of the cabin. There was no one else inside.

Van Zumwalt's wound was serious. Moving him inside his cabin, Doc Jennison went to work and washed and dressed the wound, giving Zumwalt and the free-staters a clinical lecture as he went along. Jennison explained everything and told them how to proceed if they ever had to treat such a wound.

Then, after making certain Zumwalt understood how to change the dressing, Doc Jennison warned him that proslavery settlers in Kansas Territory would find it healthier living elsewhere. At that Jennison and the others rode away to the north toward the boundary of Miami and Linn counties.

That was on February 28, 1858.

For more than three years Kansas Territory had been the scene of on-again and off-again violence between proslavery forces and those wanting Kansas to be free of slavery. The Kansas-Nebraska Act had established Kansas Territory in 1854, and it called for "popular sovereignty." It was up to the residents of the new territory to decide for themselves whether or not slavery would be permitted. As a result, supporters on both sides of the question flocked to the territory.

At first, both factions used only strong words, but violence soon followed. Some Missourians, in hopes of forcing free-state settlers to leave the territory, began to cross into Kansas to steal horses, set fires and to loot. They soon became known as "border ruffians."

It was then that free-state settlers banded together for mutual protection and defense, and some of them began their own excursions into Jackson, Cass, Bates and Vernon counties in Missouri in retaliation.

One of the free-state leaders was Doc Jennison, twenty-four years old, born in Jefferson County, New York, in 1834. When he was twelve years old, he moved with his parents to Wisconsin. After completing his medical schooling and taking a bride, Jennison moved to Kansas in 1857. He first settled at Osawatomie but later moved to Mound City.

Just how many raids into Missouri were made by Jennison and his men is unknown, but years later it was said that "the pedigree of most Kansas horses should have been recorded as 'out of Missouri by Jennison.'"

Jennison and his men probably were returning from a raid into Missouri when they visited Zumwalt that cold February day in 1858. After leaving the wounded man's cabin, Doc Jennison and the other free-staters rode north several miles. As darkness came they camped in a wooded area for the night.

Early the next morning a guard woke the sleeping men. Soon they were gathered around a large fire rubbing their hands together for warmth and waiting for their morning coffee. After breakfast, the men began to break camp in preparation for their return to Osawatomie. It was then that one of the party reported that Pat Devlin was approaching the camp.

Devlin, a rawboned redheaded young Irishman, had been with the free-staters the day before, but at some point he had ridden off on his mule. Doc Jennison, curious as to where Devlin had gone, walked out to meet him. Jennison was amazed at what he saw. Pat's mule was loaded down with all sorts of plunder. In front of Devlin, hanging from the horn of the saddle, was a big turkey, three or four chickens and a string of red peppers. Behind him was a fifty-pound shoat, a sheepskin, a pair of boots and a bag of potatoes.

"Hello, Pat, where have you been?" asked Doc Jennison.

"I've been over to Eph. Kepley's a-jay-hawking," replied Devlin.

"Jayhawking? What in thunder do you mean?" asked Jennison.

"Well, sir, in old Ireland we have a bird we call the jayhawk, that when it catches another bird it takes delight in bullyragging the life out of it, like a cat down a mouse, and me was in that same business myself," he said.

Before Jennison could say anything, Devlin added, "You call it 'foraging off the enemy,' but, begobs, I call it jayhawking."

"All right," laughed Jennison. "We'll call it 'Jayhawking' from now on."

And as this version of the story goes, from that point the sudden retaliatory raids made by free-staters became known as Jayhawking. (There are at least two other versions of this tale, only slightly different.)

Whether this is how the word first became associated with free-staters in Kansas Territory is still a matter of speculation. History records that there was a Doc Jennison and a Pat Devlin and that the word Jayhawking was used beginning about 1858 by free-staters in Kansas Territory. But there never was a bird in Ireland, or anywhere else, called the Jayhawk. On that point Pat Devlin was wrong.

During the early 1940s Paul Wellman, then a reporter for the *Kansas City Star,* wrote a letter of inquiry to the Library of Dublin in Ireland to check Devlin's story. A reply came back saying there was no such bird in Ireland, but the librarian added that the name might exist in an isolated locality as a nickname for some other species. At the end of the reply, the writer added, "May I suggest that you inquire if history relates whether the original Pat Devlin was known sometimes to have an inventive turn of mind."

Just who invented the Jayhawk and Jayhawker—which came first is unknown—is still a mystery. It probably wasn't Pat Devlin, because the term Jayhawker was in use nine years before Devlin mentioned it that February day to Jennison. In 1849 a party of pioneers crossing what is today Nebraska called themselves the "Jayhawkers of 49." It was this party, formed at Galesburg, Illinois, that later discovered Death Valley in California. One member of the party, John B. Colton, later remembered first hearing the word on the Platte River in 1849, long before

Kansas Territory was established. According to Colton, when the Argonauts returned East, the word continued in use.

It is very likely that the word *Jayhawker* was created even earlier than 1849 by the fusion of two birds' names—the bluejay or jay and the hawk.

The late John J. Ingalls, onetime United States senator from Kansas, suggested this about 1872. Ingalls wrote: "The Audubon of the 20th century, as he compiles the history of the birds of Kansas, will vainly search the ornithological biographies of his illustrious predecessors for any allusion to the jayhawk.... Were it not that nature forbids the adulterous confusion of her types, he might surmise that the jayhawk was a mule among birds, the illicit offspring of some sudden liaison or aerial intrigue, endowed with the most malign attributes of its progenitors."

Early in this century, the late Frank W. Blackmar, a professor at the University of Kansas, attempted to find out who coined the word Jayhawk. After much research, he reported: "Just when, where, and by whom the names of the two birds were joined in Jayhawk and applied to human beings, no one knows."

In 1858 the word Jayhawker was associated with the free-staters' robbing, looting and general lawlessness. But during the Civil War it took on new meaning. Doc Jennison used it in 1861 when he was commissioned a colonel by Kansas Governor Charles Robinson and charged with raising a regiment of cavalry. Jennison called his regiment the "Independent Mounted Kansas Jayhawkers," although it was officially known as the First Kansas Cavalry and later the Seventh Kansas Regiment.

During the Civil War the word Jayhawk became associated with the spirit of comradeship and the courageous fighting qualities associated with efforts to keep Kansas a free state. Following the war most Kansans were proud to be called Jayhawkers.

By 1886, the University of Kansas at Lawrence had adopted the mythical bird as part of the KU yell, and by the 1890s birds of one sort or another were used to represent the university on postcards and wall posters. In 1901 the university's yearbook became known as the *Jayhawker*. But it was not until 1910 that Henry Maloy, a student from Eureka, Kansas, created a cartoon Jayhawk. It was the basis for the modern-day bird symbolic of the University of Kansas.

But the bird has had its problems.

About 1943, someone pointed out to the Kansas Board of Education that one of the textbooks being used by schoolchildren stated that the Jayhawk was a real bird and that it was native to Kansas. The

The first caricature of the mythical Jayhawk appears to have been produced in 1910 by Henry Maloy, a University of Kansas student. The bird, *upper left,* was the basis for other drawings of the Jayhawk that followed. In 1920 someone drew the motionless Jayhawk perched on a KU monogram. Soon after, in 1923, Jimmy O'Bryon and George Hollingbery designed the quaint ducklike Jayhawk, which continued in use until about 1929. It was then that Forrest O. Calvin drew a bird representing the austere, fighting spirit of the mythical Jayhawk. Calvin's drawing continued in use until Dr. Gene "Yogi" Williams created a bird with a perky contemptuous attitude, which might become tough if bothered. This caricature continued in use during World War II and was adopted by some Kansans in military service. The caricature used today *(lower right)* was designed by Harold D. Sandy while he was a student in 1946. It remains in use today. These Jayhawks were redrawn for this book by Cynthia Dary, a daughter of the author.

board appointed a committee to look into the matter. For a time some committee members talked of prohibiting the use of any textbook using the term. By this action the board apparently hoped to rid Kansans of what they believed to be an insulting nickname.

But the effect was just the opposite. Kansans including newspaper editors rose in arms supporting the Jayhawk. The issue even gained attention outside of Kansas. One Chicago newspaper reported: "Whatever the original connotation of Jayhawker may have been, successive generations of Kansans have made it a badge of distinction. When Kansans cease to take pride in being Jayhawkers we have reached a sorry status. It would be a calamity."

The words *Jayhawker* and *Jayhawk* have survived. But their use is a bit different today compared to ninety or more years ago. To be called a Jayhawk today usually implies that one is an alumnus or friend of the University of Kansas. The word *Jayhawker,* however, is taken by many to mean any Kansan, not just those whose loyalties, particularly in athletics, lean toward the University of Kansas.

The Jayhawk is not beast, fish nor fowl. It is a myth. But just as Greek mythology often reflected Greek humor and idealism, the Jayhawk has served to express the spirit of Kansas. As the late William Ernest Hocking, professor of philosophy at Harvard, wrote in 1953: "Myths there must be, since visions of the future must be clothed in imagery."

The myth of the Jayhawk will outlive us all.

NOTES AND CREDITS

PART I

Milt Bryan's Santa Fe Trail Adventures

The account of Milton E. Bryan's adventures is based on Bryan's reminiscences. I used the original manuscript of Bryan's 1828 journey loaned to me by James Stuppy of Kansas City, Missouri, after he read a shorter version of the Bryan story that I put on paper for *Star* magazine, the *Kansas City Star,* February 8, 1976. Mr. Stuppy is Bryan's great-great-great grandson. Bryan's account was first published under the title "The Flight of Time" in *The Kansas Chief,* Troy, Kansas, June 9, 1887. An undated clipping from a Seneca, Kansas, newspaper (not identified) provided by Mr. Stuppy mentions that the reminiscences were presented as a speech by Bryan in May 1885, at Wathena, Kansas.

The late Henry Inman published an abbreviated version of Bryan's adventures in *The Old Santa Fe Trail,* New York, 1887, but Inman insisted on calling Bryan "Mr. Bryant."

Mr. Stuppy also loaned this writer Bryan's record book of his gold field days.

Additional biographical material came from a sketch of Bryan's life written early in this century by Mrs. Pauline Bryan Wild, Butte, Montana. Still other biographical material may be found in A. T. Andreas's *History of the State of Kansas,* Chicago, 1883, p. 494, and *Gray's Doniphan County History,* Bendena, Kansas, 1905, pp. 25–29.

The Massacre on Walnut Creek

Bits and pieces of this story may be found in numerous places including the *Leavenworth* (Kansas) *Daily Times,* July 29, 1864; the *Topeka* (Kansas) *Daily Times,* July 29, 1864; the *Topeka* (Kansas) *Daily Capital,* May 4, 1906; *Depredations by Kiowa and Arapaho Indians,* Ex. Doc. No. 62, 42nd Congress, 3rd Sess., House of Representatives; Will E. Stoke's *Episodes of Early Days,* Great Bend, Kansas, 1926, containing material provided by Allen W. Edwards; an unpublished manuscript entitled "Great Bend Massacre" by Melvin Good, in the manuscript files of the Kansas State Historical Society, Topeka; plus an article from the St. Louis, Missouri, *Globe-Democrat* (undated but late-nineteenth century) headlined "The Man Who Was Scalped" in the manuscript files of the Kansas State Historical Society.

A Ride for Life

I first ran across this tale in Henry Inman's little book *Stories of the Old Santa Fe Trail* published in 1881 in Kansas City. The book is now as rare as hens' teeth. From what I have since learned, it appears that Inman, a former army officer, heard the story from Henry Booth. It is confirmed, and there are other details in a biographical sketch of Booth's life in Andreas's *History of the State of Kansas,* Chicago, 1883, pp. 1351–1352.

The Crazy Bet of F. X. Aubry

A variety of sources provided information for this story including an account of the ride in the *Daily Missouri Republican,* September 23, 1848; *Outing* magazine, April, 1888; "Diaries of Francis Xavier Aubry, 1853–1854," in *Exploring Southwest Trails, 1846–1854,* Volume 7, Southwest History Series, Arthur Clark Co., Glendale, 1938; the Garden City (Kansas) *Sentinel,* October 6, 1888; Archives of the Archdiocese of Santa Fe; New Mexico State Archives, Santa Fe; *Kansas Historical Collections,* Volume 12; and my own futile search for Aubry's grave at Santa Fe, New Mexico, in 1971. A brief account of Aubry's ride appears in Donald Chaput's fine biography, *François X. Aubry,* published by Arthur Clark, Glendale, 1975. My first story of Aubry's ride was put on paper for *Star* magazine, the *Kansas City Star,* January 23, 1972.

Windwagons and Samuel Peppard

The best information came from old issues of the *Oskaloosa* (Kansas) *Times.*

Samuel Peppard's obituary was published in that paper on April 27, 1916. A story in the May 4, 1916, issue added much background and detail. One of the earliest summaries of Peppard's windwagon journey outside of newspapers may be found in Andreas's *History of the State of Kansas,* Chicago, 1883, pp. 515–516. Brief mention of what was undoubtedly Peppard's windwagon arrival at Fort Kearney may be found in *Frank Leslie's Illustrated* newspaper, July 7, 1860. Details of earlier windwagons came from many newspapers including the *Daily Missouri Republican,* April 20, April 25 and May 1, 1859; *Western Weekly Argus,* June 4, 1859; *Rocky Mountain News,* April 18, 1860; *Kansas City Journal,* March 3, 1907; *Kansas State Record,* May 26, 1860; *Council Grove Press,* July 23, 1860; *Lawrence* (Kansas) *Republican,* August 16, 1860; *The Weekly Tribune* (Liberty, Missouri), October 24, 1846; *Daily Union* (St. Louis), April 12, 1847; *Kansas Free State* (Lawrence, Kansas), February 14, 1855; *Topeka State Record,* April 14, 1860; and the *Atchison* (Kansas) *Champion,* May 19, 1860.

Bill Cody and the Pony Express

One of the earliest accounts of this ride, although short, appears in *The Life of Hon. William F. Cody known as Buffalo Bill, famous hunter, scout and guide,* published in Hartford, Connecticut, in 1879. This reputed "autobiography" was actually written by Frank E. Bliss, but it is the earliest authentic biography of Cody. Other details may be found in Alexander Majors's book *Seventy Years on the Frontier* published in 1893 and edited by Prentiss Ingraham. Cody helped to finance Majors's book. Cody's pony express days are discussed in *The Lives and Legends of Buffalo Bill* (Norman, Oklahoma, 1960) by my good friend Don Russell. Don Reynolds, curator of the Pony Express Stables Museum at St. Joseph, Missouri, was kind enough to help me obtain other information on the ride and the route Cody followed.

The Battle of Coon Creek

I used a much shorter version of this story in *The Buffalo Book.* Since then additional facts have come to light, thanks to the efforts of the late Louise Barry, who located Royall's report in 30th Cong., 1st Sess., H. Ex. Doc. No. 1 (Serial 537), pp. 141–144, 146. Newspaper accounts include St. Louis *Daily Union,* July 20 and August 23, 1848; *The Weekly Tribune,* Liberty, Missouri, July 29, 1848; and the New York *Weekly Tribune,* July 29 and August 19, 1848. One account says Royall was a nephew of Sterling Price.

A colorful firsthand account was written early in this century by James H. Birch, one of the Missouri recruits. It may be found in the *Kansas Historical Collections,* Volume 10, pp. 409–413.

PART II

The Big Springs Treasure

I first heard this tale many years ago as a boy growing up in Kansas. Once, when stopping at the only service station and general store in Big Springs, I remember hearing an old-timer tell the story to my father. The legend is still told by a few old-timers around Big Springs, not many miles west of where this was written. A brief summary of the legend was published by the *Topeka Daily Capital,* July 24, 1927, as part of an article detailing the history of the Big Springs area. The newspaper version is essentially the same story I remember hearing.

The Du Pratz Gold Mine

The main source of this legend is Lee Page du Pratz's book *History of Louisiana,* London, 1757. The map published in the book forms the basis for the tale. Additional information relating to Jesse Chisholm's search and the tradition that there was actually a buried treasure and not a gold mine was provided by James R. Mead's article, "The Little Arkansas," published on page 9 of Volume 10, *Kansas Historical Collections,* published in 1908.

Don Antonio José Chavez's Treasure

Perhaps the earliest publication of this legend, aside from newspaper stories, was in Andreas's *History of the State of Kansas,* Chicago, 1883, p. 56. It is repeated in William Connelley's *Kansas and Kansans,* Volume 1, p. 120, published in New York, 1918. A contemporary review of the legend and an account of one search for the treasure appears in the *Wichita* (Kansas) *Eagle,* May 15, 1931.

Jesus M. Martinez's Treasure

An early account of this tale appeared as an article entitled "A Strange Story" in the *Dodge City* (Kansas) *Times,* September 22, 1877. In the article the writer— not identified—observed: "This story, as told above, is an historical fact, and portions of it have been heretofore published. We can give names of men who know more about it than we do, but by request we do not publish them." Robert Wright later quoted the article in his book *Dodge City, Cowboy Capital,* Wichita, 1913, pp. 17–20.

The Dutch Oven Treasure

I first ran across this tale in a scrapbook containing Edwards County newspaper clippings in the library of the Kansas State Historical Society. A January 9, 1936, story headlined "Renew Search for Treasure Buried in Sands Near Offerle" told about Wilbur Oliphant's experiences and those of Lee Smith. A later newspaper story, published in the Kansas City *Times,* March 9, 1953, repeated the story, but claimed the treasure was buried in buckskin bags and amounted to $50,000 in gold dust. It is possible the bags were inside the Dutch oven.

A search of government records, Santa Fe Trail narratives and related documents has failed to turn up confirmation of the massacre in what is today Edwards County, Kansas. Even Robert Wright's work *Dodge City, The Cowboy Capital,* Wichita, 1913, does not include mention of this tale, although several other treasure tales are told. Dodge City is about 25 miles southwest of where the massacre supposedly occurred.

The Nemaha River Treasure

I have included my sources in the story.

PART III

The Man Who Really Tamed Abilene

Several sources are the basis for this story. Much information came from a paper written by J. B. Edwards, an early-day resident of Abilene. It was first published in the *Abilene Chronicle* in 1896 and later reprinted in the paper. Another source is an unpublished manuscript now in the files of the Kansas State Historical Society titled "The Death of Tom Smith" by Walter D. Nichols, also an early-day Abilene resident. Other bits and pieces came from news stories appearing in the *Abilene Chronicle;* the fine book *Great Gunfighters of the Kansas Cowtowns, 1867–1886* by Nyle Miller and Joseph Snell; and from *Conquering Our Great American Plains* by Stuart Henry, a brother of T. C. Henry, Abilene mayor, and the man who hired Smith as marshal. Henry's book was published in 1930. My good friend Joseph Rosa called to my attention the article in the Utah *Desert News,* December 24, 1868, which reported that Tom Smith had been sent to the Salt Lake Penitentiary.

The Collapse of the Dalton Gang

Most of the material for the story came from a rare little booklet titled *Last Raid of the Daltons and Battle with the Bandits* published in 1892 by David Steward Elliott, editor of the *Coffeyville Journal*. Elliott was an eyewitness to the shootout and wrote the booklet soon after the battle. Also of help was Elliott's story in the *Coffeyville Journal*, October 7, 1892. Emmett Dalton's 1931 interview appeared in the *Kansas City Star*, May 10, 1931.

The Shootout in Perry Tuttle's Dance Hall

Material for this tale came from the *Kansas Daily Commonwealth* (Topeka), August 22, 23 and 27, 1871. Also from the *Abilene Chronicle*, August 24, 1871, and the *Emporia* (Kansas) *News*, August 25, 1871. Judge R. W. P. Muse's "History of Harvey County Kansas, for One Decade—from 1871 to 1881" in *Edwards' Historical Atlas of Harvey Co., Kansas, 1882*, provided additional information.

Who Murdered Belle Starr?

My longtime friend, LeRoy Towns, wrote the story of A. J. Robinson's tale for *Midway*, the Topeka *Capital-Journal*, August 2, 1970. At the time Towns was editor of the Sunday supplement. He later became press secretary to Kansas Governor Robert Bennett. Towns not only gave permission to use Robinson's story here, but he provided the photographs.

Much has been written about Belle Starr. Unfortunately many accounts are based on a little book titled *Bella Starr, the Bandit Queen; or, the Female Jesse James*, first published in 1889 in New York City by Richard K. Fox and written by an anonymous writer on the *Police Gazette* staff. The book is, in the words of the late Ramon Adams, a longtime authority on outlaws, "historically worthless."

Perhaps the most accurate work on Belle Starr was written by Burton Rascoe and called *Belle Starr, "the Bandit Queen."* It was published in New York City in 1941. Another interesting volume is William Yancey Shackleford's little pamphlet *Belle Starr, the Bandit Queen; The Career of the Most Colorful Outlaw the Indian Territory Ever Knew* published in Girard, Kansas, in 1943. Shackleford reviews and compares all material on Belle Starr written before his volume was published. He makes no mention of Mrs. Devena and leaves the question of who killed Belle Starr unanswered.

The Bloody Benders

Information on the Bender family is voluminous. Much that has been written contains errors or outright fiction thereby compounding the problem of telling the true story. For instance, there is the crudely printed and illustrated little booklet, now very rare, titled *The Five Fiends,* Philadelphia, 1874. Among other things it claims there were three Bender girls—not just Kate—and that "it is certain that they have murdered over one hundred people."

For my sources I have relied on old newspaper accounts from the area plus *The Bender Tragedy* by Mary E. York, wife of Dr. W. H. York, a 42-page booklet published in Mankato, Kansas, in 1875; "The Bloody Benders" by Edith Connelley Ross, in Volume 17, *Kansas Historical Collections,* 1928; and *The Notorious Benders* by Eleanor Rorick, published in Cherryvale, Kansas, for the community's centennial in 1971. A good account of the discovery of the bodies is contained in "Another Horror," an article in the *Leavenworth* (Kansas) *Times,* May 8, 1873. The absurd story told by Captain Don Pieppo appeared in *The Commonwealth* (Topeka), August 4, 1877.

William Clarke Quantrill: Was He a Madman?

William Clarke Quantrill's story was pieced together from many sources. Some were located in the files of the Kansas State Historical Society in Topeka, but several publications in my own library provided details on Quantrill's Lawrence raid of August 21, 1863. The date of his raid is one I find easy to remember. I was born on August 21 seventy-one years after the raid. A copy of J. S. Boughton's 38-page booklet, which I prize greatly, contains eyewitness accounts of Quantrill's raid. The booklet, *The Lawrence Massacre By A Band of Missouri Ruffians Under Quantrell* [sic], was published in Lawrence in 1884. It originally sold for ten cents but is so rare today that a copy, if located, will sell for several hundred dollars. Another reliable and equally rare booklet on the raid is Hovey E. Lowman's *Narrative of the Lawrence Massacre on the Morning of the 21st of August, 1863, Prefaced with a Running History of the Early Settlement and After Experiences of the Historic City of Kansas.* This was published in Lawrence in 1864, but no complete copy is known to exist. The text in all known copies ends abruptly at the bottom of page 96. Lowman, a Lawrence newspaper editor, either ran out of time or money, and published whatever was completed. Lowman's booklet was based on a series of articles he had written for his *Kansas State Journal* newspapers beginning in December, 1863. My search has uncovered in old copies of his paper additional articles that he apparently intended to include in his book. Still another source was William E. Connelley's *Quantrill and the Border Wars* published at Cedar Rapids, Iowa, in 1910.

The Tale Texans Don't Like to Tell

Like so many tales about the old-time plains, this yarn was pulled together from various sources. Reference to the "skirmish" appears in most works covering the bloody days of Kansas Territory. The better sources include A. T. Andreas's Bourbon and Linn County sketches in *History of the State of Kansas,* Chicago, 1883, and the records of the territorial governments in the files of the Kansas State Historical Society.

One of the better accounts of the Rangers' exploits appears in T. F. Robley's *History of Bourbon County, Kansas, To the Close of 1865,* published at Fort Scott, Kansas, in 1894. William Ansel Mitchell provides additional details in his version of the story in his 1928 book *Linn County, Kansas; A History.* In nearly all accounts the Texans are called Rangers.

PART IV

Old Dan the Ox and Bob Wright

Robert Wright's reminiscences, Volume 7, *Kansas Historical Collections,* are the source.

Prairie Dog Dave

My friend Gary Leland Roberts was kind enough to loan me his research file on Morrow. Roberts wrote a biographical sketch of Dave Morrow for *Frontier Times,* October-November 1973. I found additional material in several old newspapers including the *Ford County Globe, Dodge City Times, Wichita Beacon, Topeka Daily Commonwealth* and *Newton Kansan.* I included this story in *The Buffalo Book.*

Jim Caspion's White Buffalo

The only reference to this tale that I have found appears in the *Topeka* (Kansas) *State Journal,* August 4, 1897. It too was included in *The Buffalo Book.*

The Saga of Black Kettle

Most of the material for this story comes from a small pamphlet, now rare, titled *Black Kettle,* written by Frank M. Lockard and published by R. G. Wolfe in Goodland, Kansas, about 1924. I found additional bits and pieces in the *Oberlin* (Kansas) *Herald,* May 13, 1880, and the *Norton County* (Kansas) *People,*

August 19, 1880. An earlier version of my story appeared in *Star* magazine, the *Kansas City Star,* August 13, 1972. It included a watercolor of Black Kettle painted by the late Byron B. Wolfe, who used my story as source material for the painting. It was later reproduced and tipped in a limited edition of 250 copies of *The Sketchbook of Byron B. Wolfe,* published by Lowell Press, Kansas City, 1972.

The German Sisters

The files of the Kansas State Historical Society contain a wealth of information on the story of the German sisters. In addition, many government documents, newspaper clippings and books were consulted in order that the full story could be told. The 1896 volume *From the Personal Recollections of General Nelson A. Miles* contains material as does Gen. Richard Irving Dodge's 1877 work *The Plains of the Great West.* But the most complete work is Grace E. Meredith's *Girl Captives of the Cheyennes,* published in Los Angeles in 1927. Many different accounts of what happened were published during the late nineteenth and early twentieth century. In order to set the record straight, Mrs. Meredith, a niece of the German sisters, used military and other government documents and diaries kept by the girls to write her 1927 book.

The Ride of Portugee John Phillips

Aside from the source alluded to in the story, some material came from records relating to the government's investigation of the massacre. I visited the site of Fort Kearny in 1973. At that time I attempted to retrace Phillips's route.

Plains Snake Lore

Snake stories are about as plentiful as buffalo once were on the Great Plains. These stories were gathered over a period of nearly twenty years and filed away. Some were found in the files and publications of the Kansas State Historical Society while others were obtained from friends including ranchers, farmers and history buffs who happened upon the stories.

The First "Real" Bullfight in the United States

The Dodge City newspaper *Kansas Cowboy,* July 12, 1884, provided much material for this story. The issue includes reprints of articles by correspondents sent to cover the bullfight for the *St. Louis Globe-Democrat* and the *New York Herald*. Correspondence between Kansas Governor Glick and Henry Bergh, Jr., is in the files of the Kansas State Historical Society in Topeka. See also Kirke Mechem, "The Bull Fight at Dodge," *Kansas Historical Quarterly,* 1933.

Comanche

Reference to Comanche may be found in nearly all accounts of the Battle of the Little Big Horn. The best sources, however, include Edward S. Luce's fine book *Keogh, Comanche and Custer,* St. Louis, 1939 (reprinted in Ashland, Oregon, 1974); Anthony Amaral's *Comanche,* Los Angeles, 1961; Barron Brown's *Comanche,* Kansas City, 1935; and Robert M. Mengel's *Comanche: Silent Horse On A Silent Field,* Lawrence, Kansas, 1969. The Inman material appeared in the *Topeka Daily Capital,* November 12, 1891. Biographical material on Keogh came from G. A. Hayes-McCoy's *Captain Myles Walter Keogh,* National University of Ireland, n.d. At the request of Dr. Philip S. Humphrey, director of the Museum of Natural History at the University of Kansas, I wrote a longer version of Comanche's story that was published in booklet form in 1976 on the 100th anniversary of the Battle of the Little Big Horn. A limited edition of 50 bound copies was also produced.

Lilly's Escape and Unbelievable Ride

The only other published account of this tale, so far as I know, appeared in Henry Inman's *Stories of the Old Santa Fe Trail,* published in Kansas City, Missouri, in 1881. The book, long out of print and rare, deserves to be reprinted.

PART V

The Hermit Priest of Belfry Hill

John Maloy first told this tale in the *Council Grove* (Kansas) *Republican,* February 7, 1890. Maloy had learned the story from old-timers around Council Grove. The story is repeated in Volume 16, *Kansas Historical Collections.* Another version appears in Henry Inman's *Stories of the Old Santa Fe Trail,* Kansas City, 1881. Phil LeNoir tells much of the hermit's legend in New Mexico in his article "The Hermit of Las Vegas" in the Texas Folklore Society's *Tone the Bell Easy,* Austin, 1932. LeNoir, however, does not identify the hermit by name. A more recent publication, *New Mexico Place Names,* p. 70, identifies the hermit as Juan Maria Agostini. Whether Agostini *or* Boccalini was the hermit's real name or both were false names or whether there were two hermits, one in Kansas and another in New Mexico, is unknown. But I believe the story as told here is correct regardless of the man's name.

The Day Chief Old Wolf Nearly Lost His Scalp

From what I can learn Henry Inman heard the story from Hatcher himself. It was first put down on paper by Inman in *The Old Santa Fe Trail,* New York, 1897. Its only other appearance was my own version that appeared in *Star* magazine, *The Kansas City Star,* in 1974.

Frederic Remington: Sheep Rancher and Saloon Owner

Mr. Atwood Manley, Canton, New York, an authority on Remington's early life in the East, was most helpful in providing me with leads on Remington's Kansas period. He also provided facts relating to Remington's inheritance. Other bits and pieces of the sheep ranching story came from old issues of the *Peabody* (Kansas) *Gazette* for 1883 and early 1884; from material gathered by the late Dr. Robert Taft of Lawrence, Kansas, now in the files of the Kansas State Historical Society; and from Jacob DeCon's recollections of Remington published in the *Topeka Daily Capital,* January 30, 1910.

Much of the material relating to Remington's Kansas City period came from old newspapers including the *Kansas City Star,* January 23, 1891, December 27, 1909; January 23, 1910; February 5, 1911 and March 25, 1920. Nellie Hough's article "Remington at Twenty-Three," *International Studio,* February 1923, provided additional insights.

When Abe Lincoln Came to Kansas

This version is essentially the same as my article "Lincoln's Frontier Guard," which appeared in *Civil War Times Illustrated,* August 1972. Some sources are mentioned in my article. Others include a copy of the "Roll and Other Proceedings of the Frontier Guard" in my files and Edgar Langsdorf's fine 1940 article "Jim Lane and the Frontier Guard" in Volume 9 of the *Kansas Historical Quarterly.*

Jim Lane and His Frontier Guard

Old newspaper accounts have provided much of the material for this story including the *Free Press* (Elwood, Kansas), December 3, 1859, and the *Leavenworth* (Kansas) *Daily Times,* December 8, 1859. Also, Albert D. Richardson includes some material on Lincoln's journey in his book *Field, Dungeon and Escape* published in 1865. Franklin G. Adams's reminiscences in the *Kansas Historical Collections* and Fred Brinkerhoff's research in the *Kansas Historical Quarterly,* Volume 13, 1945, provided additional material.

What Happened to Boston Corbett?

Many sources were used to piece together the Corbett tale. *Harper's Weekly,* May 13, 1865, contains an interesting account of Corbett's shooting of Booth. Additional information on Corbett's life came from the late Albert T. Reid, a native of Concordia, Kansas, who was acquainted with Corbett in Kansas. And there is Corbett's own account of the shooting of Booth. It was published, among other places, in the Abilene (Kansas) *Chronicle,* February 3, 1887.

My friend John Redjinski of the Menninger Foundation, Topeka, a collector of material on Corbett, opened his files to me. They include a history of Corbett from the files of the state hospital at Topeka. It was written by a Dr. Wentworth who treated Corbett after he was committed.

Mrs. Granville M. Bush, Lyons, Kansas, in a letter to me dated March 24, 1972, described how her father, Irvin DeFord, and her uncle, Richard Thatcher, hid Corbett in a barn near Neodesha, Kansas, after his escape from the Topeka hospital and just before he vanished forever.

Mrs. Mildred Barber of Concordia also provided material gathered in Cloud County.

The Song "Home on the Range"

Material on how John Lomax recorded the song was found in *The Southwest Review,* Dallas, Volume 31, 1945. Details of Moanfeldt's search for the authors is contained in his report to the Music Publishers Protective Association, May 1935, which is reproduced in Volume 17 of the *Kansas Historical Quarterly* where Kirke Mechem, former secretary of the Kansas State Historical Society, first pulled the story together.

In spite of the evidence, CBS News correspondent, Charles Kuralt, in a report on the Walter Cronkite network television news, December 17, 1973, reported that David Guion of Dallas, Texas, was the song's author. Before that broadcast, CBS had contacted the Kansas State Historical Society and was provided with the song's history. Kuralt apparently ignored it.

Nyle Miller, then secretary of the society, wrote in January of 1974, "To my hitherto favorite in the CBS stable of national newscasters, Charles Kuralt, I sadly ask, 'Charley, how could you?' An eighty-year-old man, the author of a hundred-year-old song? Good grief."

The First White Woman to Climb Pike's Peak

Bits and pieces of this story may be found scattered throughout the *Kansas Historical Collections* and the *Kansas Historical Quarterly.* Some of the material was located in the Colorado State Historical Society files at Denver. The letter sent by Julia Holmes to her mother was published by the *Daily Missouri Republican,* October 17, 1858. If the letter had not been published, we might not know of Julia Holmes's accomplishment.

The Legend of Smoky Hill Thompson

Bits and pieces of the "Smoky Hill" Thompson story were found in old recollections and historical volumes. The sketch of Ellsworth County, Kansas, in A. T. Andreas's *History of the State of Kansas,* Chicago, 1883, p. 1274, contains some information as does *Compendious History of Ellsworth County,* Ellsworth, 1879. Adolph Roenigk's *Pioneer History of Kansas,* Denver, 1933, contains material on Thompson including William H. Ziegler's meager recollections of "Smoky Hill." Thompson's Texas adventures came from "The Recollections of W. S. Glenn, Buffalo Hunter," edited by Rex W. Strickland, *Panhandle Plains Historical Review,* Volume 22, pp. 49–50. Additional material was located in Ida Ellen Rath's *The Rath Trail,* Wichita, 1961.

Battle at Pawnee Rock

Major Henry Inman heard and recorded this story from the lips of Kit Carson. Inman wrote that about 1865 he, Jack Henderson, Lucien B. Maxwell and a couple of Apache Indians were camped halfway up the rugged sides of "Old Baldy" in the Raton Range. He said it was a cold night and everyone was huddled around a little fire of pine knots. It was then that Carson told the story that he said he had heard from Jim Gibson, one of the participants. Inman included the story in that rare little book of his *Stories of the Old Santa Fe Trail* (Kansas City, 1881).

How Kansans Became Known as Jayhawkers

Material for this story was plentiful. The *Kansas Historical Collections,* Robley's *History of Bourbon County Kansas,* Fort Scott, 1894, and numerous old newspapers were consulted.

Index

This index is intended primarily as a reference guide to place names and leading characters. It is not an index to subject matter, nor does it cover the notes and credits.